LEVEL III PRACTICE EXAMS – VOLUME 2  S0-AVC-043

SCHWESER 2017 LEVEL III CFA® PRACTICE EXAMS VOLUME 2

©2016 Kaplan, Inc. All rights reserved.

Published in 2016 by Kaplan, Inc.

Printed in the United States of America.

ISBN: 978-1-4754-4143-7

HOW TO USE THE LEVEL III PRACTICE EXAMS

Save practice exams until last. Just do not wait too long. Complete the readings and other practice questions before the practice exams. Your final four to six weeks of preparation should focus on practice exams. You will need ample time to take, review, and retake these exams. We at Schweser provide you with six complete, six-hour exams. They are designed like the actual exam. The first three hours are constructed response, and the second three hours are 10, six-question vignettes. The CFA Institute provides the actual morning sessions of the past three years as practice. *In the LMS, we provide you full, question-by-question coverage of these past morning exams. We review the relevant taught material, but our focus shifts to extracting the key case facts and how to use them to write an effective answer in the allotted time. This is a critical exam (and career) skill.* The Institute also has item-set practice tests on its website. You will want to complete these exams and tests at least one week before the actual test so you have time to learn from your mistakes and improve. One of the worst things you can do is wait to take a practice exam just before the real exam, leaving no time to learn anything from the experience.

A good strategy is to take the CFA Institute practice tests and then take the Schweser practice exams, finishing one to two weeks before exam day. Then retake the Institute's constructed response questions and several Schweser practice exams. In particular, take the time to write out and improve your constructed response answers. Each year, we hear from candidates who did well on the afternoon session but terrible in the morning session and flunked the exam as a result. It is much harder to write a reasonable constructed response answer in the time allotted and under exam conditions than you think. The good news is it gets better with more practice, and practice the item sets as well.

Time management is critical in practice and, even more so, on the exam. Plan to work in three-hour blocks of time and not peek at the solutions. Initially the most important thing is to work carefully and don't worry how long you spend on a single question. You are learning the material and good technique. As the exam becomes closer and certainly on your second try, answer the questions in the allotted time. Some candidates say our practice exams are easier than the real exam, while others say our exams are harder. It largely comes down to how well you prepare. The CFA Institute has made it clear that the Level III exam requires more judgment and perspective than is required on Level I or II. Count on there being questions that do not look like what you studied. Think about the concepts that were repeatedly stressed in the curriculum. Give the most logical answer you can in the time and space provided for the question. Remember, others around you feel the same stress too.

Be ready for the Level III exam format. The morning session (three hours and 50% of the exam) is entirely constructed response essay format. The afternoon session (three hours and 50% of the exam) is 10 selected-response, six-question item sets, each worth 18 points. The Level III topic area weights, as presented by CFA Institute, are shown here. You will notice these guidelines are vague. *The Level III exam is very "lumpy" in terms of what specific items make it into the exam in any one year. Do not expect an even distribution of topics.*

Topic Area Weights for the Level III CFA Exam	
Topic Area	*Level III Weight*
Ethical and Professional Standards	10–15%
Economics	5–15%
Fixed Income	10–20%
Equity Investments	5–15%
Alternative Investments	5–15%
Derivatives	5–15%
Portfolio Management	40–55%

The only things you can count on at Level III are surprises. The CFA Institute has specifically stated that all areas except ethics can (and have been) tested in combined fashion. Historically:

- There have been two item sets for ethics in the afternoon. In 2015 the ethics exam weight was changed to 10–15%, so do not be surprised if there are three item sets or even some constructed response questions.
- It is more accurate to think of the exam as 100% portfolio management in orientation.
- GIPS has been 0–5% with 0 or 1 item set. It is part of the portfolio management exam weight, not ethics.

Answering constructed response questions. Follow the specific directions for each question. The question will direct "use the template provided" or "answer on the blank pages provided." It may ask you to give one, two, or three reasons; or, it may state nothing and you must give the best answer you can in the time and space allowed. If you do not read and follow the directions given, expect to fail. The CFA Institute has said it gives no points for a general display of knowledge.

Give the CFA answer. Graders use an answer key and don't give points for creative thought. The correct exam answer is the one that best reflects what was prominently taught in the assigned material and is relevant to the case facts. Creative or personal views do not receive credit. Graders are not allowed to read anything into your answer, so you must be precise. Also, organize your work and think before you write. If the graders can't find or decipher your work, you will receive no credit. Constructed response questions are typically designed to have a range of acceptable as well as unacceptable answers. Most answers receive partial credit based on how close to the acceptable they come, so show and explain your work. In constructed response, you are being graded on your work process, not just the final answer.

Don't forget to prepare for item set questions as well. These tend to be more comfortable and technical, in other words, like Level II. The practice exams will prepare you for both types of questions.

Be prepared. Get plenty of sleep the night before the exam. Bring all necessary items (including snacks) with you and arrive early enough at the test site to get a decent parking space. In fact, I recommend thoroughly checking out the site before exam day. Important! Be sure to read the CFA Institute testing policies, which can be found on the CFA Institute website. All CFA candidates are expected to know and abide by all CFA Institute testing policies and procedures as well as the CFA Institute Code of Ethics and Standards of Professional Conduct.

My thanks to the Schweser team. I would like to thank all of my colleagues at Schweser, especially Kurt Schuldes, CFA, CAIA, and Jared Heintz, Production Project Manager, for their incredible work ethic and commitment to quality. Schweser would not be the company it is, nor could it provide the quality products you see, without all the Schweser content and editing professionals.

Best Regards,

David Hetherington

David Hetherington,
CFA Vice President and Level III Manager
Kaplan Schweser

2017 Practice Exam Answers and Explanations are Online at www.schweser.com

Answers and explanations for self-grading all practice exam essays and item sets are included at the end of this book. Explanations and calculations for the *item sets* are also available online at schweser.com. They also contain embedded links to supporting curriculum material for the relevant Learning Outcome Statements. In addition, you can access Performance Tracker, a tool that will provide you with exam diagnostics to target your review effort and allow you to compare your scores to those of other candidates.

USE YOUR SCHWESER *ONLINE ACCESS* ACCOUNT

You should have received an email with login information for Online Access. This is your login to view "How to Pass the Level III CFA® Exam" and the two videos on answering constructed response questions. You can also access volumes in the Candidate Resource Library, use the Schweser Study Calendar and Performance Tracker, and (if you purchased any package) ask us questions regarding our material. Simply log in at www.schweser.com and select Online Access to use any of these features. You can access practice exam answers and explanations with the Practice Exams Vol. 1 left-hand menu item. If you need password help, go to www.schweser.com/password or use the Password Help link that appears if your login is unsuccessful.

PRACTICE EXAM ONLINE FEATURES AT A GLANCE

Answer Explanations
Our answer format contains explanations to help you understand why one answer is the best of all the choices. When using Performance Tracker, you can choose to get detailed explanations for only those item set questions you missed or for all item set questions.

Links to Curriculum
Within the answer explanations, we have embedded links to the relevant content for review. This can include multiple Learning Outcome Statements, concepts, definitions, or formulas.

Exam Diagnostics
When you access Performance Tracker, you can request a breakdown of your overall score on the afternoon session of any exam. You can even get the LOS references for questions you answered incorrectly to facilitate your review efforts.

Performance Comparison
Log in today and enjoy the benefits of the Candidate Library*, Office Hours**, the Schweser Study Calendar, expanded Practice Exam item set answers, and Performance Tracker.

* Included with the Premium and Premium Plus study packages.

** Included with the Essential study package.

PRACTICE EXAM 1 MORNING SESSION QUESTION BREAKDOWN

Question	Topic	Minutes
1	Private Wealth Management	19
2	Private Wealth Management and Asset Allocation	26
3	Trading, Monitoring, and Rebalancing	23
4	Behavioral Finance	18
5	Portfolio Management - Institutional	10
6	Portfolio Management - Institutional	11
7	Asset Allocation	14
8	Asset Allocation	14
9	Equity	21
10	Performance Evaluation/GIPS	24
	Total	180

- Asset Allocation
- Equity

PRACTICE EXAM 1 SCORE SHEET

MORNING SESSION		
Question	Maximum Points	Your Estimated Score
1A	2	0
1B	6	5
1C	6	0
1D	3	3
1E	2	2
2A	5	5
2B	6	6
2C	7	4
2D	4	1
2E	4	3
3A	4	3
3B	12	10
3C	4	4
3D	3	1
4A	10	10
4B	3	1
4C	5	2
5A	7	6
5B	3	2
6A	4	4
6B	4	2
6C	3	2
7A	5	1
7B	6	6
7C	3	2
8A	5	2
8B	5	0
8C	4	2
9A	4	4
9B	6	4
9C	6	3
9D	5	4
10A	3	3
10B	2	1
10C	3	3
10D	4	4
10E	9	5
10F	3	0
Total	180	120 = 67%

$\frac{29}{\cancel{}}$ (64%)

$\frac{60}{86}$ (70%)

85/111 (77%)

AFTERNOON SESSION		
Question	Maximum Points	Your Estimated Score
1–6	18	
7–12	18	
13–18	18	
19–24	18	
25–30	18	
31–36	18	
37–42	18	
43–48	18	
49–54	18	
55–60	18	
Total	180	40×3 = 120

67%

EXAM 1
MORNING SESSION

QUESTION 1 HAS FIVE PARTS FOR A TOTAL OF 19 MINUTES

Jane Guthrie is a social media coach. For several years she has been exclusively retained by a financially stable public corporation to provide support to its executives and advice in designing the company's social media message and presentation strategy. She is 36 years old, believes her skills are highly marketable and, if needed, she could find comparable employment elsewhere. However, her relationship with the company is on a one-year employment contract. Her goal is to retire at age 58.

Guthrie has never been married, but 10 years ago, she accepted sole responsibility for her sister's two children when her sister and the sister's husband were killed in a car accident. A relatively substantial trust was funded by the sister's life insurance and has provided for the childrens' needs through four years of college. Both children are quite gifted and will finish their undergraduate college education in a few years. Guthrie plans to establish an additional trust to provide for postgraduate education needs. She would like to establish a new trust and contribute $175,000 to the new trust within the next year.

[handwritten: Not part of TH]

Guthrie has a moderately aggressive stock and bond portfolio held in a tax-exempt account and worth USD 450,000. The funds were accumulated from after-tax contributions, and any withdrawals made before age 60 would be subject to a very high tax penalty.

[handwritten: $450,000 (tax exempt)]

Guthrie also has USD 400,000 in a fully taxable portfolio. Included in the portfolio is USD 200,000 of money market assets. Guthrie is in the 28% income tax bracket.

[handwritten: $400,000 (taxable)]

Guthrie has annual after-tax employment income of USD 150,000 and living expenses of USD 100,000. She plans to contribute the difference to her tax-exempt portfolio annually up to the limit allowed. The balance will go to her taxable portfolio at the end of each year.

[handwritten: $150,000 AT income ($100,000) expenses]

At retirement Guthrie estimates she will need USD 2,000,000.

A.   **State** and **discuss** one factor that reduces Guthrie's risk objective.

(2 minutes)

B.   **Discuss** Guthrie's:
i.   Time horizon.
ii.   Legal needs.
iii. Liquidity needs.

(6 minutes)

C.   **Calculate** the required annual return required to meet Guthrie's goals. **Show** your calculations.

(6 minutes)

D. Assuming that capital gains make up most of stock returns, are taxed at a lower rate than income return, and Guthrie is a passive investor planning to hold all securities for long periods; **state** whether Guthrie would most likely be better off to hold stocks rather than bonds in her taxable or tax-exempt portfolio and **explain** why. To answer the question, assume stocks must be held in one account and bonds in the other.

(3 minutes)

E. Assume that Guthrie plans to accumulate a USD 50,000 emergency cash reserve. **Explain** whether this should be held in her tax-exempt or taxable portfolio if the goal is to minimize taxes on the cash at withdrawal.

(2 minutes)

QUESTION 2 HAS FIVE PARTS FOR A TOTAL OF 26 MINUTES

Six years have passed, and Jane Guthrie is now 42 years old. She has had both successes and disappointments in her career. Shortly after her initial efforts at determining a required return, she lost her job. Due to a severe recession, she was underemployed for a couple of years. This occurred immediately after she funded the education trust for the children. Both children completed their initial and postgraduate education and are successfully employed. Under the terms of both trusts, the small remaining trust funds will be distributed to them at age 28.

While she was underemployed, she found a few part-time opportunities and returned to school for an MBA. During that period, she substantially reduced her portfolio. Three years ago she took a position with a small private, startup company as Senior Vice President for product marketing. This makes her an important executive in executing, though not setting, company strategy. While her immediate compensation is moderate and she has been unable to add to her portfolio from savings, she has received restricted stock grants in the company of 50,000 shares in lieu of direct monetary compensation.

She consults Kate VonLee, CFA, to assist her in developing a financial plan. Her tax-exempt portfolio is now worth USD 350,000, and her taxable portfolio is worth only USD 200,000 due to the substantial withdrawals made for living expenses and the MBA. Guthrie excluded her employer stock from both these figures. Her combined asset allocation, excluding the employer stock, is shown in Exhibit 1. Guthrie admits that her confidence in making sound financial decision was shaken over the last few years and wonders if she would have been better off to have pursued full-time work instead of an MBA. She also expresses concern that so much of her net worth is in employer stock and would like to be able to diversify that position.

Exhibit 1. Current Portfolio Allocation

Asset Class	Portfolio Allocation
Money Market	13%
Small-cap stock	30%
Large-cap stock	25%
Domestic bonds	32%

*Employer stock is excluded but has a value equal to 40% of the combined portfolio.

©2016 Kaplan, Inc.

A. **Comment** on how Guthrie's decision to pursue the MBA affected her allocation between financial and human capital over the last few years and **explain** how it could have increased her total wealth.

(5 minutes)

B. **Determine** and **explain** the asset class in Guthrie's portfolio the employer stock is most similar to and which risk bucket—personal, market, or aspirational—the stock would fall into. **Recommend** from a tactical and strategic perspective what should be done with the stock. **Explain** why.

(6 minutes)

C. Guthrie has heard about the concept of monetizing concentrated single-asset positions and asks VonLee to **explain** the following strategies and **recommend** the one that is most suitable to her situation. Assume that rumors Guthrie has heard that the company will go public are true. **Support** your recommendation with *two* reasons related directly to Guthrie's situation.

    i.   Corporate estate tax freeze.

    ii. Collateralized bank loan.

(7 minutes)

D. Fifteen years later, Guthrie is 57 years old and considering retirement. She again turns to VonLee seeking advice on whether she has the resources to retire now or if she should continue to work for another three years. VonLee runs Monte Carlo simulations to present to Guthrie. **Explain** two benefits of using Monte Carlo analysis to make this decision and **explain** what reports VonLee should show Guthrie to help Guthrie make the decision to retire now or in three years.

(4 minutes)

E. When Guthrie retires, **state** and **explain** how her portfolio return and risk objective are most likely to change.

(4 minutes)

QUESTION 3 HAS FOUR PARTS FOR A TOTAL OF 23 MINUTES

Ken Johnson manages global bond portfolios and has been asked to prepare a briefing paper relating to order execution and trading strategies. In the paper he plans to cover the role of brokers and dealers, the four components of implementation shortfall cost, and some typical situations where market or limit orders would be used.

A.   **Contrast** the role of brokers versus dealers and **discuss** how each is compensated.

(4 minutes)

B.   **Explain** the four components of implementation shortfall, **circle** whether each can be a cost, negative cost, or either. **Circle** whether each is directly observable or must be inferred from a benchmark price.

Answer Question 3-B in the template provided.

(12 minutes)

Template for Question 3-B

Component	Explain	Cost, negative cost, or can be either (circle one)	Observable or inferred (circle one)
Market impact		Cost Negative Cost Can be Either	Observable Inferred
Delay		Cost Negative Cost Can be Either	Observable Inferred
Unrealized gain/loss		Cost Negative Cost Can be Either	Observable Inferred
Explicit cost		Cost Negative Cost Can be Either	Observable Inferred

C.   Johnson reviews some recent trades he made in his portfolios.

       Trade 1: After considerable proprietary fundamental research, Johnson
               determines a corporate bond is likely to be substantially
               downgrade. The bond is only moderately liquid.

       Trade 2: A portfolio receives a substantial inflow of funds and in order to
               quickly match the duration of the portfolio's benchmark, U.S.
               Treasuries are purchased.

       Determine and **explain** whether each trade should have been a market
       or limit order.

                            (4 minutes)

D.   Johnson also decides to include a brief discussion of why he believes
       implementation shortfall is superior to volume weighted average price
       (VWAP) to avoid gaming. **Explain** how gaming can avoid showing a
       cost in VWAP analysis and how gaming would most likely affect the
       component costs of implementation shortfall.

                            (3 minutes)

QUESTION 4 HAS THREE PARTS FOR A TOTAL OF 18 MINUTES

Thomas Simms is a client manager for Bueno Capital Management and has become dissatisfied with traditional capital market theory. He believes it should be complemented with behavioral finance to gain better insights into market and client behavior. Simms is reviewing profiles he has prepared on several of his clients.

- Client 1 generally calls Simms after receiving each of his quarterly reports and suggests Simms reallocate funds out of stocks that have risen into stocks that have declined.
- Client 2 is very wealthy and likes to explain to Simms that he was too conservative when he started his career but as his wealth increased, he took more risk and that is what led to his ultimate financial success. Now he just wants to protect his capital and enjoy life.
- Client 3 used to continually object when Simms recommended increasing the equity allocation until Simms began to point out the bonds in the portfolio provide an investment base, and the equity could ultimately improve the client's long-term standard of living without risking his lifestyle.
- Client 4 is frustrating to deal with because he is only willing to consider new stocks of domestic companies but will not consider international companies, even in other highly developed markets.
- Client 5 insists that Simms use ETFs for her domestic large-cap stock allocations but use individual securities for her small-cap growth stocks.

A. For each of Simms's comments, **circle** the concept best exhibited by that client. Each concept must be used only once, and each concept must be matched to a client.
- Bounded Rationality
- Efficient Market Hypothesis
- Friedman-Savage Double Inflection Function
- Goal Based Investing
- Loss Aversion

Answer Question 4-A in the template provided.

(10 minutes)

Template for Question 4-A

Client	Concept best exhibited (circle one)
1	Bounded Rationality Efficient Market Hypothesis Friedman-Savage Double Inflection Function Goal Based Investing Loss Aversion
2	Bounded Rationality Efficient Market Hypothesis Friedman-Savage Double Inflection Function Goal Based Investing Loss Aversion
3	Bounded Rationality Efficient Market Hypothesis Friedman-Savage Double Inflection Function Goal Based Investing Loss Aversion
4	Bounded Rationality Efficient Market Hypothesis Friedman-Savage Double Inflection Function Goal Based Investing Loss Aversion
5	Bounded Rationality Efficient Market Hypothesis Friedman-Savage Double Inflection Function Goal Based Investing Loss Aversion

B. Simms is puzzled when he comes across a reference to myopic loss aversion. **Explain** any ways in which loss aversion and myopic loss aversion are similar and any ways in which they differ.

(3 minutes)

-55 y/o, wife is 52
- Good health
- over confidence
  - riskier assets
  - used options

Simms has a new client. In their first meeting, Simms learned his client was a middle-level corporate finance executive for a large corporation. The client is 55 years old, and his wife is 52. Both are in good health. In the meeting the client spent considerable time bragging about the successful strategies used in the corporation and how his personal role at the company led to the large increase in value of his stock options. When the corporation began to pursue international diversification, the client shifted a large part of his wealth into emerging market funds and tripled his money. He then further leveraged these gains with call options. He expects Simms to continue these excellent returns.

In the second meeting, Simms and the client reviewed the client's total financial situation and developed a set of portfolio objectives and constraints. The client expressed strong views that the return needs were the minimum he could accept, and the asset allocation they discussed was perfect.

After that meeting Simms reviews his firm's capital market expectations, has his assistant prepare a set of mortality table projections, and Simms estimates the client's core capital requirements to be 20% higher than the client's assets.

C. Simms is preparing for the third client meeting. **Determine** whether the client is mostly exhibiting cognitive errors or emotional biases in his thinking and **support** this with facts from the client meetings. **Recommend** and **explain** whether Simms should accommodate the client's views on required return and asset allocation or educate the client on the benefits of revising the investment plan.

(5 minutes)

QUESTION 5 HAS TWO PARTS FOR A TOTAL OF 10 MINUTES

The Astney Foundation was funded in 1951 by the heirs of a large brewing fortune. The foundation's sole purpose is to support training for gifted young skiers in the United States. Yearly grants are provided to children between the ages of 9 and 15 to cover training, living accommodations, and education at Astney Mountain School. The $25 million portfolio is expected to generate a real return of 4% and cover operating expenses of 0.75%. General inflation — *Ignore* is estimated at 2.5%, while costs covered by the foundation are expected to increase at 3.5%. The foundation is tax exempt, subject to no minimum payout requirement, and the trustees have expressed a strong desire to generate a 3% annual income return.

A.
  i. **State** the return objective of the foundation.
  ii. **Calculate** the required annual nominal return requirement. **Show** your calculations.
  iii. **Calculate** the dollar amount that can be distributed over the next year that is consistent with the foundation's long-term goals. **Show** your work.

(7 minutes)

B. **Discuss** how inflation and the foundation's time horizon affect its risk objective. **State** and **explain** how *one* other factor from the case information directly affects the risk objective.

(3 minutes)

QUESTION 6 HAS THREE PARTS FOR A TOTAL OF 11 MINUTES

Silts Life Insurance Company offers a variety of life insurance and savings plans. Due to an extended period of low interest rates and customer dissatisfaction with returns on savings, the marketing department has developed a new combination life insurance and guaranteed investment product (GIC). Customers receive five years of life insurance coverage as well as a 3% fixed rate on a five-year GIC. However, the rate will increase after two years if 5-year, A-rated bond rates increase. The rate will reset upward by the same amount as the increase in 5-year, A-rated bonds. The product has led to a 20% increase in company liabilities over the last two years, and the growth is expected to continue.

Jim Silts, CEO, is firmly convinced that interest rates are going to start rising, making the product a winner for customers and the company. To fund the liabilities and match duration, he has directed the investment department to purchase 5-year, fixed-rate bonds. Silts has also mandated the portfolio be managed in total and not segmented, explaining they offer a combined product, so viewing the portfolio in aggregate is more appropriate.

A.   Assuming that Silts is correct in his interest rate expectations, **explain** the likely affect on the company's earnings and surplus.

(4 minutes)

B.   **Explain** by giving *two* reasons directly related to the company why the segmented portfolio approach makes more sense.

(4 minutes)

C.   **Explain** how the surplus would likely be affected if Silts is wrong and rates fall.

(3 minutes)

QUESTION 7 HAS THREE PARTS FOR A TOTAL OF 14 MINUTES

Andy Beer is chief strategist for an investment advisor. The firm's asset base is more or less equally split between defined benefit pension plans and participant-directed 401(k) defined contribution plans. He recently hired John Cook as a strategy analyst. Cook is a candidate sitting for the Level III exam. Beer directs Cook to analyze real rate bonds whose principal is indexed to inflation.

[handwritten note: 50/50 b/w DB + DC]

A.   **Determine** whether real rate bonds should be regarded as a distinct asset class or considered as part of traditional fixed income. **Support** the conclusion with three reasons. **Explain** which type of portfolios managed by the firm would have the clearest use for the bonds. You must choose either the defined benefit or defined contribution plans as having the clearest use.

(5 minutes)

Beer next directs Cook to consider two other new asset classes (NAC) for inclusion in their typical DB portfolios. Cook gathers the following data:

	Typical DB Portfolio	NAC 1	NAC 2
Expected return	8.5%	6.7%	11.1%
Standard deviation	9.3%	7.5%	11.8%
Sharpe ratio	0.806	0.760	0.856

B.   Cook returns to Beer and states the NAC 2 is desirable to add, and NAC 1 is not. **Evaluate** and **explain** whether each recommendation is correct.

(6 minutes)

C.   Beer then asks Cook to **state** and **explain** whether it is more appropriate to hedge currency exposure for international bond or equity assets.

(3 minutes)

QUESTION 8 HAS THREE PARTS FOR A TOTAL OF 14 MINUTES

Andy Beer is preparing to meet with a large prospective client. The client is considering alternate methods of setting strategic asset allocation. In preparation, Beer is reviewing alternative approaches.

A. **State** and **explain** the primary problem with mean-variance optimization that can be overcome with resampling and the consequences of this problem.

(5 minutes)

B. **Discuss** how the Black-Litterman and ALM approaches to asset allocation differ or are similar.

(5 minutes)

C. **Discuss** whether it makes more sense to regard risk-free assets as an asset class in efficient frontier analysis or as the starting point of the Capital Allocation Line when determining strategic asset allocation for portfolios with ongoing and multiple-period time horizons.

(4 minutes)

QUESTION 9 HAS FOUR PARTS FOR A TOTAL OF 21 MINUTES

Keith Worthington and Jan Carlos are discussing various approaches to equity portfolio management and the tradeoff between active return versus tracking risk. Worthington states the tradeoff is that as active return increases, there will be an increase in tracking risk, resulting in no systematic change in the information ratio. Carlos states that tracking risk will be higher for enhanced indexing than for full-blown active management if the active manager is allowed to selectively hedge risk.

A.   **State** whether each comment is correct or incorrect. If it is incorrect, **explain** what is incorrect.

(4 minutes)

Worthington then brings up a recent analysis he has performed on a manager. He ran the following regression analysis on the manager's return (R_p). The factors in the analysis are small- and large-cap growth and small- and large-cap value, respectively.

$$R_p = 1.2\% - 0.61(SCG) - 0.85(LCG) + 1.23(SCV) + 1.45(LCV)$$

- Worthington goes on to state that because the largest weight is large-cap value, the best classification is that the manager is a large-cap value style manager.
- Carlos states that the analysis is consistent with a long-short portfolio, and a reasonable performance benchmark is money market return plus a spread.

B.   **Discuss** each comment and **state** what is correct and incorrect in each statement. There must be parts you agree and disagree with in each comment.

Answer Question 9-B in the template provided.

(6 minutes)

©2016 Kaplan, Inc.

Template for Question 9-B

Statement by:	Discuss what is correct	Discuss what is incorrect
Worthington		
Carlos		

C.   Carlos is considering combinations of the three investment alternatives shown in Exhibit 2. **Compute** the expected active return, active risk, and information ratio of allocating 80% to alternative 1 and 20% to alternative 2. **Show** your work.

(6 minutes)

Exhibit 2

Alternative	Active Return	Active risk
1	–0.10%	0.01%
2	2.71%	4.55%
3	1.55%	2.77%

D.   **State** whether this allocation is most likely a completeness fund approach or a core-satellite approach. **Support** your decision with two reasons.

(5 minutes)

QUESTION 10 HAS SIX PARTS FOR A TOTAL OF 24 MINUTES

Alyssa Chong and Ivan Kozlov are reviewing client return reporting requirements for their firm. One of the issues they have been asked to research is the effect of client contributions and withdrawals to a portfolio return. As an example, in the month of June, account 179E received a contribution of GBP15.0 million on June 10. The account had an ending value of 107.9 million, a beginning value of 86.3 million, and a value after the contribution of 116.2 million.

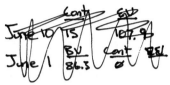

A. **Compute** the most accurate measure of return for the month to reflect the performance of the manager. **Show** your work.

(3 minutes)

B. Kozlov reviews the calculations for account 179E and states that while that is the most accurate calculation, in this case, there are several methods that could be used because they would produce reasonable approximations. **Discuss** whether Kozlov is correct in general and whether he is correct in this specific situation. **Support** your conclusions with reference to specifics of the account. No additional calculations are required.

(2 minutes)

Chong next reviews the issue of selecting valid benchmarks for portfolio performance analysis. She has identified the Wilshire 5000 as the suitable market proxy (M) for account 179E but needs to determine a style benchmark (B) for the manager of the account. She has defined the portfolio return as being composed of: M (market return), S (style = M – B), and A (manager value added). To determine a suitable benchmark, she has analyzed three possible benchmarks and regressed their returns with the manager's value added. The results are shown in Exhibit 3.

Exhibit 3

Benchmark	Value added (P – B)	Correlation of A to S
1	1.23%	0.75
2	0.97%	−0.04
3	1.83%	−0.89

C. **Determine** the most appropriate style benchmark for portfolio 179E and **support** your conclusion.

(3 minutes)

Kozlov wishes to perform attribution analysis on account 263. Account 263 is a balanced account and is composed of two sub accounts: 263E is managed by the firm's equity team and 263B by the fixed income team. He first reviews macro attribution analysis for the last quarter shown in Exhibit 4.

Exhibit 4 (in millions)

Asset category	Beginning value	Ending value	Net cash flow	Return	Benchmark return
Domestic equity	23.45	14.67	−10.82	8.97%	9.53%
Fixed income	4.92	16.49	+9.75	17.63%	15.33%
Total	28.37	31.16	−1.07	14.79%	n.a.

D.   **Determine** which investment team or teams (equity or fixed income) added value to the portfolio during the period. **Support** your conclusions with calculations.

(4 minutes)

Chong next reviews the micro attribution data of another account, 56E. That data is shown in Exhibit 5.

Exhibit 5

	Weight		Return %	
Sector	*Portfolio*	*Benchmark*	*Portfolio*	*Benchmark*
Industrials	0.176	0.197	4.50	6.70
Consumer	0.453	0.483	6.71	7.52
Finance	0.222	0.134	5.99	6.57
Energy	0.149	0.186	3.22	−4.59
Total portfolio	1.00	1.00	n.a.	4.98

E.
   i.   **Compute** the total value added by the manager.
   ii. **Compute** pure sector allocation effect.
   iii. **State** which within-sector decisions added value and which reduced value (no computations are required for part iii).

(9 minutes)

F. Kozlov reviews the data and computations for account 56E and points out the actual return for the account was 0.15% higher than just computed. Assuming all of the numbers computed are correct, **explain** what the additional 15 b.p. represents.

(3 minutes)

EXAM 1 AFTERNOON SESSION
TOPIC BREAKDOWN

Question	Topic	Minutes
1–6	Ethical and Professional Standards	18
7–12	Ethical and Professional Standards	18
13–18	Portfolio Management – Institutional/GIPS	18
19–24	Global Bonds and Fixed Income Derivatives and Risk Management Applications of Derivatives	18
25–30	Management of Active and Passive Fixed Income Portfolios and Global Bonds and Fixed Income Derivatives	18
31–36	Global Bonds and Fixed Income Derivatives	18
37–42	Alternative Investments	18
43–48	Portfolio Management – Individual	18
49–54	Risk Management Applications of Derivatives	18
55–60	Execution of Portfolio Decisions: Monitoring and Rebalancing	18
	Total	180

EXAM 1 SELECTED RESPONSE ITEM SET ANSWER SHEET

The afternoon session of the Level III exam contains 10 Selected Response Item Sets, each with six questions, and you must answer them by filling in a bubble sheet with a number 2 or HB pencil. For realism, we suggest that you use this answer sheet and darken the bubbles corresponding to your answers. This sheet will also facilitate entering your answers into our online Performance Tracker. You have 180 minutes for this session of the exam. That equates to 3 minutes per item set question, so budget your time well.

1.	(A) (B) (C)	31.	(A) (B) (C)
2.	(A) (B) (C)	32.	(A) (B) (C)
3.	(A) (B) (C)	33.	(A) (B) (C)
4.	(A) (B) (C)	34.	(A) (B) (C)
5.	(A) (B) (C)	35.	(A) (B) (C)
6.	(A) (B) (C)	36.	(A) (B) (C)
7.	(A) (B) (C)	37.	(A) (B) (C)
8.	(A) (B) (C)	38.	(A) (B) (C)
9.	(A) (B) (C)	39.	(A) (B) (C)
10.	(A) (B) (C)	40.	(A) (B) (C)
11.	(A) (B) (C)	41.	(A) (B) (C)
12.	(A) (B) (C)	42.	(A) (B) (C)
13.	(A) (B) (C)	43.	(A) (B) (C)
14.	(A) (B) (C)	44.	(A) (B) (C)
15.	(A) (B) (C)	45.	(A) (B) (C)
16.	(A) (B) (C)	46.	(A) (B) (C)
17.	(A) (B) (C)	47.	(A) (B) (C)
18.	(A) (B) (C)	48.	(A) (B) (C)
19.	(A) (B) (C)	49.	(A) (B) (C)
20.	(A) (B) (C)	50.	(A) (B) (C)
21.	(A) (B) (C)	51.	(A) (B) (C)
22.	(A) (B) (C)	52.	(A) (B) (C)
23.	(A) (B) (C)	53.	(A) (B) (C)
24.	(A) (B) (C)	54.	(A) (B) (C)
25.	(A) (B) (C)	55.	(A) (B) (C)
26.	(A) (B) (C)	56.	(A) (B) (C)
27.	(A) (B) (C)	57.	(A) (B) (C)
28.	(A) (B) (C)	58.	(A) (B) (C)
29.	(A) (B) (C)	59.	(A) (B) (C)
30.	(A) (B) (C)	60.	(A) (B) (C)

Exam 1
Afternoon Session

Questions 1–6 relate to Ethical and Professional Standards.

Rowan Brothers is a full-service investment firm offering portfolio management and investment banking services. For the last 10 years, Aaron King, CFA, has managed individual client portfolios for Rowan Brothers, most of which are trust accounts over which King has full discretion. One of King's clients for whom he has full discretion is Shelby Pavlica, a widow in her late 60s whose husband died and left assets of over $7 million in a trust. The assets are to be used solely for her benefit.

Pavlica's three children are appalled at their mother's spending habits and have called a meeting with King to discuss their concerns. They inform King that their mother is living too lavishly to leave much for them or Pavlica's grandchildren upon her death. King acknowledges their concerns and informs them that, on top of her ever-increasing spending, Pavlica has recently been diagnosed with a chronic illness, a fact previously not known by her children.

Since the diagnosis could indicate a considerable increase in medical spending, he will need to increase the risk of the portfolio to generate sufficient return to cover the medical bills and spending and still maintain the principal. King restructures the portfolio accordingly and then meets with Pavlica a week later to discuss how he has altered the investment strategy, which was previously revised only three months earlier in their annual meeting.

During the meeting with Pavlica, King explains his reasoning for altering the portfolio allocation but does not mention the meeting with Pavlica's children. Pavlica agrees that it is probably the wisest decision and accepts the new portfolio allocation adding that she will need to tell her children about her illness so they will understand why her medical spending requirements will increase in the near future. She admits to King that her children have been concerned about her spending. King assures her that the new investments will definitely allow her to maintain her lifestyle and meet her higher medical spending needs.

One of the investments selected by King for Pavlica's portfolio is a private placement offered to him by a brokerage firm that often makes trades for King's portfolios. The private placement is an equity investment in ShaleCo, a small oil exploration company. In order to make the investment, King sold

sdd VNC to buy ShaleCo

shares of a publicly traded biotech firm, VNC Technologies. King also held shares of VNC, a fact that he has always disclosed to clients before purchasing VNC for their accounts. An hour before submitting the sell order for the VNC shares in Pavlica's trust account, King placed an order to sell a portion of his position in VNC stock.

By the time Pavlica's order was sent to the trading floor, the price of VNC had risen, allowing Pavlica to sell her shares at a better price than received by King.

Although King elected not to take any shares in the private placement, he purchased positions for several of his clients, for whom the investment was deemed appropriate in terms of the clients' objectives and constraints as well as the existing composition of the portfolios. In response to the investment support, ShaleCo appointed King to their board of directors. Seeing an opportunity to advance his career while also protecting the value of his clients' investments in the company, King gladly accepted the offer. King decided that since serving on the board of ShaleCo is in his clients' best interest, it is not necessary to disclose the directorship to his clients or his employer.

NO

For his portfolio management services, King charges a fixed-percentage fee based on the value of assets under management. All fees charged and other terms of service are disclosed to clients as well as prospects. In the past month, however, Rowan Brothers has instituted an incentive program for its portfolio managers. Under the program, the firm will award an all-expense-paid vacation to the Cayman Islands for any portfolio manager who generates two consecutive quarterly returns for his clients in excess of 10%. King updates his marketing literature to ensure that his prospective clients are fully aware of his compensation arrangements.

1. In discussing Pavlica's spending and medical condition with Pavlica's children, did King violate any CFA Institute Standards of Professional Conduct?
    A. No. Because the children are the remaindermen, King is obligated to manage the trust in the best interest of both Pavlica and the children.
    B. Yes, because he violated his client's confidentiality.
    C. Yes, because he created a conflict of interest between himself and his employer.

2. In reallocating the portfolio after the meeting with Pavlica's children, did King violate any CFA Institute Standards of Professional Conduct?

    A. No, because King has discretion over the portfolio.
    B. Yes, he violated Standard III(A) Loyalty, Prudence, and Care.
    C. No, because he had a reasonable basis for making adjustments to the portfolio.

✓ 3.   In his statements to Pavlica after the reallocation, did King violate any CFA Institute Standards of Professional Conduct?

A. No.
B. Yes, because he misrepresented the expected performance of the strategy.
C. Yes, because he met with her before their annual meeting, which is unfair to clients who only meet with King annually.

✓ 4.   Did King's actions with regard to allocating the private placement and the sale of VNC stock violate any CFA Institute Standards of Professional Conduct?

	Private placement	VNC sale
A.	Yes	Yes
B.	No	No
C.	No	Yes

✓ 5.   According to the CFA Institute Standards of Professional Conduct, which of the following statements is *most correct* concerning King's directorship with ShaleCo?

A. King may not accept the directorship because it creates a conflict of interest.
B. King may accept the directorship as long as it is disclosed to clients and prospects.
C. King may accept the directorship as long as it is disclosed to his employer, clients, and prospects.

✗ 6.   Does the fee structure at Rowan Brothers and King's disclosure of the compensation structure violate any CFA Institute Standards of Professional Conduct?

(A)

	Fee structure	Disclosure
A.	No	Yes
B.	Yes	No
C.	No	No

4/6

Questions 7–12 relate to Ethical and Professional Standards.

Garrett Keenan, CFA, is employed by Gold Standard Bank (GSB), in the Capital Markets Division. The GSB Board of Directors has recently made two decisions: a leveraged co-invest fund is to be created for the benefit of senior-level employees of GSB, and a hedge fund is to be constructed which will be marketed to high net worth Trust Department clients and prospects. Both of the new entities will be fund-of-funds (FOF) managed on behalf of GSB by "third party" managers that Keenan will select.

Keenan first researched the available pool of hedge fund managers, and compiled a report on a subset that was based primarily on historical performance record. The 60 managers selected for further review were tiered into three groups according to their three-year track record. Of the 20 managers in the highest performing tier, Keenan selected 15 managers for the employee leveraged co-invest FOF. The other five managers in the top tier were selected along with the 20 hedge fund managers in the second tier for the FOF to be marketed to high net worth trust clients.

While screening hedge fund managers, Keenan came across his college friend, John Carmichael, one of the principals at the hedge fund management firm Bryson Carmichael (BC). Because BC's track record met Keenan's criteria for inclusion in one of the FOFs, BC was selected. Upon being informed of this development, Carmichael called Keenan to express his appreciation, and during that conversation, offered Keenan the use of Carmichael's mountain house resort. Over the next year, Keenan and his family spent two long weekends at Carmichael's mountain house. In appreciation for his stay, Keenan promised to take Carmichael's two children to Walt Disney World (free of charge) during their planned upcoming summer vacation (assuming Keenan's wife can take time off from her independent medical practice). Carmichael accepted this invitation, but was told by Keenan to keep the invitation confidential.

Another hedge fund manager being considered for inclusion was Barry Grant. Grant had been actively soliciting investors for his hedge fund and offered to pay Keenan a personal fee of $200 if Keenan accepted Grant's fund into one of GSB's FOFs. Because Grant's fund performance was within Keenan's acceptable guidelines, Keenan refused to accept the fee. However, Keenan told Grant that if his fund were able to beat the benchmark return by at least 1% during the first annual measurement period, he would be happy to accept his one-time fee. Keenan later mentioned this arrangement to his direct supervisor during their weekly meeting.

Once Keenan had finished the manager selection process, he was asked to offer a training seminar to the Trust Department's sales force. In that training, Keenan reviewed the agreed upon forms of compensation that the hedge funds would receive: a) a 2% fee on assets under management, and b) 20% of the returns over a high water mark. While the sales force was instructed to inform prospective FOF clients that "past performance is no guarantee of future results," Keenan recommended that the sales force emphasize positive rather than negative aspects of the fee earned on returns over the high water mark. Keenan said, "Your clients should not worry about the managers failing to outperform each year, because the profits on returns over the high water mark are how they make their real money." Keenan also instructed the sales force to emphasize the combined number of CFA charterholders on the management teams of the hedge funds in the FOF and provide a factual description of the requirements to become CFA charterholders.

As a matter of good business, GSB's compliance procedures require a quarterly review of all managers for performance assessment, style drift, and strategy changes. One year after the funds' formation, such a review showed that Carmichael's fund had by far the worst one-year return. After the review, Keenan removed the second worst performing hedge fund from the employees' leveraged co-invest FOF, but decided to give Carmichael's firm one more quarter to improve performance. As a replacement for the fund Keenan removed from its FOF, he selected a new hedge fund which invested in companies that fund managers believed were likely takeover candidates.

7. During his initial selection of the managers for the two FOFs, which of the following Standards did Keenan *least likely* violate?
   A. *Independence and Objectivity.*
   B. *Performance Presentation.*
   C. *Fair Dealing.*

8. By accepting the use of John Carmichael's mountain house, Keenan:
   A. violated the *Diligence and Reasonable Basis* Standard.
   B. violated the *Independence and Objectivity* Standard.
   C. did not violate a Standard.

9. Assuming that Grant's fund beats the benchmark return by 1.5% the first year and Keenan receives the $200 fee, the *Additional Compensation Arrangement* Standard was:
   A. not violated because the amount of the one-time fee was not material.
   B. not violated because Keenan disclosed the fee arrangement to his supervisor.
   C. violated as Keenan failed to get the written consent from Grant and his supervisor.

10. In his presentation to the bank Trust Department sales force, Keenan:
    A. violated the *Misrepresentation* Standard by describing the hedge funds' fee structure as a mechanism for delivering better returns.
    B. violated the *Misrepresentation* Standard by mentioning the number of CFA charterholders on the FOF management teams.
    C. was in compliance with the Standards.

11. As a result of the first year review and resulting change in fund managers, did Keenan violate the following Standard(s)?

	Misconduct	Loyalty to Employer
A.	Yes	Yes
B.	Yes	No
C.	No	Yes

12. By including the new fund with the takeover strategy in the FOF, Keenan:
    A. violated the *Market Manipulation* Standard.
    B. violated the *Suitability* Standard.
    C. did not violate any Standards.

Questions 13–18 relate to Portfolio Management for Institutional Investors and GIPS.

Jack Rose and Ryan Boatman are analysts with Quincy Consultants. Quincy provides advice on risk management and performance presentation to pension plans, insurance firms, and other institutional portfolio managers throughout the United States and Canada.

Rose and Boatman recently attended a meeting with one of their larger pension plan clients. In the meeting, the client asked them to review several proposals that might change the risk to the client of offering retirement plans. In reviewing the client's proposals, Rose and Boatman make the following statements.

- Rose: Both defined benefit and defined contribution plans carry similar risk to the sponsoring company and obligate the company to make contributions to benefit the participating employees of the company.
- Boatman: Cash balance and ESOP plans are also similar in that they are an exception to the general aversion to investing plan assets in the stock of the sponsor.

At the same meeting, Boatman discusses the client's traditional asset only approach to the pension plan and recommends the client adopt an asset/liability management (ALM) approach to the plan. Boatman explains the following.

1. While the plan may have maximized the portfolio's Sharpe ratio, this can still leave the surplus excessively vulnerable to a change in interest rates.

2. ALM is superior because it allows Monte Carlo simulation (MCS) to analyze how the portfolio will perform over various time periods while asset only management cannot use MCS.

3. An asset only approach often overinvests in equities while ALM frequently underinvests in real rate bonds.

Rose also has two insurance company clients. One company offers life insurance and the other offers property and casualty insurance. Rose instructs his new assistant to research some of the differences between these two types of insurance companies. The assistant begins by reviewing some terminology he has not worked with before.

- The crediting rate (the actuarially assumed rate of return necessary to meet policyholder obligations) portion of portfolio return is generally not taxed for either life or property and casualty companies.
- The underwriting cycle for property and casualty companies refers to the swing in profitability as interest rates fluctuate, coupled with a mismatch in asset and liability durations.

X
- Compared to property and casualty companies, life insurance companies have greater exposure to inflation risk and the policy payouts they will make in a given year are more predictable.

Quincy Consultants has been retained by Monroe Portfolio Managers for advice regarding performance presentation and GIPS compliance. Monroe is a large firm offering a variety of investment styles with a complex organizational structure. To meet legal requirements of some key clients, each of the four primary investment teams at Monroe is a legal entity. The teams are:

- Equity: The unit has its own investment staff and is responsible for all equity portfolios and composites. Many accounts are balanced and portfolio management decisions are made jointly by a fixed income and equity team manager. For client presentations, either manager may be designated as the client portfolio manager, but actual decisions are made jointly.
- Fixed Income: The unit has its own investment staff and is responsible for all fixed income portfolios and composites. All equity and fixed income investment decisions are the responsibility of Monroe's investment policy committee (IPC). The IPC is made up of members from both teams.
- Real Estate and Private Equity each have their own investment staff but report to a single chief investment officer (CIO), who is responsible for the investment decisions. Their CIO is completely independent of the IPC.

All four units share the same non-investment support staff and back office.

Rose and Boatman next discuss the performance presentation standards for real estate and private equity portfolios. Discussing the differences between the general provisions of the GIPS standards and those for real estate and private equity portfolios, Rose states the following:

Statement 1: The GIPS general provisions require valuation in accordance with the definition of fair value and the GIPS valuation ✓ principles. Real estate portfolios can be valued quarterly, but all real estate investments must be valued at least annually by an independent third party qualified to perform such valuations.

Statement 2: In addition to a minimum of annual valuations, private equity provisions require the annualized since-inception internal rate of return (SI-IRR) using daily cash flows. Stock distributions must be considered cash flows.

Statement 3: In presentations for real estate composites, firms are required to disclose their definition of discretion as well as their internal valuation methodologies for the most recent period presented. In addition, for real estate closed-end composites, firms must present the since-inception paid-in capital and since-inception distributions for each year.

Statement 4: The GIPS real estate requirements state that the income return and capital return must be calculated separately.

13. Which of the two statements by Rose and Boatman are *correct*?
   A. Only Rose's statement.
   B. Only Boatman's statement.
   C. Neither statement is correct.

14. Which of Boatman's comments comparing asset only with ALM is *most likely* correct?
   A. Statement 1.
   B. Statement 2.
   C. Statement 3.

15. Which of the assistant's three comments regarding terminology is *most correct*? The comment regarding:
   A. crediting rate.
   B. underwriting cycle.
   C. inflation risk and policy payouts.

16. Which of the following combinations of Monroe's teams would be *most appropriate* as a firm for GIPS reporting?
   A. Equity as a separate firm.
   B. Equity and Fixed Income combined as one firm.
   C. Equity, Fixed Income, Real Estate, and Private Equity combined as one firm.

17. Determine whether Rose's statements 1 and 2 on the GIPS standards are correct or incorrect.
   A. Only statement 1 is correct.
   B. Only statement 2 is correct.
   C. Both statements are correct.

18. Determine whether Rose's statements 3 and 4 on the GIPS standards are correct or incorrect.
   A. Only statement 3 is correct.
   B. Only statement 4 is correct.
   C. Both statements are correct.

Questions 19–24 relate to Management of Active and Passive Fixed Income Portfolios, Portfolio Management of Global Bonds and Fixed Income Derivatives, and Risk Management Applications of Derivatives.

Daniel Castillo and Ramon Diaz are chief investment officers at Advanced Advisors (AA), a boutique fixed-income firm based in the United States. AA employs numerous quantitative models to invest in both domestic and international securities.

During the week, Castillo and Diaz consult with one of their investors, Sally Michaels. Michaels currently holds a $10,000,000 fixed-income position that is selling at par. The maturity is 20 years, and the coupon rate of 7% is paid semiannually. Her coupons can be reinvested at 8%. Castillo is looking at various interest rate change scenarios, and one such scenario is where the interest rate on the bonds immediately changes to 8%.

Diaz is considering using a repurchase agreement to leverage Michaels's portfolio. Michaels is concerned, however, with not understanding the factors that impact the interest rate, or repo rate, used in her strategy. In response, Castillo explains the factors that affect the repo rate and makes the following statements:

1. "The repo rate is directly related to the maturity of the repo, inversely related to the quality of the collateral, and directly related to the maturity of the collateral. U.S. Treasury bills are often purchased by Treasury dealers using repo transactions, and since they have high liquidity, short maturities, and no default risk, the repo rate is usually quite low."

2. "The greater control the lender has over the collateral, the lower the repo rate. If the availability of the collateral is limited, the repo rate will be higher."

Castillo consults with an institutional investor, the Washington Investment Fund, on the effect of leverage on bond portfolio returns as well as their bond portfolio's sensitivity to changes in interest rates. The portfolio under discussion is well-diversified, with small positions in a large number of bonds with an average duration of 7.2. Of the $200 million value of the portfolio, $60 million was borrowed. The duration of borrowed funds is 0.8. The expected return on the portfolio is 8% and the cost of borrowed funds is 3%.

The next day, the chief investment officer for the Washington Investment Fund expresses her concern about the risk of their portfolio, given its leverage. She inquires about the various risk measures for bond portfolios. In response, Diaz distinguishes between the standard deviation and downside risk measures, making the following statements:

1. "Portfolio managers complain that using variance to calculate Sharpe ratios is inappropriate. Since it considers all returns over the entire distribution, variance and the resulting standard deviation are artificially inflated, so the resulting Sharpe ratio is artificially deflated. Since it is easily calculated for bond portfolios, managers feel a more realistic measure of risk is the semi-variance, which measures the distribution of returns below a given return, such as the mean or a hurdle rate."

2. "A shortcoming of VAR is its inability to predict the size of potential losses in the lower tail of the expected return distribution. Although it can assign a probability to some maximum loss, it does not predict the actual loss if the maximum loss is exceeded. If Washington Investment Fund is worried about catastrophic loss, shortfall risk is a more appropriate measure, because it provides the probability of not meeting a target return." ✗

AA has a corporate client, Shaifer Materials with a €20,000,000 bond outstanding that pays an annual fixed coupon rate of 9.5% with a 5-year maturity. Castillo believes that euro interest rates may decrease further within the next year below the coupon rate on the fixed rate bond. Castillo would like Shaifer to issue new debt at a lower euro interest rate in the future. Castillo has, however, looked into the costs of calling the bonds and has found that the call premium is quite high and that the investment banking costs of issuing new floating rate debt would be quite steep. As such, he is considering using a swaption to create a synthetic refinancing of the bond at a lower cost than an actual refinancing of the bond. He states that in order to do so, Shaifer should buy a payer swaption, which would give Shaifer the option to pay a lower floating interest rate if rates drop.

Diaz retrieves current market data for payer and receiver swaptions with a maturity of one year. The terms of each instrument are provided below:

Payer swaption fixed rate	7.90%
Receiver swaption fixed rate	7.60%
Current Euribor	7.20%
Projected Euribor in one year	5.90%

Diaz states that, assuming Castillo is correct about falling interest rates, Shaifer can exercise a swaption in one year to effectively call in their old fixed rate euro debt paying 9.5% and refinance at a floating rate, which would be 7.5% in one year.

? ✓ 19. Calculated in bond equivalent yield terms, Michaels's return over the next year, if interest rates change as expected, is *closest* to:
A. 2.56%.
B. −2.56%.
C. 3.50%.

X 20. Determine whether each of Castillo's statements about repos is correct or incorrect.
(c)
A. Statement 1 is correct.
B. Statement 2 is correct.
C. Neither statement is correct.

✓ 21. If the Washington Investment Fund portfolio earns the expected 8% over the next year, its net return will be *closest* to:
A. 7.14%.
B. 10.14%.
C. 11.00%.

X 22. The leveraged duration on the Washington Investment Fund portfolio is *closest* to:
(c)
A. 6.4.
B. 8.0.
C. 9.9.

$7.2 - 0.8 = 6.4$

$D_P P = D_E E + D_B B$

$(7.2)(200) = D_E(140) + 0.7(60)$

$9.9 = D_E$

✓ 23. Regarding the statements made by Diaz about downside risk measures, are the statements correct?
A. Only statement 1 is correct.
B. Only statement 2 is correct.
C. Neither statement is correct.

✓ 24. Regarding their statements concerning the synthetic refinancing of the Shaifer Materials fixed rate euro debt, are the statements correct?
A. Only Castillo is correct.
B. Only Diaz is correct.
C. Both Castillo and Diaz are incorrect.

4/6

©2016 Kaplan, Inc.

Questions 25–30 relate to Management of Active and Passive Fixed Income Portfolios and Portfolio Management of Global Bonds and Fixed Income Derivatives.

Ellen Truxel is a principal at Truxel Investment Management. Her firm uses bonds for income enhancement as well as capital gains. She occasionally uses sector-quality bets and yield curve positioning to exploit her beliefs on the relative changes in sector credit quality and the direction of interest rates. She has recently hired John Timberlake to assist her in preparing data for the analysis of bond portfolios. Timberlake is a recent graduate of an outstanding undergraduate program in finance.

Truxel is considering investing in international bonds, as this is an arena she has previously ignored. During conversations:

- Truxel says it is her understanding that changes in international bond markets have made it easier to manage the duration of an international bond portfolio.
- Timberlake notes that the European Monetary Union has increased the availability of corporate bonds, making it easier to rotate across sectors.

In the domestic arena, Truxel is considering constructing a portfolio that matches the index on quality, call, sector, and cash flow dimensions and tilts the portfolio duration by moderate amounts to take advantage of predictions of yield curve shifts.

- Truxel states that this would be referred to as enhanced indexing with minor mismatches. ✗
- Timberlake states that her relative performance may also depend on her ability to perform credit analysis. ✓

Truxel then tells Timberlake that before they venture into new areas, she wants him to prepare an analysis of their current positions. Timberlake obliges and presents the following data on Truxel's current portfolio.

Bond Rating	Percent Weight in Truxel Portfolio	Sector Effective Duration	Percent Weight in Index Portfolio
AAA	12%	5.3 = 0.636	35%
AA	30%	5.4 = 1.62	30%
A	30%	5.5 = 1.65	25%
BBB	28%	5.0 = 1.4	10%
		5.306	

25. Regarding the conversation on the attributes of international bond investing, are Truxel and Timberlake correct or incorrect?
    A. Both are correct.
    B. Neither is correct.
    C. Only Timberlake is correct.

✓ 26. Regarding the conversation on domestic bond portfolio management, are Truxel and Timberlake correct or incorrect?

~~A.~~ Both are correct.

B. Neither is correct.

Ⓒ Only Timberlake is correct.

✓ 27. Given a parallel shift in the yield curve of 60 basis points for Treasury yields, the percentage change in the value of the Truxel portfolio is *closest* to:

Ⓐ 3.2.   5.306 ~~××××~~ 0.6 = 3.2

B. 3.4.

C. 5.3.

✓ 28. If the OAS for all bond sectors changes by 60 basis points while Treasury yields remain unchanged, the approximate percent change in the Truxel portfolio is *closest* to:

Ⓐ 3.2.

B. 3.4.

C. 5.3.

✗ 29. If the OAS for all bond sectors changes by 100 basis points while Treasury yields remain unchanged, which sector or sectors would contribute the most to tracking error for Truxel's portfolio?

(B)

A. BBB.

B. AAA.

Ⓒ AA and A, which contribute about the same.

✓ 30. In evaluating relative valuation methodologies, which of the following rationales for trading in the secondary bond market is *least* appropriate?

A. Cash flow reinvestment.

B. New issue swaps.

Ⓒ Seasonality.

Questions 31–36 relate to Portfolio Management of Global Bonds and Fixed Income Derivatives.

Mark Rolle, CFA, is the manager of the international bond fund for the Ryder Investment Advisory. He is responsible for bond selection as well as currency hedging decisions. His assistant is Joanne Chen, a candidate for the Level I CFA Exam.

Rolle is interested in the relationship between interest rates and exchange rates for Canada and Great Britain. He observes that the spot exchange rate between the Canadian dollar (C$) and the British pound is C$1.75/£. Also, the 1-year interest rate in Canada is 4.0% and the 1-year interest rate in Great Britain is 11.0%. The current 1-year forward rate is C$1.60/£.

Rolle is evaluating the bonds from the Knauff company and the Tatehiki company, for which information is provided in the table below. The Knauff company bond is denominated in euros and the Tatehiki company bond is denominated in yen. The bonds have similar risk and maturities, and Ryder's investors reside in the United States.

Return on Knauff bond in euros	8.00%
Risk-free rate in the European Union	5.00%
Expected change in the euro relative to the U.S. dollar	−1.20%
Return on Tatehiki bond in yen	6.00%
Risk-free rate in Japan	2.00%
Expected change in the yen relative to the U.S. dollar	2.00%
Risk-free rate in United States	4.80%

[handwritten annotations: "3%" beside risk-free rate in the European Union; "4%" beside risk-free rate in Japan]

Provided this information, Rolle must decide which country's bonds are most attractive if a forward hedge of currency exposure is used. Furthermore, assuming that both countries' bonds are bought, Rolle must also decide whether or not to hedge the currency exposure.

Rolle also has a position in a bond issued in Korea and denominated in Korean won. Unfortunately, he is having difficulty obtaining a forward contract for the won on favorable terms. As an alternative hedge, he has entered a forward contract that commits him to sell yen in one year, when he anticipates liquidating his Korean bond. His reason for choosing the yen is that it is positively correlated with the won.

One of Ryder's services is to provide consulting advice to firms that are interested in interest rate hedging strategies. One such firm is Crawfordville Bank. One of the certificates of deposit (CDs) Crawfordville has outstanding is a jumbo CD requiring the payment of LIBOR plus 150 basis points. The chief financial officer at Crawfordville is worried that interest rates may

[handwritten notes in right margin:]

$$\text{Spot} = \frac{C\$1.75}{£}$$

Can = 4.0%
GB = 11.0%

$$F_0 = \frac{1.60}{£}$$

$$1.75 \times \frac{0.04}{0.11} = 1.6396$$

increase and would like to hedge this exposure. Rolle is contemplating either an interest rate cap or an interest rate floor as a hedge.

Additionally, Rolle is analyzing the best hedge for Ryder's portfolio of fixed-rate coupon bonds. Rolle is contemplating using either a call or a put on T-bond futures. *IRT, bond Price ↓*

31. Given the current forward rate of C\$1.60/£, the exact forward premium or discount for the £ against the C\$ is *closest* to:
   A. –9.37%.
   B. –8.57%.
   C. 8.57%.

32. Assume that Rolle is managing a U.S. based portfolio and that Rolle predicts the CAD and GBP will appreciate 2% and depreciate 2%, respectively, versus the USD. In order to maximize return, Rolle would *most likely* recommend hedging the currency exposure on:
   A. CAD bond investments.
   B. GBP equity investments.
   C. Neither currency.

33. Assuming Rolle uses forward contracts to effectively hedge the currency risk of either bond investment, determine which bond is the better investment.
   A. The Knauff bond because its return is 8.0%.
   B. The Tatehiki bond because its excess return is 4.0%.
   C. The Knauff bond because its excess currency return is 3.2%.

34. Calculate the expected return for both bonds if Rolle uses forward contracts to hedge the currency risk of the Knauff company bond and leaves the Tatehiki company bond unhedged.

	Knauff bond	Tatehiki bond
A.	6.8%	8.1%
B.	6.8%	8.8%
C.	7.8%	8.1%

35. The hedge that Rolle uses to hedge the currency exposure of the Korean bond is *best* referred to as a:
   A. proxy hedge.
   B. forward hedge.
   C. minimum variance hedge ratio.

36. The *best* hedges of the Crawfordville position and the Ryder portfolio are:

	Crawfordville	Ryder
A.	Cap	Call
B.	Cap	Put
C.	Floor	Call

Handwritten margin notes:
$$\frac{K}{8 + (4.8 - 5)} = 7.8\%$$
$$\frac{T}{6 + 2} = 8\%$$
5/6

Questions 37–42 relate to Alternative Investments for Portfolio Management.

Cynthia Farmington, CFA, manages the Lewis family's $600 million securities portfolio. Farmington and the Lewis family have agreed that they should hire a manager of alternative investments to manage a portion of the portfolio containing those assets. As part of the hiring process, they attempted to perform the necessary due diligence. They assessed each manager's organization, the relative efficiency of the markets each manager has invested in, the character of each manager, and the service providers, such as lawyers, that each manager has used. In particular, they hoped to find a manager who has run an operation with low employee turnover, has invested in efficient and transparent markets, has sound character, and has utilized reputable providers of external services.

Eventually, Farmington hires the firm owned and managed by Bruce Carnegie, CFA, to diversify the Lewis portfolio into alternative investments. Carnegie will manage the portion of the portfolio containing these assets, and Farmington will continue to manage the remainder of the portfolio in a mix of approximately 50/50 high-grade stocks and bonds. Over the past ten years, the stock portion of the portfolio has closely tracked the S&P 500 and the bond portfolio has closely tracked a broad bond index.

Carnegie and Farmington meet to discuss how Carnegie should proceed. Farmington mentions that she and the Lewis family have agreed that the main goal of alternative investments that Carnegie will manage in the $600 million securities portfolio should be to enhance the return of the overall portfolio. Diversification is only a secondary goal. In particular, Farmington says the Lewis family has expressed an interest in having the portfolio take positions in private equity. Farmington says that she envisions that Carnegie should take five positions of about $5 million each in distinct private equity investments, and each position should have a short time horizon of about two years.

Farmington states that she has grown very dependent on benchmarks for her investing activities, and she has concerns with respect to how she and Carnegie will monitor the success of the portfolio allocation in private equity. She has read that there can be a problem with the valuation of private equity indices in that they depend on price-revealing events like IPOs, mergers, and new financing. Thus, the repricing of the index occurs infrequently. Carnegie concludes that the solution is to follow the commonly accepted practice of creating their own private equity benchmark.

Farmington asks Carnegie to explain the choices that exist in the private equity market. Carnegie explains that there are two basic categories: venture capital funds and buyout funds. Farmington asks that Carnegie explain the pros and cons of one over the other. Carnegie states that although buyout funds would probably have lower return potential, they tend to have fewer losses, earlier cash flows, and less error in the measurement of the returns.

Carnegie comments that before he proceeds he will need to communicate with the clients. Farmington says this communication is not necessary because the Lewis family has largely followed her advice with very few questions. Even when the market has fallen and the portfolio has not done well, the Lewis family has not asked for any changes.

X 37. With respect to the criteria that Farmington used to choose a manager
(B) of alternative assets, which of the following is not a due diligence checkpoint? Finding a manager who:
A. has low staff turnover.
B. invests only in efficient and transparent markets.
C. has stable providers of external services.

X 38. Given that Farmington states that increased return is more important
(B) than diversification, the choice to focus on private equity is:
A. not appropriate because private equity offers good diversification, but the returns are comparatively low.
B. appropriate because private equity offers a high return but relatively low diversification.
C. appropriate because private equity offers both a high return and good diversification.

V 39. Regarding Farmington's recommended private equity allocations and time horizon, which of her guidelines is *least* appropriate?
A. The horizon is too short.
B. Too few positions for proper diversification.
C. Too much invested given the size of the overall portfolio.

V 40. With respect to the issue of benchmarks, Farmington made an observation concerning the potential problem with benchmarks, and Carnegie offered a solution. With respect to their discussion, are Farmington and Carnegie correct or incorrect?
A. Only Farmington is correct.
B. Only Carnegie is correct.
C. Both are correct.

X 41. Regarding Carnegie's statement comparing buyout funds to venture
(A) capital funds, the statement is true:
A. even though venture capital funds tend to have lower average returns than buyout funds.
B. with regard to mega-cap buyout funds only, because middle-market buyout funds' returns tend to be delayed.
C. with regard to middle-market buyout funds only, because mega-cap buyout funds' returns tend to be more uncertain.

X

42.

(c)

With respect to the special issues that an alternative investment manager should address with a private wealth client, from the conversation between Farmington and Carnegie, Carnegie will need to discuss all of the following with the possible exception of:

A. tax issues.

B. other closely held investments.

C. decision risk.

Questions 43–48 relate to Private Wealth Management.

Bill Ogilvey, CFA, manages money for clients residing in various countries. Some of them reside in countries that do not currently have tax-advantaged accounts. Ogilvey keeps current on the tax laws to be able to quickly advise his clients if and when new tax-advantaged accounts become available.

Ogilvey often counsels his clients with regard to how they should manage their investment accounts for tax purposes. One of his newest clients, Tilly Beamer, lives in a country with a tax regime that has a flat rate for ordinary income, dividends, and capital gains, but provides favorable treatment for interest income. Her portfolio is in a taxable account and is equally allocated among interest-paying assets, dividend-paying assets, and non-dividend-paying growth stocks.

Flat

Beamer is interested in Ogilvey's advice about her retirement planning and which tax-advantaged account(s) would be most beneficial to her. Beamer is young and her income is modest, but she has a high degree of job security and expects her income to increase dramatically over the upcoming ten years. Her objective is to fund a retirement income approximately equal to her wage income at retirement. She is specifically concerned with managing her risk exposure and wonders how a planned reduction in her portfolio risk will affect her expected returns, investment time horizon, and tax drag.

Ogilvey has another client, Steven Vance, who lives in a country with a heavy capital gains tax regime. The current tax law in Vance's country does not provide for tax-advantaged accounts, but that is expected to change, as tax-exempt accounts may soon become available.

To fund a new tax-exempt account, Vance will need to sell some stock, and he is concerned with the ramifications of reorganizing gains. In specific, Vance has a position in TTT stock, which he accumulated over several years at successively higher prices. If this position is liquidated, taxes will be payable on his investment gains. He asks Ogilvey his advice concerning the best way to handle the sale of the shares and how to measure the tax consequences of realizing the gains.

X 43.　The tax regime in Beamer's country can be *best* classified as:
(A)
　　A. Flat and Heavy.
　　(B) Flat and Light.
　　C. Heavy Capital Gain Tax.

✓ 44.　Assume that Beamer's interest paying assets are held in a taxable
　　account. The account is currently worth €1,000,000, the pretax interest
　　income is 7%, and the tax rate, assessed annually, is 25%. If there are
　　no deposits or withdrawals from this account and compounding is
　　annual, in 15 years the value of the account will be approximately:
　　A. €2,069,274.
　　(B) €2,154,426.
　　C. €2,759,032.

$$\left(1 + 0.07 \times (1-0.25)\right)^{15} \times 1,000,000$$

X 45.　Beamer's plan to reduce her investment risk will *most likely*:
? (c)
　　A. decrease her investment horizon because the resulting tax drag will
　　　　be less than the applicable tax rate.
　　(B) increase her investment horizon but result in tax drag that is less
　　　　than the applicable tax rate.
　　C. increase both her investment horizon and result in tax drag that
　　　　exceeds the applicable tax rate.

✓ 46.　Assume that Vance sells some of his TTT stock. The pretax return on the
　　TTT stock averaged 12% per year over 10 years, the capital gains tax rate
　　is 35%, and the cost basis is $250,000. <u>What is the after-tax gain on the
　　investment?</u>
　　A. $254,700.
　　(B) $342,200.
　　C. $592,200.

$$250,000 \times 1.12^{10} = 776,462 - 250,000 = 526,462$$
$$\times 35\%$$
AT Gain $\boxed{342,200}$
$$+ 250,000$$
$$\overline{592,200}$$

X 47.　Which of the following is *closest* to the percentage tax drag Vance will
(B)
　　experience with sale of the TTT stock?
　　(A) 25%.
　　B. 35%.
　　C. 40%.

$$\frac{776,462}{250,000} = 3.1058^{0.1} = 12\%$$

$$\left(\frac{592,200}{250,000}\right)^{0.1}$$
$$= 9.01\%$$

✓ 48.　Suppose that Vance's after-tax proceeds on his TTT stock sale were
　　$150,000, his cost basis was $60,000, the pre-tax return was 13%, and
　　the holding period was 9 years. The <u>accrual equivalent after-tax return is
　　closest</u> to:
　　(A) 10.7%.
　　B. 17.7%.
　　C. 27.8%.

$$\left(\frac{150,000}{60,000}\right)^{\frac{1}{9}} - 1 =$$

(3/6)

Questions 49–54 relate to Risk Management Applications of Derivatives.

Elkridge Inc., based in St. Paul, Minnesota, is one of the largest manufacturers and distributors of baby care products in the U.S. The company recently filled two new senior level investment strategist positions by hiring Andrea Willow and Craig Townsend directly out of graduate school. While both Willow and Townsend have similar strengths, they have very different outlooks on the markets, including the short-term outlook. Willow firmly believes that the stock market is poised to increase, but is pessimistic about the bond market. In contrast, Townsend is optimistic about the bond market, but feels that stocks are overbought and about to correct.

As part of their first major assignment, Willow and Townsend have been asked to analyze and evaluate two of Elkridge's major investment portfolios. Exhibit 1 provides statistics on Portfolio 1, an actively managed portfolio, along with data on six-month S&P futures and bond futures contracts which the company is considering as a means to manage portfolio risk.

Exhibit 1. Portfolio 1 and Futures Contracts

Portfolio 1 (Actively Managed)	
Size	$168 million
Allocation	70% stocks, 30% bonds
Beta (stock portion)	0.85
Target Modified Duration (bond portion)	4.3
Effective Duration (Cash equivalents and any hedged positions)	0.25
6-month S&P Futures	
Current Price	1526.00
Beta	0.92
Multiplier	250
6-month Bond Futures	
Current Price	96,500
Implied Modified Duration	5.2
Yield Beta	0.94

Exhibit 2 provides statistics on Portfolio 2 and the terms of a potential swap (Swap A) that Elkridge is interested in using to lower the portfolio's modified duration.

Exhibit 2. Portfolio 2 and Swap Contract

Portfolio 2	
Size	$96 million
Allocation	100% bonds
Modified Duration	6.3
Target Modified Duration	4.5
Swap A	
Tenor	1 year **3**
Payment Frequency	Quarterly
Long Float Duration	0.125
Short Fixed Duration	0.875 **2.625**

In reviewing Portfolio 1, Willow recommends using 187 S&P futures contracts to adjust portfolio beta to 1.41 to take advantage of projected stock market increases. Also reviewing Portfolio 1, Townsend would like to see the company reallocate its holdings to 55% stocks and 45% bonds by using bond futures contracts to capitalize on his projections for bond market increases.

Six months later, the bond futures contract price has fallen 6%. Over that same time, the stock market has risen 2.2%, the stocks in Portfolio 1 have generated a total return of $2,199,120, and the S&P futures contracts are priced at 1547.00. However Willow is surprised to find the effective beta (realized hedged beta) did not meet her target of 1.41. She and Townsend discuss possible reasons this could have happened:

Reason 1. The beta of her stocks showed mean reversion.

Reason 2. The futures contract was initially mispriced.

Willow and Townsend then formulate two hypothetical situations with identical facts except:

Situation 1. Purchase 6-month contracts to increase equity exposure by $10,000,000 (not a synthetic position).

Handwritten notes:
168mm × 0.7 = 117,600,000
2,199,120
1.87%
1.87/2.2 = 0.85
1547−1526 = 21 × 250 = 5,250 × 187 = 981,750
2199120 + 981,750 = 3,180,870 / 117mm = 2.7/2.2 = 1.23

Situation 2.   The $10,000,000 will not be received for 6 months and the contracts are being purchased to create a $10,000,000 synthetic position.

Among its liabilities, Elkridge has a $50 million floating-rate bond issuance outstanding with coupons paying LIBOR + 1% (resetting semiannually). The firm would like to pay a fixed rate instead and is looking at engaging in a $50 million notional, 4-year, semi-annual swap (Swap B) where it would receive LIBOR.

49.   Assume the company had followed Willow's recommendation for Portfolio 1. Calculate effective beta and determine which of the two reasons for effective beta diverging from the target is *most likely*?

Effective Beta	Reason
A. 0.87	1
B. 1.23	1
C. 1.23	2

50.   Assume that Elkridge has followed Townsend's advice. Using the data and assumptions in Exhibit 1, after six months, the loss on the bond futures position is *closest* to:
   A. $1,105,890.
   B. $1,175,370.
   C. $1,250,640.

51.   Suppose Elkridge considers futures contract transactions to implement the strategies espoused by Willow and Townsend. A potential goal (means) of these transactions and the individual strategist's viewpoint supported by that goal would be to:
   A. decrease target beta by selling stock futures, as supported by Willow.
   B. increase stock exposure by buying stock futures, as supported by Townsend.
   C. increase modified duration by buying bond futures, as supported by Townsend. ✔

52.   The number of contracts purchased for Situation 2 compared to Situation 1 would *most likely* be:
   A. greater.
   B. equal.
   C. less.

✓ 53. In regard to its floating-rate bond issuance, in what direction must Elkridge feel interest rates are moving and what fixed rate will it pay on Swap B to have a net cost of funds of 7.25%?

	Rate Direction	Fixed Rate
A.	Fall	8.25%
B.	Rise ✓	6.25%
C.	Rise	8.25%

(B. is circled)

? 54. Extending the tenor of Swap A to three years, assuming a short fixed duration of 2.625, would result in a notional principal of:

A. $69,120,000.
B. $76,800,000.
C. $230,400,000.

(A. is circled)

$$\frac{4.5 - 6.3}{2.625}$$

---

(50) 70/30 → 55/45   B↑15% × 168 = 25,200,000

$$\frac{5.2 - \varnothing}{4.3} \quad \frac{4.3 - \varnothing}{5.2} \times \frac{25,200,000}{96,500} \times 0.94 = 205 \text{ contracts}$$

$$96,500 \times (1 - 0.06) = \$90,710$$

$$\text{Loss} = 5,790 \times 205 = 1,175,370$$

(5/6)

Questions 55–60 relate to Execution of Portfolio Decisions: Monitoring and Rebalancing.

Wealth Management's top economist, Frederick Milton, is an economic cycle forecaster. Milton's economic forecasts indicate an economic upswing that will impact all goods and services sectors. Milton presents his economic findings to the rest of Wealth Management's professionals at their monthly meeting. All are excited about Milton's forecast of an improving economic condition that should translate into a steadily rising stock market.

Nathaniel Norton and Timothy Tucker have confidence in Milton's capabilities and decide to meet with their clients. Their first meeting is with Elizabeth Mascarella to whom Norton recommends a dynamic asset allocation strategy to take advantage of Milton's forecast. However, Mascarella is concerned because the somewhat persistent back-and-forth of economic activity has translated into an oscillating stock market. Mascarella questions Norton's recommendation and asks Tucker which strategy should be followed if the market continues as it has, instead of making such "wonderful" strides.

It is one year later and Frederick Milton's economic forecast has been correct, and the market has trended upward as expected. Mascarella's strategic allocation to equity, which was $600,000 of a total portfolio of $1,000,000, has increased 20%. Her overall portfolio, which contains equity, debt, and some cash, is now valued at $1,150,000. Tucker meets with Mascarella and indicates it may be time to rebalance her portfolio.

55. Assuming a steadily rising market, the *best* strategy for Mascarella is:
    A. buy and hold.
    B. constant mix.
    C. constant proportion portfolio insurance.

56. Determine the preferred dynamic rebalancing strategy if the market is expected to be highly volatile, but more or less flat.
    A. Buy and hold.
    B. Constant mix.
    C. Constant proportion portfolio insurance.

57. Which of the following statements about CPPI strategies is probably *least* correct?
    A. CPPI strategies represent the purchase of portfolio insurance because they buy stocks as they rise and sell them as they fall.
    B. CPPI strategies offer good upside potential because they increase exposure to risky assets as the market rises.
    C. Due to the concave nature of CPPI strategies, they offer good downside protection.

✓ client

58. ✓ Mascarella has instructed Tucker to rebalance annually to maintain a corridor of ± 5% for equity. Given the constraint, Tucker should:
   A. reallocate approximately $70,000 of the increase in equity to debt and cash.
   B. reallocate the entire $120,000 increase in equity to debt and cash.
   C. make no adjustments.

(handwritten notes, right margin)
orig = 60% equity
= 600,000
New = 600 × 1.2 = 720,000
$\frac{720,000}{1,150,000}$ = 62.6%

59. ✓ Tucker has tried to make Mascarella understand the benefits of percentage-of-portfolio rebalancing relative to calendar rebalancing. Which of the following statements made by Tucker is probably *least* correct?
   A. Calendar rebalancing provides discipline while requiring less monitoring. ✓
   B. Percentage-of-portfolio rebalancing minimizes the amount by which the allocations stray from their strategic levels. ✓
   C. Combining calendar and percentage of portfolio rebalancing would be the most costly.

60. ✓ Which of the following would generally suggest a narrower tolerance band?
   A. Assets in the portfolio tend to be illiquid.
   B. Highly volatile assets.
   C. Correlated portfolio assets.

(handwritten, circled) 6/6

END OF AFTERNOON SESSION

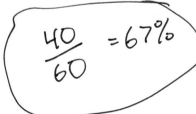

(handwritten, circled) $\frac{40}{60}$ = 67%

Practice Exam 2 Morning Session Question Breakdown

Question	Topic	Minutes
1	Private Wealth Management	21
2	Behavioral Finance and Portfolio Management – Institutional	27
3	Fixed Income and Equity Portfolio Management and Alternative Investments	10
4	Economic Analysis	28
5	Equity Portfolio Management	23
6	Asset Allocation	22
7	Portfolio Management – Institutional	14
8	Global Investment Performance Standards	12
9	Performance Evaluation and Attribution	14
10	Portfolio Management – Institutional and Equity Portfolio Management	9
	Total	180

Practice Exam 2 Score Sheet

MORNING SESSION		
Question	Maximum Points	Your Estimated Score
1A	3	2
1B	4	4
1C	6	5
1D	4	4
1E	4	2
2A	6	
2B	11	
2C	10	
3	10	
4A	5	
4B	4	
4C	5	
4D	8	
4E	6	
5A	4	
5B	7	
5C	12	
6A	9	
6B	7	
6C	6	
7	14	
8	12	11
9A	8	8
9B	3	
9C	3	
10A	6	
10B	3	
Total	180	

AFTERNOON SESSION		
Question	Maximum Points	Your Estimated Score
1–6	18	
7–12	18	
13–18	18	
19–24	18	
25–30	18	
31–36	18	
37–42	18	
43–48	18	
49–54	18	
55–60	18	
Total	180	

Exam 2
Morning Session

QUESTION 1 HAS FIVE PARTS FOR A TOTAL OF 21 MINUTES

LT Horizon

Barney Smythe, 40, and his wife Heather, 39, are considering what to do with a recent windfall they received after the untimely death of Heather's mother. The windfall is estimated to be $2,500,000 (after taxes). Barney is currently a supervising mechanic at a local luxury car dealership and has a salary of $48,750 annually. Heather has been a stay-at-home mom since she was injured. The Smythes have two children, Lenny, 12, and Buford, 10. By design, the Smythes owe no debt and pay their expenses on a monthly basis. Family expenses last year amounted to approximately $150,000.

- Age 40, 39
- $2.5mm inheritance
- $1.25mm cash
- Salary (48,750)
- Expenses (150,000)
- 2 kids (12, 10)

In addition to the inheritance they will receive, the Smythes have an additional $1,250,000 in cash equivalents. The savings are what remain from a large settlement the Smythes received when Heather was injured on the job five years ago. Barney and Heather have approached Net Worth Enhancers, PC, for assistance in managing their portfolio. The Smythes made the following statements at a recent client discovery meeting:

- "One of our goals at this stage in our lives is to pay for the college education of our children. We would like both of them to go to Heather's alma mater, which is a prestigious liberal arts institution."
- "We expect our annual expenses to increase at the general rate of inflation of 2%."

  Inflation = 2%
- "We want to retire at 65 and be able to live comfortably, but not extravagantly."

  Retire @ 65
- "We are taxed at 25% on both income and capital gains."
- "We believe our portfolio should never suffer an annual loss of more than 5%. In addition, we do not want to invest in any individual investment or security that is too risky."
- "We do not foresee any unusual expenses over the short term. As always, we would like to have enough cash on hand for emergencies."

A.   **Determine** the Smythes' willingness to take risk and justify your answer with *two* reasons based on their situation.

(3 minutes)

B.   **Justify** with *one* reason *each* why the Smythes' have higher and lower ability to take risk based on their situation.

(4 minutes)

C.   **State** the Smythes' return objective(s) and **calculate** the required after-tax nominal return for the coming year.

(6 minutes)

D. **Determine** the Smythes' liquidity needs and time horizon.

(4 minutes)

E. **Justify** whether the Smythes *most likely* have high or low needs for life insurance and annuities at this time. Consider *each* insurance product separately.

(4 minutes)

QUESTION 2 HAS THREE PARTS FOR A TOTAL OF 27 MINUTES

Matrix Corporation is a multidivisional company with operations in energy, telecommunications, and shipping. Matrix sponsors a traditional defined benefit pension plan. Plan assets are valued at $5.5 billion, while recent declines in interest rates have caused plan liabilities to balloon to $8.3 billion. Average employee age at Matrix is 57.5, which is considerably higher than the industry average, and the ratio of active to retired lives is 1:1. Joe Elliot, Matrix's CFO, has made the following statement about the current state of the pension plan.

Underfunded

Age > industry avg

Active : retired = 1 (high)

"Recent declines in interest rates have caused our pension liabilities to grow faster than ever experienced in our long history, but I am sure these low rates are temporary. I have looked at the charts and estimated the probability of higher interest rates at more than 90%. Given the expected improvement in interest rate levels, plan liabilities will again come back into line with our historical position. Our investment policy will therefore be to invest plan assets in aggressive equity securities. This investment exposure will bring our plan to an over-funded status, which will allow us to use pension income to bolster our profitability."

A. **Critique** Elliot's statement with respect to investing Matrix's plan assets by addressing the following three points:

    i. The behavioral fallacy Elliot is most likely exhibiting is: illusion of control, myopic loss aversion, or sample size neglect.
    ii. Plan risk and return objectives.
    iii. Using pension plan income to bolster firm profitability.

(6 minutes)

B.   Based on the information provided, **formulate** a return objective and a risk objective for the Matrix Corporation pension plan. (No calculations required.)

Answer Question 2-B in the template provided.

(11 minutes)

Template for Question 2-B

Investment Policy Statement for Matrix Corporation	
Risk	
Return	

C.   Based on the information provided, **formulate** an appropriate constraints section for the investment policy statement for the pension fund.

Answer Question 2-C in the template provided.

(10 minutes)

Template for Question 2-C

Constraints	Time Horizon	
	Liquidity	
	Legal/ Regulatory	
	Taxes	
	Unique	

©2016 Kaplan, Inc.

QUESTION 3 HAS ONE PART FOR A TOTAL OF 10 MINUTES

John Carpenter is considering using fixed income securities, hedge funds, and international stocks as vehicles for his more wealthy clients. Before doing so, he consults with Tom McKnealey, who is president of Benchmark Associates, a firm that specializes in the construction of benchmarks for portfolio managers. During a meeting with Carpenter, McKnealey makes the following statements about the proper construction of benchmarks for fixed income, hedge fund, and international stock portfolio managers:

- "The popularity bias can cause problems for measuring value-weighted hedge fund benchmark performance. The popularity bias argues that out-performing hedge funds as well as hedge fund styles tend to attract additional funding, so as they grow in popularity their performance tends to have a greater and greater impact on the value-weighted index's measured performance. This creates a double impact on the value-weighted hedge fund index return; the individual funds have good returns, and their increasing size means they have a greater weight in the index. The result is that the index's return has an upward bias. This bias, however, can be counteracted by utilizing two indices, one long and one short. Since most hedge fund managers attempt to generate alpha through both long and short positions, they can have a net zero weight or even a net negative weight. A single, long-only benchmark will not capture the performance of both strategies."

- "If an investor is averse to market value risk, the bond benchmark used should have a long maturity so they can lock in a yield to maturity."

- "The recommended solution to the 'free float' problem in international markets is to determine the amount of shares to be floated by an issuer in the upcoming year and use that to recalculate the issuer's weight in market capitalization weighted indices."

- "For bond investors such as foundations who desire a stable stream of income, long-term bond benchmarks should be used."

Determine which of McKnealey's statements are correct or incorrect, and if incorrect, **justify** your response.

Answer Question 3 in the template provided.

(10 minutes)

Template for Question 3

Comment	Is this statement correct or incorrect? (circle one)	Explanation, if incorrect
✓ "The popularity bias can cause problems for measuring value-weighted hedge fund benchmark performance. The popularity bias argues that out-performing hedge funds as well as hedge fund styles tend to attract additional funding, so as they grow in popularity their performance tends to have a greater and greater impact on the value-weighted index's measured performance. This creates a double impact on the value-weighted hedge fund index return; the individual funds have good returns, and their increasing size means they have a greater weight in the index. The result is that the index's return has an upward ✓ bias. This bias, however, can be counteracted by utilizing two indices, one long and one short. Since most hedge fund managers attempt to generate alpha through both long and short positions, they can have a net zero weight or even a net negative weight. A single, long-only benchmark will not capture the performance of both strategies."	Correct Incorrect	

Comment	Is this statement correct or incorrect? (circle one)	Explanation, if incorrect
"If an investor is averse to market value risk, the bond benchmark used should have a long maturity so they can lock in a yield to maturity."	Correct Incorrect	
"The recommended solution to the 'free float' problem in international markets is to determine the amount of shares to be floated by an issuer in the upcoming year and use that to recalculate the issuer's weight in market capitalization weighted indices."	Correct Incorrect	
"For bond investors such as foundations who desire a stable stream of income, long-term bond benchmarks should be used."	Correct Incorrect	

QUESTION 4 HAS FIVE PARTS FOR A TOTAL OF 28 MINUTES

William Barkley and David McFalls are economists for Irvington Advisors, a U.S.-based firm. Irvington provides independent economic and investment advice to portfolio managers, research analysts, and others.

Barkley has compiled the following data for equity returns in an emerging market:

	Normal conditions, 80% probability	*High volatility conditions, 20% probability*	*Unconditioned expectations, 80/20 average*
Risk-free rate	3%	4%	3.20%
Estimated world market risk premium	8%	−5%	5.40%
Beta	1.1	1.3	1.14
Estimated emerging market return	3 + 1.1(8) + 1 = 12.80%	4 + 1.3(−5) + 1 = −1.5%	9.94
Alpha	1%	1%	1%

A.   McFalls points out that there is a problem in Barkley's analysis. McFalls calculates the expected unconditioned return estimate as 3.20 + 1.14(5.40) + 1 = 10.36%. **Explain** how systematic and unsystematic risk are reflected in Barkley's analysis. **Comment** on the implications of this issue.

(5 minutes)

B. Barkley has found it difficult to gather data on alternative investments for emerging markets. He has been able to estimate an initial value 10 years ago and a current value. He is confident in both numbers, and he assumes income returns are evenly distributed throughout the 10-year period. **Explain** how smoothing and regime change could affect his expected return and risk estimates derived from the data.

(4 minutes)

McFalls has gathered the following data for another emerging market. He has selected time periods for historical data he believes are relevant to future conditions.

	Historical Data	*Current Conditions*	*Expected Conditions*
A rated government bond yield	6.8%	4.8%	
Average equity market total return	9.5%	Past 12 months: 2.1%	
Average inflation	4.5%	Past 12 months: 2.5%	3.3%
Average P/E	12.5	13.5	13.2
Average dividend yield	2.5%		1.7%
Average real economic growth	6.2%		4.1%

C.

    i.   **Calculate** the historical equity risk premium and use it to calculate the appropriate equity discount rate based on current bond market conditions.

         (2 minutes)

    ii. **Calculate** the equity risk premium and the appropriate expected equity return based on Grinold-Kroner assuming a 1% reduction in shares outstanding.

         (3 minutes)

McFalls sees the variations in estimated equity return produced by various models as an opportunity and decides to use business cycle analysis to gage the relative attractiveness of the equity market. He gathers economic data for the last four years with year 4 the oldest data and year 1 the most recent.

	Year			
Economic Indicator	*4*	*3*	*2*	*1*
Inflation	1.80%	1.75%	2.0%	2.5%
Consumer confidence index	0	−0.1	+1.1	+2.5
Inventory, % change	−1%	1.1%	3.4%	9.3%
30 − 1 year government bond yield	1.1%	2.7%	2.5%	0.1%
Unemployment	6.5%	5.5%	4.5%	4.0%

D.   **Determine**, based on business cycle analysis, whether the outlook for the equity market is favorable or unfavorable and **support** your conclusion with three reasons.

         (8 minutes)

Barkley and McFalls are discussing alternative approaches to forecasting markets and exchange rate movements.

Statement 1: Barkley states that if interest rates in country A exceed those in country B by 3% and real rates in both countries are equal, then the currency of country B is likely to appreciate.

A > B

Statement 2: McFalls states that under those same conditions, the currency of country A should appreciate.

Statement 3: Both agree that countries with higher real growth, inflation, and savings deficits have an incentive to maintain the value of their currency.

E. **State** and **explain** why each statement is most likely consistent with the purchasing power parity (PPP), relative economic strength (RES), or savings-investment imbalances (SII) approach to forecast exchange rate movements. Each statement must have a different label, and each label must be used only once.
(6 minutes)

QUESTION 5 HAS THREE PARTS FOR A TOTAL OF 23 MINUTES

Aaron Bell, a portfolio manager, is focusing his attention on investment style, and whether style should be a factor in investment decision making. Bell decides to play it safe and investigate how he can use different instruments related to style indices or indexing strategies to see if he can add value to his customers' portfolios.

A.   **Explain** holdings-based style analysis. **Discuss** *one* disadvantage and *one* advantage of holdings-based style analysis over returns-based style analysis.

(4 minutes)

B.   **Explain** returns-based style analysis. **Reproduce** the general form of the regression equation used for returns-based style analysis, including any constraints, and label *each* component of the equation. **Discuss** *one* disadvantage and *one* advantage of returns-based style analysis over holdings-based style analysis.

(7 minutes)

C.   Bell is considering indexing strategies and a colleague has suggested three alternatives: full replication; stratified sampling; and optimization. **Explain** *each* along with the conditions under which each would be appropriate to use and provide *one* disadvantage for *each*.

(12 minutes)

QUESTION 6 HAS THREE PARTS FOR A TOTAL OF 22 MINUTES

Wyatt Washington is the portfolio manager for Mark Beitia, a recent retiree. He is currently exploring a change in Beitia's strategic asset allocation. He gathers data on the expected returns, standard deviations, and correlations for five assets. Using these market expectations, he derives an efficient frontier. Washington uses the following information in his construction of the asset allocation:

- Beitia's asset base = $5,000,000.
- Expected annual after-tax spending amount = $150,000.
- Estimate of future inflation = 3.5%.
- Beitia will donate $750,000 to his alma mater over the coming year in one lump sum.
- Risk-free rate = 4.0%.
- Beitia's tax rate = 25%.
- Beitia's risk aversion value = 5.0.

Washington and Beitia discuss appropriate tax assumptions for the portfolio. There will be no tax benefit for the donation; however, they expect some tax sheltering by deferring gains and through tax location of assets. For the initial analysis, they assume the component of return equal to inflation will not be subject to tax.

Washington forms four corner portfolios from his efficient frontier and calculates the following expected returns and standard deviations:

Corner Portfolio	Expected Before Tax Return	Expected Std. Dev.	Sharpe Ratio	Weights in assets 1 to 5				
				1	2	3	4	5
1	6.50%	4.10%	0.610	0%	20%	80%	0%	0%
2	7.75%	5.80%	0.647	0%	15%	85%	0%	0%
3	9.70%	7.80%	0.731	60%	10%	30%	0%	0%
4	13.50%	10.60%	0.896	100%	0%	0%	0%	0%

A.   **Calculate** the required before-tax return for Beitia's portfolio and Beitia's expected utility from holding each of the corner portfolios.

(9 minutes)

B.   Assuming that Washington combines two corner portfolios to meet Beitia's desired return (calculated in Part A), **calculate** the weights of the appropriate corner portfolios that will be used (assume no borrowing or short-selling) and the resulting portfolio standard deviation.

(7 minutes)

C.   Assuming that Washington combines a corner portfolio with the risk-free asset to meet Beitia's desired return (calculated in Part A), **calculate** the weights of the appropriate corner portfolio and the risk-free asset that will be used (assume no borrowing) and the resulting portfolio standard deviation.

(6 minutes)

QUESTION 7 HAS ONE PART FOR A TOTAL OF 14 MINUTES

A1 Casualty, Inc. writes property and casualty insurance policies for individuals, homeowners, and small businesses located in the Southeastern portion of the United States. For the last three years, market forces have caused A1 to more competitively price their policies to increase underwriting volume. This competitive pricing environment coincides with a somewhat slowing general business cycle. Two months ago, a massive hurricane hit the panhandle of Florida and southeast Alabama, causing unprecedented damages to property. Approximately 50% of A1's homeowners' policies are written in that geographic region, but as of yet, claims processing has been much less than expected from the area. Stan Carnay, A1's CEO, has been busy preparing the latest investment portfolio report for the Board of Directors' meeting in two weeks and has asked Eileen Carlyle, CFA, A1's most recent addition to the investment group, for assistance in updating a decades-old investment policy statement. In preliminary discussions, Carlyle indicated the following:

(margin note: Higher return target →)

- "Underwriting activity, although somewhat improved over the past decade, has not been as profitable as expected during the last three years. The competitive marketplace in which we operate has directly impacted our ability to profitably price our insurance products."

- "We should count our blessings that so few claims from the recent hurricane have been submitted. Actuarial estimates indicate our potential exposure from this weather event is approximately $75 million, which represents 75% of our surplus portfolio. Since claim submission has been almost non-existent, we can transition our investment portfolio into a greater proportion of common stock, taking our stock to surplus ratio from 90% to close to 100%. That action should help strengthen our long-term competitive position."

(margin note: Long tail risk)

- "Recent economic conditions have slowed, but numerous other comparable casualty companies are optimistic that economic conditions will improve over the next 9 to 12 months. Although market economists continue forecasting a slightly longer downturn in the national economy, we consider those forecasts overly pessimistic."

Without using calculations, **formulate** an investment policy statement appropriate for A1.

Answer Question 7 in the template provided.

(14 minutes)

Template for Question 7

Investment Policy Statement for A1 Casualty	
Objectives	Return Objectives
	Risk Tolerance
Constraints	Time Horizon
	Liquidity
	Legal/Regulatory
	Taxes
	Unique Circumstances

QUESTION 8 HAS ONE PART FOR A TOTAL OF 12 MINUTES

Bailey Investments is a U.S.-based investment management firm. The firm and composite began operations on January 1, 2009. Their client base has grown considerably over the last few years and in order to ensure accurate and consistent performance data they have decided to pursue GIPS® compliance. The following includes composite data and notes relating to the first presentation for one of their composites in which they claim GIPS compliance.

Year	Total Return (%)	Benchmark Return (%)	Number of Portfolios	Composite Dispersion (%)	Total Firm Asset ($ millions)
2010	6.54	7.25	15	2.5	86
2011	8.74	9.25	19	3.2	135
2012	9.45	8.67	28	4.1	276
2013	7.53	7.45	35	4.5	332

Bailey Investments claims compliance with the Global Investment Performance Standards (GIPS®) and has prepared and presented this report in compliance with the GIPS Standards.

Notes:

1. Valuations are obtained by Reuters and computed using the U.S. dollar.

2. Bailey Investments is a dedicated equity portfolio manager that invests entirely in U.S. securities and has no affiliates.

3. The benchmark composition is 100% S&P 500. The annualized compound benchmark return is 8.15%. The annualized compound composite return is 8.06%.

4. Composite dispersion is the annualized monthly standard deviation of composite returns.

5. No modifications to the composites as presented here have occurred as a result of changes in personnel or for any other reason at any time.

6. Performance results are presented before management and custodial fees but after all trading commissions.

7. The composite includes discretionary and non-discretionary fee-paying portfolios.

List *four* non-compliant items in the presentation. For *each*, **state** the necessary corrective action.

Answer Question 8 in the template provided.

(12 minutes)

Template for Question 8

Errors in presentation and corrective action.
1.
2.
3.
4.

QUESTION 9 HAS THREE PARTS FOR A TOTAL OF 14 MINUTES

One year has passed since HNW Advisors first started operations. Their overall equity portfolio has returned 28.2% versus a return of 22.4% for the S&P 500. The standard deviation of the S&P 500 is 20%, and Maggie Day, CFA, has estimated the standard deviation of HNW Advisor's equity portfolio at 45%. HNW Advisor's equity portfolio has a beta of 1.35, and the risk-free rate is 4.4%.

A major HNW client is attempting to evaluate the relative performance of HNW's equity fund. The client is unsure whether the Sharpe measure or the Treynor measure is appropriate for the HNW portfolio.

A.   Using the Sharpe and Treynor measures for the HNW portfolio and the S&P 500, **compute** how HNW has performed relative to the S&P 500.

(8 minutes)

B.   Day also performs a similar analysis on another portfolio. The other portfolio has a slightly positive alpha but significantly underperforms based on the M^2 ratio. **Explain**, in terms of systematic and unsystematic risk, what these ratios indicate.

(3 minutes)

[handwritten margin notes:]

S+P
Return - 22.4%
θ = 20%

HNW
Return = 28.2%
θ = 45%
b = 1.35

rf = 4.4%

C. **Compute** M^2 for the HNW portfolio. **Explain**, in terms of relative returns and volatility, the circumstances under which M^2 for HNW would equal M^2 for the market.

(3 minutes)

QUESTION 10 HAS TWO PARTS FOR A TOTAL OF 9 MINUTES

Tom Groh is the President of Opportunity Banks. Opportunity has historically operated in the northeastern United States, with most of its business in Maryland, Delaware, and New Jersey. Opportunity has been in business since 1987 and has built its business on making mortgages and construction loans to residential developers. Opportunity has been very profitable, because developers value the services the bank provides. This allows Opportunity to price their construction loans with higher interest rates. Opportunity services and retains ownership of the its loans. It historically has had a near-zero leverage-adjusted duration gap.

In the most recent fiscal year, Opportunity has experienced important changes in their business as follows:

1. Due to pressure from local activists, Opportunity has stepped up lending in low-income areas. Groh expects the default rate on these loans to be higher than the loans currently in their portfolio.

2. Opportunity has bought a regional bank with operations in North Carolina, South Carolina, and Georgia. The acquired bank's loan portfolio consists mostly of commercial loans to small, local businesses.

3. A recent downturn in interest rates has caused many of Opportunity's variable rate mortgages to be refinanced to 15- and 30-year fixed-rate mortgages. Opportunity has retained the business of most of its customers who have refinanced.

A. In each of the scenarios provided, **determine** *one* effect on the risk objective of the bank's security portfolio. **Evaluate** *each* scenario in isolation from the others.

Answer Question 10-A in the template provided.

(6 minutes)

Template for Question 10-A

Scenario	Effect on Securities Portfolio Policies
1. Due to pressure from local activists, Opportunity has stepped up lending to low-income areas. Groh expects the default rate on these loans to be higher than the loans currently in their portfolio.	
2. Opportunity has bought a regional bank with operations in North Carolina, South Carolina, and Georgia. The acquired bank's loan portfolio consists mostly of commercial loans to small, local businesses.	
3. A recent downturn in interest rates has caused many of Opportunity's variable rate mortgages to be refinanced to 15- and 30-year fixed rate mortgages. Opportunity has retained the business of most of its customers who have refinanced.	

B.   Groh is advising one of the bank's clients on the management of the client's family trust. Previously the family trust hired a portfolio manager whose fee was a fixed 1% of assets. The family is now considering another portfolio manager who is paid a lower fixed 0.30% of assets but also charges 20% of any excess return above their benchmark. **Discuss** *one* advantage and *two* disadvantages of the new manager's fee structure.

(3 minutes)

END OF MORNING SESSION

EXAM 2 AFTERNOON SESSION
TOPIC BREAKDOWN

Question	Topic	Minutes
1–6	Ethics and Professional Standards	18
7–12	Ethics and Professional Standards	18
13–18	Management of Active and Passive Fixed Income Portfolios, Portfolio Management of Global Bonds and Fixed Income Portfolios, and Risk Management Applications of Derivatives	18
19–24	Portfolio Management of Global Bonds and Fixed Income Derivatives and Risk Management	18
25–30	Management of Active and Passive Fixed Income Portfolios and Portfolio Management of Global Bonds and Fixed Income Derivatives	18
31–36	Alternative Investments for Portfolio Management	18
37–42	Portfolio Management of Global Bonds and Fixed Income Derivatives, Equity Portfolio Management, and Risk Management Applications of Derivatives	18
43–48	Management of Active and Passive Fixed Income Portfolios, Risk Management, and Risk Management Applications of Derivatives	18
49–54	Execution of Portfolio Decisions: Monitoring and Rebalancing	18
55–60	Portfolio Management of Global Bonds and Fixed-Income Derivatives and Performance Evaluation and Attribution	18
	Total	180

Exam 2 Selected Response Item Set Answer Sheet

The afternoon session of the Level III exam contains 10 Selected Response Item Sets, each with six questions, and you must answer them by filling in a bubble sheet with a number 2 or HB pencil. For realism, we suggest that you use this answer sheet and darken the bubbles corresponding to your answers. This sheet will also facilitate entering your answers into our online Performance Tracker. You have 180 minutes for this session of the exam. That equates to 3 minutes per item set question, so budget your time well.

#					#			
1.	A	B	C		31.	A	B	C
2.	A	B	C		32.	A	B	C
3.	A	B	C		33.	A	B	C
4.	A	B	C		34.	A	B	C
5.	A	B	C		35.	A	B	C
6.	A	B	C		36.	A	B	C
7.	A	B	C		37.	A	B	C
8.	A	B	C		38.	A	B	C
9.	A	B	C		39.	A	B	C
10.	A	B	C		40.	A	B	C
11.	A	B	C		41.	A	B	C
12.	A	B	C		42.	A	B	C
13.	A	B	C		43.	A	B	C
14.	A	B	C		44.	A	B	C
15.	A	B	C		45.	A	B	C
16.	A	B	C		46.	A	B	C
17.	A	B	C		47.	A	B	C
18.	A	B	C		48.	A	B	C
19.	A	B	C		49.	A	B	C
20.	A	B	C		50.	A	B	C
21.	A	B	C		51.	A	B	C
22.	A	B	C		52.	A	B	C
23.	A	B	C		53.	A	B	C
24.	A	B	C		54.	A	B	C
25.	A	B	C		55.	A	B	C
26.	A	B	C		56.	A	B	C
27.	A	B	C		57.	A	B	C
28.	A	B	C		58.	A	B	C
29.	A	B	C		59.	A	B	C
30.	A	B	C		60.	A	B	C

Exam 2
Afternoon Session

Questions 1–6 relate to Ethical and Professional Standards.

Theresa Bair, CFA, a portfolio manager for Brinton Investment Company (BIC), has recently been promoted to lead portfolio manager for her firm's new small capitalization closed-end equity fund, the Horizon Fund. BIC is an asset management firm headquartered in Holland with regional offices in several other European countries.

After accepting the position, Bair received a letter from the three principals of BIC. The letter congratulated Bair on her accomplishment and new position with the firm and also provided some guidance as to her new role and the firm's expectations. Among other things, the letter stated the following:

> "Because our firm is based in Holland and you will have clients located in many European countries, it is essential that you determine what laws and regulations are applicable to the management of this new fund. It is your responsibility to obtain this knowledge and comply with appropriate regulations. This is the first time we have offered a fund devoted solely to small capitalization securities, so we will observe your progress carefully. You will likely need to arrange for our sister companies to buy and sell Horizon Fund shares between themselves and at no risk over the first month of operations. This will artificially support the price of the shares to allow the fund to trade closer to its net asset value, giving the perception that our fund is more desirable than other small-cap closed-end funds."

Bair heeded the advice from her firm's principals and collected information from qualified advisors on the laws and regulations of three countries: N, S, and D. Assume all of the investors in the Horizon Fund will be from these areas. Based on her research, Bair has determined:

- N allows crossing trades in the fund between firm clients even though this is prohibited between clients in D. BIC will internally match buy and sell orders between clients in N whenever possible, but not in D. This will reduce costs for clients in N whose orders are crossed and lower total fund expenses for all clients, which will benefit the fund's overall performance.

- For clients located in D, account statements that include the value of the clients' holdings, number of trades, and average daily trading volume will be generated on a monthly basis as required by D's securities regulators. Clients in N will only receive such reports quarterly as consistent with that country's requirements.
- For clients located in S, the fund will not disclose differing levels of service that are available for investors based upon the size of their investment. This policy is consistent with the laws and regulations in N. D's securities regulations do not cover this type of situation.

Three months after the inception of the fund, its market value has grown from $200 million to $300 million, and Bair's performance has earned her a quarter-end bonus. It is now the end of the quarter, and Bair is participating in conference calls with companies in her fund. Bair calls into the conference number for Sunrise Petroleum. The meeting doesn't start for another five minutes, however, and as Bair waits, she hears the CEO and CFO of Sunrise discussing the huge earnings restatement that will be necessary for the financial statement from the previous quarter. The restatement will not be announced until the year's end, six days from now. Bair does not remind the officers that she can hear their conversation.

Once the call has ended, Bair rushes to BIC's compliance officer to inform him of what she has learned during the conference call. Bair ignores the fact that two members of the firm's investment banking division are in the office while she is telling the compliance officer what happened on the conference call. The investment bankers then proceed to sell their personal holdings of Sunrise Petroleum stock. After her meeting, Bair sells the Horizon Fund's holdings of Sunrise Petroleum stock.

1. Do the suggestions in the letter from the principals of BIC violate any CFA Institute Standards of Professional Conduct?
    A. Yes, the principals are pressuring Bair to perform.
    B. Yes, the suggested trades are intended to manipulate market data in order to attract investors for the fund.
    C. No, even though Bair is responsible for knowing the laws, the compliance officer is responsible for making sure the firm is in compliance.

2. With regard to the treatment of clients in N and D, do the policies that Bair has selected regarding crossing trades and client statements for the Horizon Fund violate any CFA Institute Standards of Professional Conduct?

	N	D
A.	No	Yes
B.	Yes	No
C.	No	No

3. With regard to the treatment of clients in S, does the policy that Bair has selected regarding levels of service for the Horizon Fund violate any CFA Institute Standards of Professional Conduct?
A. Yes, Bair's policy will violate Standard III(B) Fair Dealing.
B. No, because disclosure in S would disadvantage clients residing in other countries.
C. No, because disclosure in any country would break the confidentiality that Bair owes to her clients.

4. After her conference call with Sunrise Petroleum, Bair should have:
A. included the information in a research report to make it public before selling the holdings from the Horizon Fund.
B. attempted to have Sunrise publicly disclose the earnings restatement before informing the compliance officer of the information.
C. informed the compliance officer and then publicly disclosed the information in a research report before selling the Sunrise stock.

5. By selling their personal holdings of Sunrise Petroleum, did the employees of BIC's investment banking division violate any CFA Institute Standards of Professional Conduct?
A. Yes, because they breached their fiduciary duty and were disloyal to Sunrise.
B. Yes, because they were front running the information by trading for their own benefit before BIC's clients.
C. Yes, because they knowingly traded on information that, if it had been publicly known, would have affected the price of Sunrise stock.

6. By selling the Horizon Fund's shares of Sunrise Petroleum, did Bair violate any CFA Institute Standards of Professional Conduct?
A. Yes, Bair violated Standard II Integrity of Capital Markets.
B. No, because she ensured public dissemination of the earnings restatement information before she traded the shares.
C. Yes, because waiting to trade the stock would severely disadvantage investors in her fund and would have violated her duty of loyalty to her clients.

Questions 7–12 relate to Ethical and Professional Standards.

Johnny Bracco, CFA, is a portfolio manager in the trust department of Canada National (CNL) in Toronto. CNL is a financial conglomerate with many divisions. In addition to the trust department, the firm sells financial products and has a research department, a trading desk, and an investment banking division.

Part of the company's operating procedures manual contains detailed information on how the firm allocates shares in oversubscribed stock offerings. Allocation is effected on a pro rata basis based upon factors such as the size of a client's portfolio, suitability, and previous notification to participate in IPOs. Additionally, company policy discloses to clients that any trade needs to meet a minimum transaction size in an effort to control trading costs and to comply with best execution procedures.

One of Bracco's trust accounts is the Carobilo family trust, which contains a portion of nondiscretionary funds managed by Stephen Carobilo. Carobilo has a friend who runs a brokerage firm called First Trades, to which Carobilo tells Bracco to direct trades from the nondiscretionary accounts. Bracco has learned that First Trades charges a slightly higher trading fee than other brokers providing comparable services, and he discloses this to Carobilo.

Due to high prices and limited supplies of oil, Bracco has been following companies in the energy sector. He believes this area of the economy is in turmoil and should present some mispricing opportunities. One company he has been researching is the Stiles Corporation, which is working on a new type of hydrogen fuel cell that uses fusion technology to create energy. To date, no one has been able to successfully sustain a fusion reaction for an extended period of time. Bracco has been in close contact with Stiles' pubic relations department, has toured their laboratories, and has thoroughly researched fusion technology and Stiles' competitors. Bracco is convinced from his research, based upon various public sources, that Stiles is on the verge of perfecting this technology and will be the first firm to bring it to the marketplace. Jerry McNulty, CFA and vice president of the investment banking division of CNL, has been working with Stiles to raise new capital via a secondary offering of Stiles common shares. One day Bracco happened to be in a stall in the bathroom when McNulty and a colleague came in and discussed the fact that Stiles had perfected the fuel-cell technology, which will greatly increase the price of Stiles' stock.

A routine audit by the quality control department at CNL discovered trading errors in several of Bracco's accounts involving an oversubscribed IPO. Some accounts received shares they should not have and others did not receive shares they should have. Bracco and his supervisor Jaime Gun, CFA, are taking responsibility to reverse the incorrect trades. Bracco told Gun, "I'll correct the trades based on our clients' investment policy statements, previous notification of intent, and according to the company's formula for allocating shares on a pro rata basis. In so doing, we will fairly allocate shares so even small accounts that did not meet minimum size requirements will receive some shares of the IPO." Gun adds that we must go further and credit short-term interest back to the accounts that should not have received the shares.

That evening, Bracco and his wife attended the company holiday party for CNL employees and their spouses. Jerry McNulty, whose wife was ill and could not come to the party, arrived drunk from a meeting with Stiles' upper management. During the party McNulty made inappropriate advances toward many of the female employees and joked about the inadequacies of Stiles' managers.

While cleaning up after the party, a janitor found McNulty's pocket notebook that he apparently dropped accidentally during the party. In the notebook, McNulty wrote the recommended amount and date of the secondary offering as well as several details on the nature of the new product. Not knowing exactly what to do with the notebook, the janitor gave it to Burt Sampson, CFA, a trader at CNL. Later that night, Sampson called many of his relatives and friends and told them about the upcoming offering. First thing the following Monday morning, McNulty submitted an order to buy the stock for his personal portfolio.

7.   Has Bracco violated any soft dollar standards regarding the Carobilo family trust? Bracco has:
   A. violated soft dollar standards because he did not satisfy the requirement of best execution.
   B. violated the soft dollar standards because client brokerage is to be used only for research purposes to benefit the client.
   C. not violated any soft dollar standards since Carobilo requested that the trades be sent to a specific broker.

8.   If after overhearing McNulty's conversation in the bathroom Bracco placed trades to purchase shares of the Stiles Corporation for some of his clients, would Bracco have violated any of the Standards of Professional conduct?
   A. No, because the information regarding the Stiles Corporation was not acquired in a breach of confidence.
   B. No, because he did not base the trade solely on the information he overheard.
   C. Yes, because he is not allowed to trade on material, nonpublic information.

9.   Regarding the statements made by Bracco and Gun on how to correct the trading errors:
   A. only Gun's statement is correct.
   B. only Bracco's statement is correct.
   C. both are correct or both are incorrect.

10. Did McNulty's behavior at the holiday party violate the:

	Code of Ethics?	Standards of Professional Conduct?
A.	Yes	Yes
B.	No	Yes
C.	Yes	No

11. Based solely on the information provided in the last paragraph, determine whether McNulty and/or Sampson violated the Code and Standards.

	McNulty	Sampson
A.	No	No
B.	Yes	Yes
C.	No	Yes

12. Under the provision of the Asset Manager Code (AMC), in order to minimize the likelihood of some of the recent problems, CNL must do all of the following except:
    A. establish written policies to ensurer fair and equitable trade allocation.
    B. appoint a qualified compliance officer.
    C. prohibit employees from trading in securities in which the firm has positions or investment banking relationships.

Questions 13–18 relate to Fixed Income Portfolio Management and Risk Management Applications of Derivatives.

Tiffany Morrison, CFA, a manager for Sierra Fund, is investigating the use of relative value methodologies for global corporate bond portfolio management. As a recent college graduate, Bernard Tabler has been assisting Morrison in data gathering and analysis.

Morrison is a firm believer that corporate yield spreads have a tendency to revert to their historical mean values. Accordingly, Tabler has compiled relevant information for three corporate issues. Morrison and Tabler use the information below to conduct mean reversion analysis.

Bond Issue	Current Spread	Mean Spread for Past 12 Months	Standard Deviation of Spread
VV	125	98	28
XX	100	75	15
YY	85	100	10

Note: All spreads are expressed in basis points.

Morrison's research has also included a study of the implications of secular and cyclical changes in the primary corporate bond market. As a result of her research, she states that the implication of both cyclical and secular changes in the primary corporate bond market for fixed-income portfolio management is that effective duration and aggregate interest rate risk will increase. Tabler adds that it also appears that credit-based derivatives will increasingly be used to achieve desired exposure to credit sectors, issuers, and structures.

During the presentation to a client, Morrison discusses corporate curve analysis. She states that corporate spread curves tend to change with the economic cycle, so in order to properly conduct this analysis the analyst must examine credit and yield curves carefully. Tabler adds that corporate spreads usually narrow during upturns and widen during downturns.

Morrison is also considering using repurchase agreements to fund some overnight investment activities. Watching the financial news, she observes that the Federal Reserve has increased the federal funds rate to combat potential inflation. She notes that this will increase the borrowing costs of investment strategies using repurchase agreements. Tabler chimes in that the strategy's interest cost could be reduced by using hot collateral such as on-the-run U.S. Treasuries. Morrison does not understand that comment and responds, "aren't on-the-run Treasuries in abundant supply?" Tabler correctly explains to her that due to their use in various trading strategies, the demand for on-the-run Treasuries can exceed supply and those issued can be in higher relative demand than other securities.

Morrison is providing advice to a client on the best way to hedge a floating rate loan using a swap. The client is paying 120 basis points over LIBOR. Morrison suggests that the client enter a 5-year LIBOR-based swap. The swap fixed rate is 100 basis points over the U.S. Treasury rate. The floating rate is LIBOR flat. LIBOR is 5.60% and the Treasury rate is 5.20% when this swap is being considered.

13. Based on the mean-reversion analysis only, which of the three bonds is the most attractive candidate for Morrison to purchase for the Sierra Fund?
   A. VV.
   B. XX.
   C. YY.

14. Regarding their statements on the implications of secular and cyclical changes in the primary corporate bond market, **determine** if Morrison and Tabler are correct or incorrect.
   A. Only Morrison is correct.
   B. Only Tabler is correct.
   C. Both are incorrect.

15. Over lunch, Morrison and Tabler get into a heated debate over the relative performance of callable and non-callable bonds in a dynamic interest rate environment. In terms of relative performance, determine which of the following relationships is *least* accurate.
   A. If rates are significantly greater than coupon rates, embedded call options are practically worthless, so callable bonds perform as if they are non-callable.
   B. As interest rates increase, the option to call a callable bond decreases. If required returns are below coupon rates and expected to increase, non-callable bonds are probably better investments than callable bonds.
   C. The value of a callable bond is significantly affected by the value of the embedded call option. For example, as its required return falls below (increases above) its coupon rate, the value of the embedded option consumes an increasing (a decreasing) proportion of the total value of the bond.

16. Regarding their statements on corporate curve analysis, are Morrison and Tabler correct or incorrect?
   A. Both are correct.
   B. Neither is correct.
   C. One is correct.

17. Regarding their statements on investment strategies using repurchase agreements, are Morrison and Tabler correct or incorrect?
   A. Only Morrison is correct.
   B. Only Tabler is correct.
   C. Both are correct.

18. In the swap hedge of the floating rate loan, the net fixed rate that the client will pay is *closest* to:
    A. 5.8%.
    B. 7.4%.
    C. 7.8%.

Questions 19–24 relate to Portfolio Management of Global Bonds and Fixed-Income Derivatives and Risk Management.

Carl Cramer is a recent hire at Derivatives Specialists Inc. (DSI), a small derivatives trading and consulting firm that advises a variety of institutions on the management of credit risk. Some of DSI's clients are very familiar with risk management techniques, whereas others are not. Cramer has been assigned the task of creating a handbook on credit risk, its possible impact, and its management. His immediate supervisor, Christine McNally, will assist Cramer in the creation of the handbook and will review it. Before she took a position at DSI, McNally advised banks and other institutions on the use of value at risk (VAR) as well as credit value at risk (CVAR).

In Cramer's handbook draft, he states that:

Statement 1:   VAR can be useful for pension plans because it assigns a probability to a specified loss in surplus. The portfolio manager can incorporate this in client meetings to facilitate a discussion of whether the level of risk taken is reasonable.

Statement 2:   VAR is also useful because it can easily aggregate estimates made by individual units within the firm. For example, credit analysts can determine the firm's CVAR while the firm's economic outlook determines expected change in interest rates and associated market value changes. The ability to simply combine views is a strength of decentralized risk management.

Cramer's next task is to address the basic dimensions of credit risk. Cramer states that:

Statement 3:   Current credit risk is low when the probability of default is low. However, because circumstances can change, the current credit risk is not fixed but can fluctuate over time.

Statement 4:   In contrast, potential credit risk is fixed and limited to the par value of a bond because only par can ultimately be received by the investor.

As DSI has clients with a variety of forward contracts, Cramer then addresses the credit risks associated with forward agreements. McNally encourages Cramer to include an example of credit risk and forward contracts in the handbook. She offers the following:

A 9-month forward contract sold by Palmer Securities has six months remaining until the delivery date. The initial contract price was 50. The underlying asset has no cash flows or storage costs and is now priced at 50.

Cramer realizes that many of DSI's derivative positions are OTC and determining market value and credit risk will be difficult. The credit quality of counterparties will vary widely. In addition, a wide variety of hedging transaction are available, and the area is rapidly evolving, with minimal standardization of terminology. While these risks can be measured using VAR and related techniques, he assigns McNally to propose methods that will lower risk to DSI as opposed to just measuring the risk.

A DSI client, Weaver Trading, has a bond they are concerned will increase in credit risk. Weaver has asked Cramer to recommend the most appropriate instrument to hedge this risk. Cramer assigns McNally to follow up on this question.

Later that week, Cramer and McNally visit a client's headquarters and discuss the potential hedge of a bond issued by Cuellar Motors. Cuellar manufactures and markets specialty luxury motorcycles. The client is considering hedging the bond using a credit spread forward because he is concerned that a downturn in the economy could result in a default on the Cuellar bond. The client holds $2 million in par of the Cuellar bond, and the bond's coupons are paid annually. The bond's current nominal spread over the U.S. Treasury rate is 2.5%. The characteristics of the forward contract are shown below.

Information on the Credit Spread Forward

Contract spread	3%
Risk factor	10
Spread at maturity	4.5%
Notional principal of credit spread forward	$2 million

19. Determine which of Cramer's statements regarding VAR and CVAR are correct or incorrect.

	Statement 1	Statement 2
A.	Correct	Correct
B.	Correct	Incorrect
C.	Incorrect	Incorrect

20. Determine which of Cramer's statements regarding credit risk are correct or incorrect.

	Statement 3	Statement 4
A.	Correct	Correct
B.	Correct	Incorrect
C.	Incorrect	Incorrect

21. Determine whether the forward contract sold by Palmer Securities has current and/or potential credit risk to either the long or short position.
    A. The contract has current credit risk only.
    B. The contract has potential credit risk only.
    C. The contract has both potential credit risk and current credit risk.

22. To meet his assignment to lower risk to DSI, McNally proposes three actions that DSI can take. Which will *most likely* meet this objective?
    A. Require netting of all cash flows with any counterparty.
    B. DSI will set up an enhanced derivatives products company for all DSI derivatives trades.
    C. DSI will use standard Treasury bond futures contracts rather than OTC derivatives to control credit risk and minimize counterpart risk.

23. Of the following, determine which will be the *best* hedge for Weaver Trading.
    A. Purchase a credit default swap.
    B. Purchase a credit spread call option.
    C. Sell a credit spread put option.

24. Assuming the $2 million in par of the Cuellar bond is hedged using the credit spread forward, the payoff to the buyer or seller from the credit spread forward contract is closest to:
    A. $300,000 to the seller.
    B. $300,000 to the buyer.
    C. $100,000 to the buyer.

Questions 25–30 relate to Fixed Income Portfolio Management.

Jack Thomas and Tim Bentley are analysts for Bond Analytics (BA). BA provides bond analysis for mutual fund managers, hedge fund managers, and institutional money managers in the United States. BA specializes in the valuation of international bonds and callable bonds, using intrasector analysis to find undervalued bonds. In addition to valuing the bonds, they also advise clients on whether to hedge currency risk for international bonds. Thomas has been a particularly strong advocate of hedging the currency risk of international bonds, especially in emerging markets, using forward contracts when they are available.

At a morning meeting, Thomas and Bentley are trying to decide whether to hedge the currency risk of a large issue of bonds from a Thai manufacturer of pressed steel, Nakhon Metals. The client considering purchasing the bonds is a large U.S. mutual fund, Epsilon Funds. Epsilon has started to explore the possibility of earning higher returns through currency management using forward contracts. Thomas and Bentley discuss the various hedges of currency risk for the Nakhon Metals bond. One possibility is using a forward hedge position on the Thai baht. A second possibility is using forward contracts where the baht is delivered for Korean won. Thomas states that the second hedge would be pursued if the won was expected to appreciate more against the U.S. dollar than the baht. In the second hedge, the manager would sell won for dollars at the future spot rate.

Thomas and Bentley gather the following information on the expected changes in the various currencies, the 1-year cash rates in the respective countries, and the expected return on the Nakhon bond.

Yield on Nakhon Metals bond in Thai baht terms	5.20%
Cash rate in Thailand	2.50%
Expected change in the baht relative to the U.S. dollar	2.80%
Cash rate in Korea	3.20%
Expected change in the won relative to the U.S. dollar	6.40%
Cash rate in Japan	4.20%
Expected change in the yen relative to the U.S. dollar	3.50%
Cash rate in United States	6.50%

Additionally, the Nakhon Metals bond has a duration of 7.30 and is being compared against a bond denominated in U.S. dollars, issued by Powhatan Industries. The Powhatan bond has a duration of 4.2 and a yield of 4.50%. Whichever bond is purchased will be held for the next year. Thomas projects that the yield for the Nakhon Metals bond is expected to increase by 15 basis points, while the yield on the Powhatan Industries bond is expected to stay constant.

The following day, Thomas and Bentley discuss the market for and valuation of callable and long duration bonds. They believe that interest rates are temporarily low and for this reason want to be careful about their bond investments. Although they could hedge interest rate risk, they prefer not to because they believe it reduces the ultimate long-term return.

Thomas says that due to secular changes in the bond market, bonds with structures are expected to become more scarce. As this happens, they will become relatively more expensive. Bentley states that bonds with very long durations also trade at a premium because they are scarce as well.

Thomas states that the performance of callables and non-callables may differ when interest rates change due to the inherent call risk. He discusses the relative performance under two scenarios:

- Scenario A: Interest rates are near coupon rates and fall for both callables and non-callables by the same amount.
- Scenario B: Interest rates are historically very low and rise for both callables and non-callables by the same amount.

25. The second hedge that Thomas recommends for the Nakhon Metals bond is *most likely* an example of which of the following currency hedging strategies?
    A. Cross hedge.
    B. Minimum variance hedge.
    C. Forward hedge.

26. Based on their cash rates determine which of the currencies (Thai baht, Korean won, and Japanese yen) should trade at forward discount to the dollar.
    A. Only the yen should trade at a forward discount.
    B. The baht and the won should trade at a forward discount.
    C. None of the currencies should trade at a forward discount.

27. Based on interest rate expectations and ignoring currency effects, determine whether the Nakhon Metals bond or Powhatan Industries bond should be more attractive over the one-year time horizon.
    A. The Nakhon Metals bond should be more attractive.
    B. The Powhatan Industries bond should be more attractive.
    C. Neither bond should be more attractive.

28.   After Thomas and Bentley review the cash rates and expectations data they have gathered on the won, baht, yen, and dollar, Thomas says, "I'm going to recommend to my U.S. managers that they remain unhedged in Japanese bond investments because they'll pick up an additional currency return versus hedging the yen back to dollars."

Bentley replies, "You're off your bean, old boy. The difference in the cash rates in the dollar and the yen is already reflected in their spot and forward rates. Since you have to exchange dollars for yen now and yen for dollars later, you won't gain anything that isn't already incorporated into the currencies."

Based on cash rates and expectations data provided above, determine whether Thomas and Bentley are correct or incorrect.
A. Only Bentley is correct.
B. Only Thomas is correct.
C. Both are incorrect.

29.   Determine whether Thomas and Bentley are correct or incorrect regarding their statements about the scarcity and pricing of callable and long duration bonds.
A. Only Thomas is correct.
B. Only Bentley is correct.
C. Both are correct.

30.   Which of the following *best* describes the relative performance of callables and non-callables under the two scenarios?
A. Callables will outperform non-callables under both scenarios.
B. Callables will outperform non-callables under scenario A only.
C. Callables will outperform non-callables under scenario B only.

Questions 31–36 relate to Alternative Investments for Portfolio Management.

William Bliss, CFA, runs a hedge fund that uses both managed futures strategies and positions in physical commodities. He is reviewing his operations and strategies to increase the return of the fund. Bliss has just hired Joseph Cantori, CFA, to help him manage the fund because he realizes that he needs to increase his trading activity in futures and to engage in futures strategies other than passively managed positions. Cantori is a registered commodity trading advisor (CTA) who generally uses a contrarian strategy to manage futures. Bliss also hired Cantori because of Cantori's experience with swaps, which Bliss hopes to add to his choice of investment tools.

Bliss explains to Cantori that his clients pay 2% on assets under management and a 20% incentive fee. The incentive fee is based on profits after having subtracted the risk-free rate, which is the fund's basic hurdle rate, and there is a high water mark provision. Bliss is hoping that Cantori can help his business because his firm did not earn an incentive fee this past year. This was the case despite the fact that, after two years of losses, the value of the fund increased 14% during the previous year. That increase occurred without any new capital contributed from clients. Bliss is optimistic about the near future because the term structure of futures prices is particularly favorable for earning higher returns from long futures positions.

Cantori says he has seen research that indicates inflation may increase in the next few years. He states this should increase the opportunity to earn a higher return in commodities and suggests taking a large, margined position in a broad commodity index. This would offer an enhanced return that would attract investors holding only stocks and bonds. Bliss mentions that not all commodity prices are positively correlated with inflation, so it may be better to choose particular types of commodities in which to invest. Furthermore, Bliss adds that commodities traditionally have not outperformed stocks and bonds either on a risk-adjusted or absolute basis. Cantori says he will research companies who do business in commodities because buying the stock of those companies to gain commodity exposure is an efficient and effective method for gaining indirect exposure to commodities.

Bliss and Cantori next discuss some of the issues that may affect client decisions to invest in Bliss's fund. Cantori states that if they begin marketing to sophisticated institutional portfolios, they can expect increased due diligence questions. They may be questioned on the portfolio's risk management procedures.

- Bliss states they must tighten up their risk budgeting process and impose tighter limits on the amount of futures trades they do with each dealer while implementing payment netting across all futures positions.
- Cantori states that this will be even more important in commodity swaps where the fund receives a commodity return and pays LIBOR because maximum potential credit risk exposure typically continues up to swap expiration.

Bliss points out that sophisticated investors in the hedge fund will be more focused on risk adjusted performance ratios such as Sharpe, Sortino, and Treynor.

31. Given the information, the *most likely* reason that Bliss's firm did not earn an incentive fee in the past year was because:
   A. of a high water mark provision.
   B. the return did not exceed the risk-free rate.
   C. the 2% asset-under-management fee is greater than the risk-free rate.

32. Assuming Cantori continues to follow a contrarian futures trading strategy, his strategy can *best* be described as a:
   A. market trading strategy.
   B. discretionary trading strategy.
   C. systematic trading strategy.

33. Bliss is optimistic about the near future because the term structure of futures prices is particularly favorable for earning higher returns from long positions. This would be the case if the term structure is:
   A. in contango.
   B. relatively flat.
   C. in backwardation.

34. The points made by Cantori and Bliss during their discussion of commodity returns given high inflation expectations were correct with the exception of:
   A. Cantori's assertions concerning the indirect method of investing in stocks to gain commodity exposure.
   B. Bliss's assertion that not all commodities are positively correlated with inflation.
   C. Cantori's assertion that a broad index would benefit from inflation.

35. Regarding the statements made by Bliss and Cantori on risk budgeting:
   A. both are correct.
   B. only Cantori is correct.
   C. both are wrong.

36. Regarding Bliss's comments on return ratios, the ratio *least appropriate* to the hedge fund is likely to be the:
   A. Sharpe.
   B. Sortino.
   C. Treynor.

Questions 37–42 relate to Global Bonds and Fixed-Income Derivatives, Equity Portfolio Management, and Risk Management Applications of Derivatives.

Jerry Edwards is an analyst with DeLeon Analytics. He is currently advising the CFO of Anderson Corp., a multinational manufacturing corporation based in Newark, New Jersey, USA. Jackie Palmer is Edwards's assistant. Palmer is well versed in risk management, having worked at a large multinational bank for the last ten years prior to coming to Anderson.

Anderson has accepted a $2 million note with a duration of 4.0 from Weaver Tools as payment for a shipment delivered to Weaver last week. Weaver markets tools and machinery from manufacturers of Anderson's size. Edwards states that in order to effectively hedge the price risk of this instrument, Anderson should sell a series of interest rate calls. Palmer states that an alternative hedge for the note would be to enter an interest rate swap as the fixed-rate payer.

As well as selling products from a Swiss plant in Europe, Anderson sells products in Switzerland itself. As a result, Anderson has quarterly cash inflows of 12,000,000 Swiss franc (CHF). In order to convert these cash flows into dollars, Edwards suggests that Anderson enter into a currency swap without an exchange of notional principal. Palmer contacts a currency swap dealer with whom they have dealt in the past and finds the following exchange rate and annual swap interest rates:

Exchange Rate (CHF per dollar)	1.24
Swap interest rate in U.S. dollars	2.80%
Swap interest rate in Swiss franc	6.60%

Discussing foreign exchange rate risk in general, Edwards states that it is transaction exposure that is most often hedged because the amount to be hedged is contractual and certain. Economic exposure, he states, is less certain and thus harder to hedge.

To finance their U.S. operations, Anderson issued a $10 million fixed-rate bond in the United States five years ago. The bond had an original maturity of ten years and now has a modified duration of 4.0. Edwards states that Anderson should enter a 5-year semiannual pay floating swap with a notional principal of about $11.4 million to take advantage of falling interest rates. The duration of the fixed-rate side of the swap is equal to 75% of its maturity or 3.75 (= 0.75 × 5). The duration of the floating side of the swap is 0.25. Palmer states that Anderson's position in the swap will have a negative duration.

For another client of DeLeon, Edwards has assigned Palmer the task of estimating the interest rate sensitivity of the client's portfolios. The client's portfolio consists of positions in both U.S. and British bonds. The relevant information for estimating the duration contributions of the bonds and the portfolio's total duration is provided below.

U.S. dollar bond	$275,000 market value
British bond	$155,000 market value
British yield beta	1.40
Duration of U.S. bond	4.0
Duration of British bond	8.5

Edwards also asks Palmer to review a client's immunized bond portfolio and recommend any appropriate strategy changes. The portfolio funds a multiyear USD liability and the liability duration is slightly below the asset duration. Palmer reviews DeLeon's interest rate outlook, which is for falling interest rates, and recommends increasing the portfolio asset duration. He also recommends using the British bond as part of the strategy based on its wide yield spread and a reasoned analysis the spread will contract.

37. Regarding their statements concerning the hedge of the Weaver Tools note, determine if Edwards and Palmer are correct or incorrect.
   A. Both are correct.
   B. Only Palmer is correct.
   C. Only Edwards is correct.

38. If Anderson enters a properly structured currency swap to convert the CHF 12,000,000 to dollars, the amount they will receive is *closest* to:
   A. $4,105,572.
   B. $7,071,429.
   C. $9,677,419.

39. Regarding Edward's statements concerning the transaction exposure of currency risk, which of the following *best* describes his statement?
   A. It is inaccurate because transaction exposure is very uncertain.
   B. It accurately describes firms' currency exposures and hedging practices.
   C. It is inaccurate because firms more frequently hedge translation exposure.

40. Regarding their statements concerning the hedge of the U.S. dollar-denominated bond Anderson issued, determine whether Edwards and Palmer are correct or incorrect.
   A. Only Edwards is correct.
   B. Only Palmer is correct.
   C. Both are correct.

41. Which of the following is *closest* to the duration contribution of the British bond and the portfolio's total duration from a U.S. perspective?

British bond	Portfolio duration
A. 2.19	4.75
B. 3.06	5.62
C. 4.29	6.85

42. Assuming the market information and expectations given are correct, which of Palmer's recommendations for the immunized portfolio are *most likely* correct? The two recommendations are to be considered separately.

    A. Both are correct.
    B. The asset duration recommendation.
    C. Both are incorrect.

©2016 Kaplan, Inc.

Questions 43–48 relate to Management of Active and Passive Fixed Income Portfolios, Risk Management, and Risk Management Applications of Derivatives.

Mary Thomas works for Kershaw-Ross, a large investment bank located in London. Kershaw-Ross provides advice to portfolio managers, securities dealers, and hedge funds. Jack Bentley is Thomas's assistant.

Washington Capital Management (WCM), one of Thomas's clients, has a $5 million position in fixed-rate U.S. Treasury bonds with a duration of 6.7. WCM has stressed they do not want to immediately sell the bonds but do want to hedge the interest rate risk while maintaining high liquidity in all portfolio positions. Thomas directs Bentley to develop several strategies that will meet WCM's objectives of hedging and liquidity. Bentley proposes the follow ideas:

[Handwritten: Dont sell / hedge IR risk / Maintain liq.]

Strategy 1: Sell 40 T-bond contracts. The contracts have a duration of 7.9 and a full price of 98,752.

[Handwritten: $\frac{0-6.7}{7.9} \times \frac{5,000,000}{98,752} = 43$]

Strategy 2: Enter an appropriately sized interest rate swap to receive floating versus pay fixed.

Strategy 3: Sell puts on interest rates and buy puts on on bond futures contracts.

Thomas is analyzing the portfolio for one of his investors, Canopy Managers. Last year the portfolio had a market value of $4,881,000 and a dollar duration of $157,200. The current figures for the portfolio are provided below:

	Market Value	Duration	Dollar Duration
Bond 1	$780,000	4.5 *×0.01=*	$35,100
Bond 2	$2,500,000	3.4	$85,000
Bond 3	$524,000	2.7	$14,148
Bond 4	$413,000	1.9	$7,847
Portfolio	$4,217,000		$142,095

Canopy would like to alter the current dollar duration of the portfolio to last year's duration, and they would like to do so with the least amount of cash possible and a controlling position in one of the bonds.

Several months later, Canopy Managers asymmetrically adjusts portfolio duration by purchasing six-month call options on bonds for $225,000. Several days after the option purchase, the bonds underlying the options have appreciated $250,000 and the effective delta of the options during the same period was 0.7.

The next week, Thomas and Bentley visit the headquarters of Capital Pension Management, one of Kershaw-Ross's largest clients. Capital is using contingent immunization to immunize a liability, but management is concerned about a possible rise in interest rates. *Rates ↑, Bonds ↓, Yields ↑*

- Thomas states that if she were to recommend the most effective strategy to Capital, she would recommend that they use bonds with high yields because immunization will be cheaper.
- Bentley interjects that the risk from nonparallel shifts in the yield curve can be minimized by concentrating the cash flows around the horizon date.

Due to their tremendous success, Kershaw-Ross has outgrown their current headquarters and is going to expand their current building. Thomas's team has been charged with securing financing for the renovations. They currently are considering a remodeling and addition that would cost approximately £5,000,000.

Thomas has secured the financing necessary for the renovations at a floating interest rate of LIBOR plus 150 basis points, with payments made quarterly over three years. Thomas believes that Kershaw-Ross should be able to complete the renovation of the building and close on the loan in one year. She is concerned, however, that interest rates will increase in the interim and has obtained a swaption to hedge the loan. She states that Kershaw-Ross should *pay Fixed* use a payer swaption to hedge the loan. Bentley evaluates the forecasts for future swap fixed rates as well as the current terms of various swaptions, which are provided below:

Fixed rate for a 1-year payer swaption	= 8.50%
Fixed rate for a 1-year receiver swaption	= 8.60%
Projected swap fixed rate in one year	= 9.30%
Fixed rate for a 4-year payer swaption	= 9.40%
Fixed rate for a 4-year receiver swaption	= 9.70%
Projected swap fixed rate in four years	= 9.80%

43. Do Bentley's strategy 1 and 2 meet WCM's objectives?
    A. Neither meet the objectives.
    B. Only strategy 1 meets the objectives.
    C. Only strategy 2 meets the objectives.

44. What name is most commonly used to describe strategy 3 and will it meet WCM's objectives?
    A. Collar and no.
    B. Collar and yes.
    C. Bull spread and yes.

45. To adjust the dollar duration of the Canopy portfolio to last year's level, the amount Canopy will need to purchase of Bond 1, acting as a controlling position, is *closest* to:
    A. $335,667.
    B. $862,916.
    C. $1,115,667.

46. The potential credit risk to Canopy of the bond call options is *closest* to:
    A. $175,000.
    B. $400,000.
    C. $475,000.

47. Regarding their statements concerning the strategy of Capital Pension Management, determine whether Thomas and Bentley are correct or incorrect.
    A. Only Thomas is correct.
    B. Only Bentley is correct.
    C. Both are correct.

48. Assuming that their interest rate forecast is correct and they use the appropriate hedge, calculate Kershaw-Ross's first quarterly payment on the building expansion loan.
    A. £125,000.
    B. £126,250.
    C. £136,250.

Questions 49–54 relate to Execution of Portfolio Decisions: Monitoring and Rebalancing.

Somerset Investment Limited is a Singapore-based money management firm that is conducting an appraisal of its investment performance. Cameron Li, CFA, has been charged with conducting the appraisal and is to report back to upper management with his findings.

Li is convinced that trade executions play a substantial role in overall portfolio performance, particularly for funds that have a relatively high level of turnover during the year. As a result, he is seeking methods that will allow him to evaluate the quality of trade executions.

He knows that the firm's traders use both market and limit orders, and he is wondering if a framework can be developed to ensure that the best order type is used under the specific circumstances for each trade. When he consults with the firm's head trader, Rick Gleeson, Gleeson tells him that market orders have price uncertainty but no execution uncertainty, while limit orders eliminate price uncertainty but have execution uncertainty. According to Gleeson, rebalancing and liquidity-motivated trades should use limit orders while value-motivated and information-motivated trades should use market orders.

Li knows that bid-ask spreads are a major component of trading costs and asks Gleeson for some recent trade data that he can use for analysis and presentation to management. He receives the following data relating to a series of buy trades for Sumatra Natural Resources (SNR), with all currency values in Singapore dollars:

Trades of Sumatra Natural Resources

Time	Bid Price	Ask Price	Execution Price	Shares Bought	
10:30	$22.18 22.27	$22.36	$22.33	900	30%
11:15	$22.23 22.33	$22.43	$22.43	600	20%
13:45	$22.29 22.385	$22.48	$22.47	700	23.3%
15:00	$22.37 22.50	$22.63	$22.65	800	26.7%

(handwritten: MP above Bid Price column; 3,000 below Shares Bought)

Gleeson also tells Li that the portfolio manager had originally made the decision to purchase 5,000 SNR at 10:00 a.m. when the price was $22.36. The closing price for the day was Gleeson's last trade at $22.65, at which point the order for the remaining 2,000 shares was cancelled.

49. Which of the following *correctly* summarizes Gleeson's comments concerning the differences between market and limit orders?
    A. He is correct concerning the nature of uncertainty; he is correct concerning when the order types should be used.
    B. He is correct concerning the nature of uncertainty; he is incorrect concerning when the order types should be used.
    C. He is incorrect concerning the nature of uncertainty; he is correct concerning when the order types should be used.

50. Concerning the Sumatra Natural Resources price and execution data, the average effective spread and weighted average effective spread are *closest* to:

	Average effective spread	Weighted average effective spread
A.	0.1957	0.1975
B.	0.0971	0.0908
C.	0.1975	0.1957

51. Assume that the four trades in Sumatra Natural Resources are the only trades in the security for the day. Determine which of the following statements concerning the volume weighted average price (VWAP) is *most* correct.
    A. The VWAP for the day is 22.470, and the trader's goal would be to have an average cost that is less than the VWAP.
    B. The VWAP for the day is 22.468, and the trader's goal would be to have an average cost that is greater than the VWAP.
    C. The VWAP for the day is 22.468, and the trader's goal would be to have an average cost that is less than the VWAP.

52. Calculate the implementation shortfall assuming total commissions paid by Gleeson when he purchased the 3,000 SNR were $210.
    A. 0.303%.
    B. 0.996%.
    C. 2.027%.

53. Which of the following statements concerning implementation shortfall and VWAP is incorrect?
    A. Implementation shortfall is greater than zero if any portion of the original order goes unfilled and is cancelled.
    B. For small trades in non-trending markets, VWAP is more appropriate than implementation shortfall.
    C. Implementation shortfall can be adjusted to accurately account for movements in the general market.

54. Determine which of the following statements concerning an algorithmic trading strategy is _most_ incorrect. An algorithmic trading strategy:
   A. ensures that the portfolio does not become over-concentrated (in specific assets or sectors) because it is based on quantitative rules.
   B. involves the use of automated processes based on quantitative measures, such as the ratio of the trade size to average daily volume, to guide trading decisions.
   C. known as simple logical participation, breaks trades into small pieces to avoid detection and to minimize market impact costs.

Questions 55–60 relate to Portfolio Management of Global Bonds and Fixed-Income Derivatives and Performance Evaluation and Attribution.

Holsten, Inc. Pension Plan (HIPP), based in the United States, has gathered the following information to assess the performance of two of its international equity portfolio managers.

Portfolio Data (in millions) – Manager A:

Country	Beginning Portfolio Value	Ending Portfolio Value	Portfolio Return in Local Currency
U.K.	£30	£35	16.7%
Germany	€30	€32	6.7%
Total Portfolio (based on beginning weights in USD)			60% U.K., 40% Germany

Portfolio Data (in millions) – Manager B:

Country	Beginning Portfolio Value	Ending Portfolio Value	Portfolio Return in Local Currency
U.K.	£20	£23	15.0%
Germany	€40	€43	7.5%
Total Portfolio (based on beginning weights in USD)			43% U.K., 57% Germany

Market Data:

	Beginning Values	Ending Values
USD/GBP	2.0000	2.2222
USD/EUR	1.3333	1.4286
JPY/USD	101.47	102.22
U.K. Index in GBP	100.00	115.00
German Index in EUR	100.00	105.00

Jane Smith, CFA, is one of the trustees for HIPP. Smith has considerable international investment experience and has been asked by another trustee to explain some comments made by Manager B. Manager B said that market conditions were unusual because real risk-free interest rates in Germany, Japan, and the United States were equal. Plus, expected inflation rates in the three countries were also equal. The trustee wants to know how the manager would have used such data to make currency hedging decisions. Smith decides to explain the issues by discussing an investment in the U.K. Index.

The other trustees have also asked Smith to review some of the issues that they will need to consider when developing customized benchmarks for the plan's international portfolio managers. In a subsequent meeting, Smith makes the following two statements:

Statement 1: International equity indexes are generally weighted using the market capitalization of the countries in the index, although the relative GDP/GNP of the countries in the index can also be used.

Statement 2: For each international equity manager, we will need to determine whether to develop a benchmark based on country or region, industry, and/or investment style. The best benchmarks are based on investment style as these benchmarks allow managers to invest across industries and countries.

HIPP's trustees are also assessing the performance of the plan's fixed-income portfolio manager. The bond manager's portfolio generated a return of 8.75% during the period. One of the trustees, John Johnson, CFA, an experienced fixed-income analyst, has constructed a Treasury-bond proxy portfolio that matches the duration of the fixed-income manager's actual performance benchmark. This Treasury proxy portfolio had the following returns that will be used to determine the sources of the bond manager's returns:

Expected one-year return on the Treasury bond proxy portfolio 9.0%

Actual one-year return on the Treasury bond proxy portfolio   7.5%

In addition, Johnson has computed a price for each security in the fixed-income portfolio at the beginning and end of the period based on the corresponding Treasury spot rate for its maturity and has calculated a total portfolio return for the period of 8.25% based on these prices. He has also determined that the portfolio's return from sector/quality management is 0.25%. Johnson makes the following two statements during the trustee meeting:

Statement 3: Total bond-portfolio returns come from the external interest rate environment and from active portfolio management. Studies have shown that a superior bond-portfolio manager can consistently add value to the portfolio through active management techniques such as sector/quality management, security selection, and interest rate management.

Statement 4:   Bond returns come primarily from the external interest
rate environment. Returns from the external interest rate
environment include returns from the default-free benchmark
with no changes in forward rates and returns from changes in
forward rates.

55.   What is the return for a U.S. investor of Manager A?
A. 2.8%.
B. 10.8%.
C. 23.5%.

56.   Relative to each other, which manager added the most (or lost the
least) value from exposure to the GBP and EUR?

	GBP	EUR
A. Manager:	A	B
B. Manager:	A	A
C. Manager:	B	A

57.   When Smith explains the investment choices for HIPP of investing in
the U.K. Index, given the market data and other information provided
by the manager, she will conclude it would have been best to:

	Sell GBP forward versus buy USD?	Sell GBP forward versus buy JPY?
A.	No	No
B.	Yes	No
C.	Yes	Yes

58.   Are Smith's statements regarding custom benchmarks for the plan's
international portfolio managers accurate?
A. Both statements are accurate.
B. Only Statement 1 is accurate.
C. Only Statement 2 is accurate.

59.   What is the bond portfolio's return from maturity management and
return from bond selection management?

	Maturity Management	Bond Selection
A.	0.50	0.50
B.	0.75	0.25
C.	0.75	0.50

60.   Are Johnson's statements regarding bond portfolio returns accurate?
A. Only Statement 3 is accurate.
B. Only Statement 4 is accurate.
C. Neither statement is accurate.

END OF AFTERNOON SESSION

PRACTICE EXAM 3 MORNING SESSION QUESTION BREAKDOWN

Question	Topic	Minutes
1	Behavioral Finance and Private Wealth Management	13
2	Private Wealth Management	15
3	Asset Allocation, Alternative Investments, and Private Wealth Management	10
4	Alternative Investments	18
5	Alternative Investments	10
6	Economic Concepts	9
7	Performance Evaluation and Attribution	24
8	Portfolio Management – Institutional	15
9	Portfolio Management – Institutional	10
10	Asset Allocation and Alternative Investments	9
11	Portfolio Management – Institutional, Portfolio Management – Individual, Behavioral Finance, Asset Allocation, Equity	26
12	Execution of Portfolio Decisions	12
13	Portfolio Management – Individual	9
	Total	180

PRACTICE EXAM 3 SCORE SHEET

MORNING SESSION		
Question	Maximum Points	Your Estimated Score
1A	4	
1B	4	
1C	5	
2A	7	
2B	5	
2C	3	
3A	4	
3B	3	
3C	3	
4A	6	
4B	3	
4C	2	
4D	3	
4E	4	
5A	3	
5B	4	
5C	3	
6A	3	
6B	2	
6C	4	
7A	10	
7B	8	
7C	6	
8A	9	
8B	6	
9A	6	
9B	4	

MORNING SESSION (CONTINUED)		
Question	Maximum Points	Your Estimated Score
10A	4	
10B	5	
11A	14	
11B	8	
11C	4	
12A	4	
12B	4	
12C	4	
13	9	
Total	180	

AFTERNOON SESSION		
Question	Maximum Points	Your Estimated Score
1–6	18	
7–12	18	
13–18	18	
19–24	18	
25–30	18	
31–36	18	
37–42	18	
43–48	18	
49–54	18	
55–60	18	
Total	180	

Practice Exam 3
Morning Session

QUESTIONS 1, 2, AND 3 RELATE TO CURT WESTIN AND WESTIN CONSULTING. A TOTAL OF 38 MINUTES IS ALLOCATED TO THESE QUESTIONS. *CANDIDATES SHOULD ANSWER THESE QUESTIONS IN THE ORDER PRESENTED.*

QUESTION 1 HAS THREE PARTS FOR A TOTAL OF 13 MINUTES

Curt Westin is a widowed father with two teenage children and an elderly mother. He is 45 years old. His wife passed away last year. His two sons, Kyle and Jared, are 15 and 11, respectively. The two boys are expected to go to college—Kyle in three years and Jared in seven years. Westin's mother, Helen, is 68 years old and in good health. Helen will live with the family until Jared leaves for college.

The Westins live comfortably because Curt Westin owns 100% of the shares of a business consulting firm that provides a fairly steady income. Westin takes a before-tax salary, currently $200,000 a year, and keeps his salary in line with the business. He operates the business to show roughly a zero profit. Westin created the business with his wife ten years ago, after he and his wife left a prestigious consulting firm. The company is set up as a limited liability company and is known as Westin Consulting. Most of his clients are private companies, including new ventures and potential buyouts. The corporate tax rate is 25.0%. The company has been growing 3.0% per year steadily and he expects this to continue. The company is currently valued at $2.5 million; practically all of this value is related to Westin as an asset. Westin has not decided whether to sell his business when he chooses to retire. He is weighing various succession and exit options including keeping it in the family.

In establishing Westin Consulting ten years ago, both Westin and his wife were known to have taken calculated risks to build their company. Westin's consulting company is now well established and is known for sound business advice and use of innovative and disciplined approaches. Westin values information, gathers relevant facts, and makes reasoned decisions.

He finished paying off his home mortgage two years ago; the current market value of the property is $1.0 million. He plans to continue living there. Other assets include $1.5 million in new cash after-tax from life insurance proceeds. An additional $500,000 exists in cash equivalents held in a money market fund. A 401(k) plan is worth $3.0 million and a separate taxable portfolio is valued at $1.5 million.

Westin has decided to seek financial planning and advice from Michelle Hyde, CFA. She is a partner in Stussy, Hyde, and Walley, an investment firm that specializes in high net worth individuals.

Westin: "I would like to know what percent of my capital gains would effectively be consumed by taxes if we pay taxes at the end of every year for the next 25 years. I see this as a worst case stress test of a high taxes scenario. It will help me evaluate your analytic and communication skills"

Hyde: "I'll run this scenario, provided I can use our analyst's assumptions."

Analysts at Stussy, Hyde, and Walley have provided the following projected information: expected inflation 3.0%, federal and state tax liability 35.0% of income, and 25.0% tax on all investment gains.

A.   **Identify** Westin's investor personality type: adventurer, celebrity, guardian, individualist, or straight arrow, based on the Bailard, Biehl and Kaiser Model (BB&K). **State** *three* characteristics of the personality type exhibited by Westin using specific facts from the case.

(4 minutes)

B.   **Calculate** the proportion of potential investment gains consumed by taxes on the taxable portfolio based on an expected return of 8.0% (all generated from capital gains) to accommodate Westin's request. Show your work.

(4 minutes)

At a subsequent meeting, Westin asks Hyde whether it makes financial sense to continue a temporary $1,500,000 life insurance policy he took out a few years ago. It is a term policy with a guaranteed annual renewal for the next eight years, but at an increasing premium. Westin and Hyde discuss the issue and agree to make certain assumptions. Westin wants to replace his current before tax salary of $200,000 for five years. The salary is paid at the end of the year and will increase by 3% a year thereafter. Given the risky nature of the business, an 11% discount rate is suitable. There are no tax issues to consider and no financial penalties if the current insurance policy is canceled.

C.   Based on Westin and Hyde's assumptions, **calculate** the amount of insurance Westin would need. Show your calculations. **State** and **justify** based on Westin's situation whether Hyde should recommend Westin continue or discontinue having life insurance. Do not use the calculation amount as a justification. Assume Westin could continue the existing policy or take out a new policy for any desired amount.

(5 minutes)

QUESTION 2 HAS THREE PARTS FOR A TOTAL OF 15 MINUTES

Westin tells Hyde that his primary goals are to continue his family's quality of life, ensure that his children get an education, provide for a comfortable retirement for his mother, and have enough money left over for a comfortable retirement in 25 years. As a secondary goal, Westin also wants to purchase a boat and a vacation home at some time. He also wants to set aside $400,000 now for the boat and vacation home for purchase within the next ten years.

Education costs are expected to increase at 6.0%, twice the rate of inflation. Total annual college expenses (tuition, books, housing, and other costs) are now over $60,000. College fees are due at the beginning of period so Kyle's fees for Year 3 will be paid at the end of Year 2. The total estimated value of the college costs for both children in today's dollars is $628,042.

His mother, Helen, has stated that she would like to live in a retirement community with her friends after the boys leave for college. This can be funded by setting aside $463,462 today.

Westin has discussed the risk of his business and his desire to be certain he meets his objectives. Hyde suggests building a set-aside layer in an "investment portfolio pyramid" using cash equivalents and dedicated bonds for (1) college funding; (2) his mother's retirement funding; and (3) personal expenses (boat and vacation home). Any additional funds should be allocated to the taxable portfolio as funds cannot be added to the 401(k).

At a subsequent meeting, Westin and Hyde agree to be conservative and value Westin's company after his retirement at zero, because there is no exit plan. They agree that Westin's salary can provide for his other after-tax living expenses as long as the portfolio generates a real $80,000 after-tax annual flow to fund his retirement. They agree that the funds in the set-aside layer of the pyramid are to be excluded from the funds generating the $80,000.

A.   **State** Westin's return objectives. **Calculate** the after-tax nominal
       return needed for the current year. Fully support the analysis with facts
       relevant to Westin and **show** all relevant calculations.

                          (7 minutes)

B.   **Evaluate** Westin's willingness and ability to tolerate risk and **state** an
       overall risk objective.

                          (5 minutes)

C. **Identify** the *two* stages in the time horizon of Westin's portfolio. The stages you identify must reflect significant changes in the likely required return from the portfolio. **Discuss** how return needs are *most likely* to change between the two stages. Do not consider the portions of the portfolio in the set aside layer.

(3 minutes)

QUESTION 3 HAS THREE PARTS FOR A TOTAL OF 10 MINUTES

After the previous analysis, Westin and Hyde determine that a 7.4% pre-tax return target is more appropriate and that all other facts are the same. Hyde provides the following asset allocation information.

Exhibit 1. Capital Market Expectations

Asset Class	Expected Return	Expected Standard Deviation
Cash Equivalents	3.0%	0.5%
Investment-Grade U.S. Bonds	5.5%	9.5%
U.S. Equities	8.5%	17.5%
International Equities	10.5%	22.5%
Real Estate (REITs)	9.5%	8.5%
Private Equity	12.5%	40.0%

Westin wants to explore alternative investments as an option as he believes that expected returns are worth the additional risk. Hyde believes Westin is suitable to invest in alternative investments provided that it is not a significant allocation. Hyde also recommends both the 401(k) and the taxable portfolio have the same asset allocation approach for both; Westin likes the idea, as he sees no value in complicating the matter as long as his investment objectives are met. Hyde lists the following to accommodate current market conditions and investment objectives:

* Up to 10.0% allocation in alternative investments—private equity and real estate are under consideration.
* Fixed income exposure of at least 25% for diversification.
* Some international equities exposure.
* Sharpe ratio greater than 0.35.
* Standard deviation of better than 13%.

While discussing alternative choices, Hyde and Westin had the following comments:

Westin: "Do I need more exposure to real estate? I already have a house. I like private equity a lot. It is an investment type I understand as part of my business. We should put all 10% of the allocation portion in it."

Hyde: "I'm not sure that is a good idea. I think we should look at your current assets compared to the alternative investments."

Exhibit 2 displays Hyde's analysis of asset allocation alternatives based upon the desired return requirements, and constraints.

Exhibit 2. Asset Allocation Options

	Portfolio and Allocations (%)			
Asset Class	A	B	C	D
Cash equivalents	10.0	7.5	5.0	5.0
U.S. fixed income	37.5	32.5	30.0	25.0
U.S. equities	42.5	45.0	42.5	45.0
Non-U.S. equities	7.5	10.0	17.5	20.0
Real estate (REITs)	2.5	2.5	5.0	0.0
Private equity	0.0	2.5	0.0	5.0
Total	**100.0**	**100.0**	**100.0**	**100.0**
Portfolio Measures	A	B	C	D
Expected returns	7.00	7.44	7.73	8.08
Expected standard deviation	11.09	12.16	12.87	14.35
Sharpe ratio	0.361	0.365	0.367	?

A. **Select** the *most* appropriate portfolio for Westin that follows the established guidelines. **Justify** your selection on the basis of *three* items from Exhibit 2 and Westin's IPS. These allocations exclude the set-aside layer of the portfolio. Do not consider the set-aside assets in your analysis.

Answer Question 3-A, in the template provided.

(4 minutes)

Template for Question 3-A

Select the most appropriate portfolio for Westin. (Write one letter below)	Justify your selection on the basis of three items from Exhibit 2 and Westin's IPS.

B. **Justify** Hyde's objections to Westin's comments on alternative investments.

(3 minutes)

C. **State** whether you agree or disagree with Hyde's comment regarding the 401(k) and taxable portfolio and his intent to use the same asset allocation for each. **Support** your decision with two reasons.

(3 minutes)

QUESTION 4 HAS FIVE PARTS FOR A TOTAL OF 18 MINUTES

Max Cady is the chairman of the investment committee of Mitchum University (MU). The MU endowment is currently invested primarily in stocks (65% of assets) and bonds (25% of assets) with the remainder in cash. Cady would like to further diversify the MU endowment by adding an asset class—commodities. In particular, Cady is interested in gaining exposure to the energy sector. Rising energy costs have been a budgetary problem for MU, and Cady would like to derive some benefit from higher energy prices. Cady is uncertain as to how MU could best add the desired exposure to energy, and he has contacted Greg Peck, CFA, who serves as a consultant to the MU endowment.

Peck has suggested three alternatives:

1. Trading long futures contracts on oil or some other energy-related commodity.

2. Overweighting energy stocks in the existing MU portfolio.

3. Buying exchange traded funds (ETFs) that exclusively invest in long futures positions on the broad commodity market.

Peck has provided Cady with a breakdown of commodity futures returns over the past 30 days for three upcoming oil futures contracts, shown in Exhibit 1.

Exhibit 1

Contract Maturity	Futures Price June 15	Futures Price May 15	Change in Spot Price
July	$83.25	$82.55	+$0.50
October	$82.35	$81.70	+$0.50
January	$81.75	$81.20	+$0.50

Cady is evaluating his alternatives.

A.   For each of the three alternatives suggested by Peck, **select** whether the approach is a direct or an indirect commodity investment, and **comment** on how well it achieves Cody's objectives.

(6 minutes)

Answer Question 4-A in the template provided.

Template for Question 4-A

Alternative	Type (circle one)	Comment
Trading long futures contracts on oil or some other energy-related commodity.	Direct Indirect	
Overweighting energy stocks in the existing MU portfolio.	Direct Indirect	
Buying exchange traded funds (ETFs) that exclusively invest in long futures positions on the broad commodity market.	Direct Indirect	

B. **Calculate** the roll return, for the period May 15 to June 15, for the oil futures contracts maturing in July, October, and January, based on the data in Exhibit 1.

(3 minutes)

Template for Question 4-B

Contract	Roll yield calculation
July	
October	
January	

C. **Identify** the current oil futures pricing situation as backwardation or contango, and **justify** your response with *one* reason.

(2 minutes)

Template for Question 4-C

Futures pricing	Justification
Backwardation	
Contango	

D. Cady has been reviewing the recent performance of the GSCI, and has found that for the last 12 months, the GSCI has had a roll return of 6.4% and a spot return of 10.2%. If the collateral return on the GSCI over the past 12 months was 7.1%, **calculate** the total return on the GSCI.

(3 minutes)

E. **Discuss** the potential benefits to the MU endowment of adding energy-related commodities as an asset class, in terms of:
    i. Inflation hedging.
    ii. Diversification.

(4 minutes)

QUESTION 5 HAS THREE PARTS FOR A TOTAL OF 10 MINUTES

Juan Ketter, CFA, specializes in real estate and real estate manager reviews for Fund Evaluators, Inc. (FEI). FEI was recently retained Von Wilstrom Real Estate Management (VWREM) to review performance results and make other recommendations. To assist in his analysis, Ketter is assigned a new employee to assist in data collection. The new employee has a strong background in marketable securities but is new to real estate management. Working together they compile the data on the Von Wilstrom Fund, a mutual fund that invests in apartment REITs and indexes to use for performance comparison. That data is shown in Exhibit 1. After looking at the data the new employee observes that:

> "Based solely on the data in the exhibit, it would appear that direct investment in real estate tends to be more volatile than indirect investment."

A summary of the performance of the fund and various benchmarks is provided below:

Exhibit 1: Performance Statistics

	Average Return	Standard Deviation
Von Wilstrom Fund	12%	28%
NAREIT index	20%	20%
NCREIF index	13%	10%
Apartment REITs	10%	30%
Office REITs	14%	26%

Ketter's supervisor, Eileen Davies, also reviews the data and concludes that the Von Wilstrom Fund performed poorly during the evaluation period.

A. **Identify** whether you agree or disagree with the new employee's assessment of direct and indirect real estate investments. **Explain** any special issues that must be considered in interpreting the data.

(3 minutes)

B. **Explain** *one* advantage and *one* disadvantage of directly investing in real estate.

　©2016 Kaplan, Inc.

Answer Question 5-B in the template provided.

(4 minutes)

C.   **Select** whether Ketter should agree or disagree with Davies's conclusion about the performance of the Von Wilstrom Fund, and **justify** your response with *one* supporting reason.

Answer Question 5-C in the template provided.

(3 minutes)

Template for Question 5-B

Advantage/ Disadvantage	Explanation
Advantage	
Disadvantage	

Template for Question 5-C

Decision	Justification
Agree Disagree	

QUESTION 6 HAS THREE PARTS FOR A TOTAL OF 9 MINUTES

Alan Carroll, CFA, is an analyst for MacroFund, a global macro hedge fund. Carroll has been asked to value the national stock market index for Mantrovia, a small developing nation, to determine whether the fund should take a position in the market.

Carroll begins his valuation by analyzing Mantrovia's growth rate. Over the last five years, the average real GDP growth rate has been 9.25%. Carroll estimates that the real growth rate will remain the same for next year, but will decrease at a steady rate over the next ten years to what will be the country's long-term sustainable growth rate. Carroll forecasts the components of the sustainable growth rate provided in the following table:

	Estimated Sustainable Rates
Growth in total factor productivity	1.0%
Growth in capital stock	4.0%
Growth in labor input	0.7%
Output elasticity of capital	0.3

Mantrovia's aggregate stock market index is currently at 645, and the most recent aggregate dividend was 31. Carroll estimates that the real required rate of return is 9%.

A.   For each of the three following factors, **identify** the direction of the change in the factor that would be consistent with a *decrease* in the real economic growth rate.
  i. Production efficiency
  ii. Environmental controls
  iii. Size of working age population

Answer Question 6-A in the template provided.

(3 minutes)

Template for Question 6-A

Factor	Factor Change (circle direction)
Production efficiency	Increase / Decrease
Environmental controls	Increase / Decrease
Size of working age population	Increase / Decrease

B.   Using the components of the sustainable growth rate provided in the table,
      calculate Mantrovia's expected sustainable growth rate in real GDP.

                              (2 minutes)

C.   **Estimate** the intrinsic value of Mantrovia's equity market and **identify** if
      it is overvalued, fairly valued, or undervalued.

                              (4 minutes)

QUESTION 7 HAS THREE PARTS FOR A TOTAL OF 24 MINUTES

The Sterling Foundation is evaluating its equity portfolio performance over the past year. For the third consecutive year, the portfolio has posted a double digit overall return. Still, the trustees of the foundation would like a more detailed analysis of their returns. The portfolio is allocated into three segments—domestic large capitalization stocks, domestic small capitalization stocks, and international stocks. The Rawls Group, a consulting firm, makes the asset allocation decision among the three segments at the beginning of each year. The segment weights and returns for the past year are provided in the following table.

	Weights		Returns	
Asset Class	Portfolio	Benchmark	Portfolio	Benchmark
Large cap stocks	0.60	0.50	12.5%	10.0%
Small cap stocks	0.25	0.30	16.0%	18.5%
International stocks	0.15	0.20	10.0%	9.0%
	1.00	1.00		

In order to help evaluate the foundation's equity performance, the trustees have asked for an attribution analysis.

A.   **Calculate** the overall returns over the past year for both the Sterling Foundation equity portfolio and the benchmark portfolio, and **state** whether Sterling has outperformed or underperformed the benchmark.

Answer Question 7-A in the template provided.

(10 minutes)

B.   **Calculate** both the pure sector allocation effect and the within-sector selection effect of Sterling's performance relative to the benchmark.

Answer Question 7-B in the template provided.

(8 minutes)

Template for Question 7-A

Portfolio	Calculation	Return
Sterling		
Benchmark		
Circle One		
Outperform		
Underperform		

Template for Question 7-B

Effect	Calculation	Final Answer
Pure sector allocation effect		
Within-sector selection effect		

C. Based on your answers to Parts A and B, **evaluate** Sterling's performance relative to the benchmark.

(6 minutes)

Questions 8 and 9 relate to Smith Hospital Corporation. A total of 25 minutes is allocated to these questions. *Candidates should answer these questions in the order presented.*

Smith Hospital Corporation (SHC) is a publicly traded company that operates acute care hospitals across the United States. A national nursing shortage has hindered SHC's ability to take full advantage of growth opportunities. To attract and retain qualified nurses, SHC offers a variety of benefits including a defined benefit pension plan. The defined benefit pension plan was created 15 years ago and its assets are currently valued at $100 million. At present, 80% of plan assets are held in publicly traded equities, with the remaining 20% invested in bonds. Benefit payments are fixed at the date the employee retires and do not provide annual cost of living adjustments. Exhibit 1 provides details about the SHC Pension Plan.

Exhibit 1: SHC Pension Plan for the current year

	Current Year
Average active participants' age	31 years old
Ratio of active to inactive participants	8 to 1
Actuarial value of plan liabilities	$100 million
Average employment service	5.5 years

Sarah Weekly, CFA, is the chief financial officer for SHC and oversees the company's pension plan. Weekly believes that the SHC Pension Plan's asset allocation affects the overall company's risk profile. Stating that the plan's portfolio allocation should more closely reflect plan liabilities, Weekly proposed the following revised asset allocation for the pension plan portfolio:

- Nominal Bonds—85%
- Real Rate Bonds (TIPS)—5%
- Equities—10%

In a meeting with upper management, Weekly also proposed the company modify the exiting plan to assist in the nurse recruitment process by increasing future employee benefits. She proposes that all future retirees will receive cost of living adjustments in their payouts. This will affect all payouts other than payouts for current retirees. Exhibit 2 provides information on how this will change the present value of future plan liabilities. Weekly goes on to state that future wage inflation is 60% correlated with the CPI and future real wage growth is 75% correlated with the equity market. Weekly also suggests that SHC start a defined contribution plan to complement the existing defined benefit pension plan.

Exhibit 2: SHC Pension Plan Projections

Liability Exposure	PV of Liability (millions)
Current retirees	$10
Deferred retirees	$20
Active accrued	$22
Future wage inflation	$35
Future real wage growth	$25

QUESTION 8 HAS TWO PARTS FOR A TOTAL OF 15 MINUTES

A. Using the information in Exhibit 1 and current plan provisions, **state** for each asset class in the proposed asset allocation whether the proposed allocation should be increased or decreased. **Justify** each decision with one reason specific to the SHC Pension Plan.

(9 minutes)

B. Based on Weekly's proposal to modify the existing defined benefit plan to provide cost of living adjustments and using the information in Exhibit 2, **calculate** the dollar amount to allocate to real rate bonds, nominal bonds, and equities in the pension plan if the plan were fully funded.

(6 minutes)

QUESTION 9 HAS TWO PARTS (A, B) FOR A TOTAL OF 10 MINUTES

While Weekly is convinced the new asset liability relative management (ALM) approach the company has adopted for the pension plan is appropriate, she recognizes it can be more complex to implement than an asset only management strategy. To prepare senior management for the challenge, she has prepared a list of factors that describe a low-risk investment in the ALM strategy:

1. A 0.0 standard deviation of return and correlation with other assets.
2. A high correlation with plan liabilities.
3. Equities.

She also lists non-market consideration that will increase the difficulty of mimicking the plan liabilities:

1. An increase in the percentage of employees who take early retirement.
2. A work force that is younger than in a typical pension plan.
3. A pre-announced, gradual change in government-provided retirement benefits that leaves employees more dependent on the company pension plan.

A.   **Select** and **explain** from Weekly's list:
   i. The factor that best describes a risk-free asset for the pension plan.
   ii. The non-market consideration that will not directly increase the difficulty of mimicking plan liabilities.

(6 minutes)

B.   In reference to the defined contribution plan suggested by Weekly, **list** *two* responsibilities of the plan sponsor and *two* responsibilities of the participant.

(4 minutes)

Answer Question 9-B in the template provided.

Template for Question 9-B

Defined contribution pension plan	List two responsibilities for each
Plan sponsor	1. 2.
Participant	1. 2.

QUESTION 10 HAS TWO PARTS FOR A TOTAL OF 9 MINUTES

Hugo Gamez, CFA, manages portfolios for high net worth investors. Gamez established an aggressive asset mix that includes a 10% allocation to international investments for those of his clients who are willing to accept greater risk. However, Gamez's international equity investments are only in developed markets, with no exposure to emerging markets. The recent strong performance produced by emerging market equities has sparked client interest in the investment class. Gamez is impressed with the fact that emerging market countries account for 85% of the world's population and 48% of the global economic output. However, Gamez is concerned about the high risk level of emerging market investments and whether they would be suitable for his clients. After reviewing Exhibits 1 and 2, Gamez states that as a result of the lack of diversification benefits, the rationale for investing in emerging markets no longer holds and thus precludes adding any emerging market equities to client portfolios.

Exhibit 1: Data from Most Recent Five Years

	Correlation				Annualized Returns	Standard Deviation
	MSCI Emerging	MSCI World ex-U.S.	U.S. Large Cap	U.S. Small Cap		
MSCI Emerging	1.00				19.3%	21.0%
MSCI World ex-U.S.	0.87	1.00			4.9%	15.6%
U.S. Large Cap	0.81	0.88	1.00		0.5%	14.9%
U.S. Small Cap	0.83	0.83	0.84	1.00	8.2%	19.2%

Exhibit 2: Data from Preceding Five Years

	Correlation				Annualized Returns	Standard Deviation
	MSCI Emerging	MSCI World ex-U.S.	U.S. Large Cap	U.S. Small Cap		
MSCI Emerging	1.00				−4.2%	27.2%
MSCI World ex-U.S.	0.82	1.00			7.5%	15.1%
U.S. Large Cap	0.71	0.78	1.00		18.3%	16.0%
U.S. Small Cap	0.67	0.67	0.65	1.00	10.3%	21.3%

A. Gamez is interested in the process of market integration. **Explain** how returns and volatility of return are affected as a country transitions from emerging to developed market status.

(4 minutes)

B.   **State** whether you agree or disagree with Gamez's statement that the rationale for investing in emerging markets no longer holds and **justify** your selection with *two* reasons. (Refer to Exhibits 1 and 2.) No calculations required.

(5 minutes)

Answer Question 10-B in the template provided.

Template for Question 10-B

Circle one	Justify with two reasons
Agree Disagree	

QUESTION 11 HAS THREE PARTS FOR A TOTAL OF 26 MINUTES

Great Northern Company, a U.S.-based global manufacturer of consumer products, recently established a foundation to provide financial and leadership support for nonprofit organizations dedicated to improving the quality of life in the communities where Great Northern Company operates. The foundation will contribute to the global social concerns found in their home communities through grants, volunteerism and leadership. The foundation has been established in the country of Grik. Great Northern selected Grik for both the amount of business conducted in the country and the fact that Grik levies no taxes on foundations, unlike some other countries.

Great Northern funded the foundation with $1.5 billion in cash and will make annual contributions based on the company's profitability. The board of directors has determined that the foundation should be viewed as a perpetual institution subject to the following two constraints. The foundation's investments must pass a socially responsible investing (SRI) screen developed by its board of trustees. In addition, the board requires that the portfolio invest 60% of its assets in non-U.S. investments to meet the constraint of investing in communities where Great Northern operates. The foundation expects to fund annual grants totaling 5.0% of total assets. In addition to the spending requirement, there is an annual expense ratio of 2%.

The board of trustees hired a consulting firm, which has provided five possible asset allocations including eight potential asset classes. The consultant provided Exhibit 1 below highlighting the return expectations for each portfolio, along with a Sharpe ratio for each. The expected inflation rate is 2.75%. The board established a guideline that a minimum of 5% must be invested in each of the asset classes.

Exhibit 1: Great Northern Foundation's Strategic Asset Allocation

Asset Class (U.S. only unless noted otherwise)	Alternative Portfolios Asset Allocation Percentages				
	A	B	C	D	E
Stocks	5.0	5.0	5.0	5.0	5.0
International stocks	30.0	5.0	15.0	20.0	20.0
Fixed income	5.0	5.0	5.0	5.0	20.0
International fixed income	30.0	55.0	45.0	20.0	40.0
Private equity	7.0	5.0	5.0	15.0	5.0
Real estate	13.0	15.0	15.0	20.0	5.0
Hedge funds	5.0	5.0	5.0	10.0	5.0
Natural resources	5.0	5.0	5.0	5.0	0.0
Current income (%)	4.0	5.3	5.1	3.5	5.0
Total return (%)	10.8	9.8	10.1	12.9	10.0
Sharpe ratio	0.9	1.0	0.7	1.1	0.9

A.   **Prepare** an investment policy statement using the objectives and constraints format for the Great Northern Foundation's portfolio.

Answer Question 11-A in the template provided.

(14 minutes)

Template for Question 11-A

Objectives	Comments
1. Return	
2. Risk tolerance	

Constraints	Comments
1. Liquidity	
2. Time horizon	
3. Taxes	
4. Unique circumstances	

B.   Based on Exhibit 1 and the objectives and constraints determined in Part A, **select** the best asset allocation for Great Northern Foundation's portfolio. **Support** your conclusion with *three* reasons.

(8 minutes)

C.   **Discuss** *two* potential problems that could occur in the Foundation's portfolio as a result of the constraints imposed by the board of directors.

(4 minutes)

QUESTION 12 HAS THREE PARTS FOR A TOTAL OF 12 MINUTES

The board of directors for Shark Mutual Funds is conducting its scheduled annual meeting. An agenda item for the meeting is the discussion of best execution. The board hired an outside consultant to review the mutual funds' trading execution. The board is hoping the consultant will help Shark comply with guidelines established in their last SEC audit.

In attendance are John Sullivan, CFA, Shark's head equity trader, and Susan Ullom, CFA, head of equities for Shark. The consultant's presentation praised the company's trading effort. She stated that for 92% of the buy tickets, the purchase price for the security was less than the value-weighted average price (VWAP) and that for 95% of the sell tickets, the selling price for the security was greater than the VWAP. Sullivan was happy with the results, especially in light of the fact that Shark's mutual funds range in style from momentum investing to value investing. However, these results are in direct conflict with Ullom's perceptions of Shark's trading efficiency. Ullom and her portfolio management staff have criticized the trading effort for the poor execution prices. Ullom believes that poor trading has contributed to the Funds' underperformance with respect to their benchmarks.

A.   **Discuss** *two* problems with the consultant's use of the VWAP benchmark as the correct pricing benchmark for Shark's mutual funds.

(4 minutes)

B.   Trades can be motivated by value or by news (i.e., information).
      Describe each of these motivations, and **identify** the *most* appropriate
      order type for each.

(4 minutes)

C.   A board member questions the consultant as to how best execution can
      be determined. **Identify** *four* characteristics of best execution.

(4 minutes)

QUESTION 13 HAS ONE PART FOR A TOTAL OF 9 MINUTES

Bill Thacker, CFA, is a portfolio manager for Andrews Advisors, a U.S.-based firm. Thacker is discussing with junior employees how to construct and revise investment policy statements. During their meeting, Thacker makes the following comments:

> "Many of our investors use a mental accounting or pyramiding approach to investment planning. Even though this approach might help them achieve a degree of self-control, it is a form of emotional bias that must be overcome for clients to effectively meet their long-term goals."

> "An investment policy statement should be reviewed and considered for possible revision periodically, or whenever an investor experiences a change in personal circumstances or when external conditions change significantly. For example, a change in tax laws may trigger an investment policy statement review."

> "We have a lot of clients I would classify as independent individualists. Due to their tendency toward emotional decisions, they can be very difficult to advise."

State whether *each* of these comments is correct or incorrect. If incorrect, **explain** why.

Answer Question 13 in the template provided.

(9 minutes)

Template for Question 13

Comment	Is the statement correct or incorrect? (circle one)	Explanation, if incorrect
"Many of our investors use a mental accounting or pyramiding approach to investment planning. Even though this approach might help them achieve a degree of self-control, it is a form of emotional bias that must be overcome for clients to effectively meet their long-term goals."	Correct Incorrect	
"An investment policy statement should be reviewed and considered for possible revision when an investor experiences a change in personal circumstances or when external conditions change significantly. For example, a change in tax laws may trigger an investment policy statement review."	Correct Incorrect	
"We have a lot of clients I would classify as independent individualists. Due to their tendency toward emotional decisions, they can be very difficult to advise."	Correct Incorrect	

END OF MORNING SESSION

Exam 3 Afternoon Session
Topic Breakdown

Question	Topic	Minutes
1–6	Ethics and Professional Standards	18
7–12	Ethics and Professional Standards	18
13–18	Capital Market Expectations/Equity Portfolio Management	18
19–24	Management of Active and Passive Fixed Income Portfolios	18
25–30	Asset Allocation, Global Bonds and Fixed Income Derivatives, Risk Management, and Risk Management Applications of Derivatives	18
31–36	Fixed Income Portfolio Management	18
37–42	Economic Concepts, Global Bonds and Fixed Income Derivatives, Risk Management, and Risk Management Applications of Derivatives	18
43–48	Risk Management	18
49–54	Fixed Income Derivatives and Risk Management Applications of Derivatives	18
55–60	Performance Evaluation and Attribution	18
	Total	180

EXAM 3 SELECTED RESPONSE ITEM SET ANSWER SHEET

The afternoon session of the Level III exam contains 10 Selected Response Item Sets, each with six questions, and you must answer them by filling in a bubble sheet with a number 2 or HB pencil. For realism, we suggest that you use this answer sheet and darken the bubbles corresponding to your answers. This sheet will also facilitate entering your answers into our online Performance Tracker. You have 180 minutes for this session of the exam. That equates to 3 minutes per item set question, so budget your time well.

#	A	B	C		#	A	B	C
1.	Ⓐ	Ⓑ	Ⓒ		31.	Ⓐ	Ⓑ	Ⓒ
2.	Ⓐ	Ⓑ	Ⓒ		32.	Ⓐ	Ⓑ	Ⓒ
3.	Ⓐ	Ⓑ	Ⓒ		33.	Ⓐ	Ⓑ	Ⓒ
4.	Ⓐ	Ⓑ	Ⓒ		34.	Ⓐ	Ⓑ	Ⓒ
5.	Ⓐ	Ⓑ	Ⓒ		35.	Ⓐ	Ⓑ	Ⓒ
6.	Ⓐ	Ⓑ	Ⓒ		36.	Ⓐ	Ⓑ	Ⓒ
7.	Ⓐ	Ⓑ	Ⓒ		37.	Ⓐ	Ⓑ	Ⓒ
8.	Ⓐ	Ⓑ	Ⓒ		38.	Ⓐ	Ⓑ	Ⓒ
9.	Ⓐ	Ⓑ	Ⓒ		39.	Ⓐ	Ⓑ	Ⓒ
10.	Ⓐ	Ⓑ	Ⓒ		40.	Ⓐ	Ⓑ	Ⓒ
11.	Ⓐ	Ⓑ	Ⓒ		41.	Ⓐ	Ⓑ	Ⓒ
12.	Ⓐ	Ⓑ	Ⓒ		42.	Ⓐ	Ⓑ	Ⓒ
13.	Ⓐ	Ⓑ	Ⓒ		43.	Ⓐ	Ⓑ	Ⓒ
14.	Ⓐ	Ⓑ	Ⓒ		44.	Ⓐ	Ⓑ	Ⓒ
15.	Ⓐ	Ⓑ	Ⓒ		45.	Ⓐ	Ⓑ	Ⓒ
16.	Ⓐ	Ⓑ	Ⓒ		46.	Ⓐ	Ⓑ	Ⓒ
17.	Ⓐ	Ⓑ	Ⓒ		47.	Ⓐ	Ⓑ	Ⓒ
18.	Ⓐ	Ⓑ	Ⓒ		48.	Ⓐ	Ⓑ	Ⓒ
19.	Ⓐ	Ⓑ	Ⓒ		49.	Ⓐ	Ⓑ	Ⓒ
20.	Ⓐ	Ⓑ	Ⓒ		50.	Ⓐ	Ⓑ	Ⓒ
21.	Ⓐ	Ⓑ	Ⓒ		51.	Ⓐ	Ⓑ	Ⓒ
22.	Ⓐ	Ⓑ	Ⓒ		52.	Ⓐ	Ⓑ	Ⓒ
23.	Ⓐ	Ⓑ	Ⓒ		53.	Ⓐ	Ⓑ	Ⓒ
24.	Ⓐ	Ⓑ	Ⓒ		54.	Ⓐ	Ⓑ	Ⓒ
25.	Ⓐ	Ⓑ	Ⓒ		55.	Ⓐ	Ⓑ	Ⓒ
26.	Ⓐ	Ⓑ	Ⓒ		56.	Ⓐ	Ⓑ	Ⓒ
27.	Ⓐ	Ⓑ	Ⓒ		57.	Ⓐ	Ⓑ	Ⓒ
28.	Ⓐ	Ⓑ	Ⓒ		58.	Ⓐ	Ⓑ	Ⓒ
29.	Ⓐ	Ⓑ	Ⓒ		59.	Ⓐ	Ⓑ	Ⓒ
30.	Ⓐ	Ⓑ	Ⓒ		60.	Ⓐ	Ⓑ	Ⓒ

Exam 3
Afternoon Session

Questions 1–6 relate to Ethical and Professional Standards.

Shirley Riley, CFA, has just been promoted from vice president of trading to chief investment officer (CIO) at Crane & Associates, LLC (CA), a large investment management firm. Riley has been with CA for eight years, but she has much to learn as she assumes her new duties as CIO. Riley has decided to hire Denny Simpson, CFA, as the new compliance officer for CA. Riley and Simpson have been reviewing procedures and policies throughout the firm and have discovered several potential issues.

Communications with Clients

Portfolio managers are encouraged to communicate with clients on a regular basis. At a minimum, managers are expected to contact clients on a quarterly basis to review portfolio performance. Each client must have an investment policy statement (IPS) created when their account is opened, specifying the objectives and constraints for their portfolio. IPSs are reviewed at client request at any time. When market conditions or client circumstances dictate a change in the investment style or strategy of a client portfolio, the client is notified immediately by phone or email and the client's IPS is revised as necessary before any changes are made.

Employee Incentive Program

CA offers several incentive programs to employees. One of the most popular of these programs is the CA IPO program. Whenever CA is involved in an initial public offering (IPO), portfolio managers are allowed to participate. The structure is simple—for every 100 shares purchased on behalf of a client, the manager is awarded five shares for his own account. The manager is thus rewarded for getting an IPO sold and at the same time is able to share in the results of the IPO. Any time shares are remaining 72 hours before the IPO goes public, other employees are allowed to participate on a first-come, first-serve basis. Employees seem to appreciate this opportunity, but CA does not have exact numbers on employee participation in the program.

Private Equity Fund

CA has a private equity fund that is internally managed. This fund is made available only to clients with more than $5 million in assets managed by CA, a policy that is fully disclosed in CA's marketing materials. Roughly one-third of the fund's assets are invested in companies that are either very small capitalization or thinly traded (or both). The pricing of these securities for monthly account statements is often difficult. CA support staff get information from different sources—sometimes using third party services, sometimes using CA valuation models. In some instances, a manager of the private equity fund will enter an order during the last trading hour of the month to purchase 100 shares of one of these small securities at a modest premium to the last trade price. If the trade gets executed, that price can then be used on the account statements. The small size of these trades does not significantly affect the fund's overall position in any particular company holding, which is typically several thousand shares.

Soft Dollar Usage

Several different managers at CA use independent research in developing investment ideas. One of the more popular research services among CA managers is "Beneath the Numbers (BTN)," which focuses on potential accounting abuses at prominent companies. This service often provides early warnings of problems with a stock, allowing CA managers the opportunity to sell their clients' positions before a negative surprise lowers the price. Stocks covered by BTN are typically widely held in CA client accounts. Managers at CA have been so happy with BTN that they have also subscribed to a new research product provided by the same authors—"Beneath the Radar (BTR)." BTR recommends small capitalization securities that are not large enough to attract much attention from large institutional investors. The results of BTR's recommendations are mixed thus far, but CA managers are willing to be patient.

As they discuss these issues, Riley informs Simpson that she is determined to bring CA into full compliance with the CFA Institute's "Asset Manager Code of Professional Conduct." The following questions should be answered with the Asset Manager Code as a guide.

1. Indicate whether CA's policies related to investment policy statement (IPS) reviews and notification of changes in investment style/strategy are consistent with the Asset Manager Code of Professional Conduct.
   A. Both policies are inadequate.
   B. Both policies are consistent with the Asset Manager Code of Professional Conduct.
   C. The IPS review policy is inadequate, but the policy on communicating changes in style/strategy is adequate.

2.   Indicate whether CA's policies related to its IPO program, specifically allowing portfolio manager participation and employee participation, are consistent with the Asset Manager Code of Professional Conduct.
   A. Policies on both portfolio manager and employee participation in IPOs are not consistent with the Asset Manager Code of Professional Conduct.
   B. The employee participation in IPOs policy is consistent with the Asset Manager Code, as is the portfolio manager's policy on participation in IPOs.
   C. The portfolio manager's policy on IPOs is not consistent with the Asset Manager Cod; however, the employee policy on IPOs is consistent with the Asset Manager Code.

3.   Participation in CA's private equity fund is limited to clients with $5 million under management. This policy:
   A. does not violate the Asset Manager Code of Professional Conduct.
   B. would be acceptable so long as a similar investment vehicle was made available to all clients.
   C. is not consistent with the Asset Manager Code of Professional Conduct.

4.   In discussing the pricing of thinly traded securities in the private equity fund, Riley suggested that CA should choose one pricing method and apply it consistently, thus avoiding the need to disclose specific pricing methods to clients. Simpson responded that using third party sources or internal valuation models was acceptable, so long as the pricing sources are fully disclosed to clients. Indicate whether Riley's comment and/or Simpson's responses are *correct* or *incorrect*.
   A. Both Riley's comment and Simpson's response are correct.
   B. Riley's comment is not correct; however, Simpson's response is correct.
   C. Riley is correct, while Simpson is not correct.

5.   Trading stocks during the last trading hour of a month to establish a fair market price:
   A. does not violate the Asset Manager Code of Professional Conduct.
   B. is acceptable so long as the trade is not material relative to the overall CA position in the security.
   C. is not consistent with the Asset Manager Code of Professional Conduct.

6. Simpson has verified that CA has adequate disclosures of its soft dollar usage. Given that full disclosure is made to clients, indicate whether CA's use of soft dollars for BTN and BTR are consistent with the Asset Manager Code of Professional Conduct.
    A. Given the adequate disclosures, use of soft dollars for both BTN and BTR is acceptable.
    B. Use of soft dollars for BTN is acceptable, but not for BTR.
    C. Neither of these publications provide direct benefit to the client; thus, neither may be paid for with soft dollars.

Questions 7–12 relate to Ethical and Professional Standards.

Stephanie Mackley is a portfolio manager for Durango Wealth Management (DWM), a regional money manager catering to wealthy investors in the southwestern portion of the United States. Mackley's clients vary widely in terms of their age, net worth, and investment objectives, but all must have at least $1 million in net assets before she will accept them as clients.

Many of Mackley's clients are referred to her by Kern & Associates, an accounting and consulting firm. DWM does not provide any direct compensation to Kern & Associates for the referrals, but Mackley, who is the president of her local CFA Society, invites Kern & Associates to give an annual presentation to the society on the subject of tax planning and minimization strategies that Kern & Associates provides for its clients. Kern & Associates' competitors have never received an invitation to present their services to the society. When Mackley receives a referral, she informs the prospect of the arrangement between DWM and Kern & Associates.

DWM maintains a full research staff that analyzes and recommends equity and debt investments. All of the in-house research is provided to the firm's portfolio managers and their clients. In addition, DWM provides a subscription service to outside investors and portfolio managers. Aaron Welch, CFA, a private contractor, researches and reports on high-tech firms in the United States and other developed countries for several portfolio management clients. One of his latest reports rated InnerTech, Inc., a small startup that develops microscopic surgical devices, as a strong buy. After reviewing the report carefully, Mackley decides to purchase shares of InnerTech for clients with account values over $6 million. After careful review of each client, she determines that accounts with less than this amount cannot accept the risk level associated with InnerTech stock.

Two days after purchasing InnerTech for her clients, the stock nearly doubles in value, and the clients are ecstatic about the returns on their portfolios. Several of them give her small bouquets of flowers and boxes of chocolates, which she discloses to her supervisor at DWM. One client even offers her the use of a condo in Vail, Colorado, for two weeks during ski season if she can reproduce the results next quarter. Mackley graciously thanks her clients and asks that they refer any of their friends and relatives who are in need of asset management services. She provides brochures to a few clients who mention they have friends who would be interested. The brochure contains a description of Mackley's services and her qualifications. At the end of the brochure, Mackley includes her full name followed by "a Chartered Financial Analyst" in bold font of the same size as her name. Following is an excerpt from the brochure:

"DWM can provide many of the investment services you are likely to need. For those services that we do not provide directly, such as estate planning, we have standing relationships with companies that do provide such services. I have a long history with DWM, serving as an investment analyst for six years and then in my current capacity as a portfolio manager for 12 years. My clients have been very satisfied with my past performance and will likely be satisfied with my future performance, which I attribute to my significant investment experience as well as my participation in the CFA Program. I earned the right to use the CFA designation thirteen years ago. All CFA charterholders must pass a series of three rigorous examinations that cover investment management and research analysis."

Two weeks later, some of Mackley's clients request that she provide supporting documentation for the research report on InnerTech so they can familiarize themselves with how DWM analyzes investment opportunities. Mackley asks Welch for the documents, but Welch is unable to provide copies of his supporting research since he disposed of them, according to the company's policy, one week after issuing and distributing the report. Mackley informs Welch that obtaining the supporting documents is of the utmost importance because of one of the clients requesting the materials. She explains that Craig Adams is about to inherit $20 million and, as a result, will be one of the firm's most important clients. Welch agrees to recreate the research documents in order to support the firm's relationship with Adams.

7. Does the arrangement between Mackley and Kern & Associates violate any CFA Institute Standards of Professional Conduct?
    A. Yes.
    B. No, because the referral agreement is fully disclosed to all clients and prospects before they employ Mackley's services.
    C. No, because Mackley only accepts clients with net assets above $1 million who are likely to know that the arrangement is common in the industry.

8. Were any CFA Institute Standards of Professional Conduct violated in conjunction with Welch's report on InnerTech and Mackley's initial purchase of InnerTech stock?

	Welch	Mackley
A.	No	Yes
B.	Yes	No
C.	Yes	Yes

9. According to the Standards of Professional Conduct, Mackley must do which of the following regarding the gifts offered to her by her clients? She may:
   A. not accept use of the condo without prior disclosure to her employer in writing.
   B. not accept the gifts or use of the condo without disclosing them to her employer in writing.
   C. accept the gifts and use of the condo as they represent little or no monetary value to her or cost to her clients.

10. Does Mackley's signature at the end of her brochure violate any CFA Institute Standards of Professional Conduct?
    A. Yes. Including "a Chartered Financial Analyst" after her name is a violation.
    B. No. Although writing out "a Chartered Financial Analyst" is discouraged, doing so does not represent a violation.
    C. Yes. Mackley may include "a Chartered Financial Analyst" in bold type only if the rest of her name is also in bold type.

11. In her marketing brochure, did Mackley violate any CFA Institute Standards of Professional Conduct in her reference to her past and future investment performance or her description of the CFA Program?

	Performance	CFA Program
A.	Yes	Yes
B.	No	Yes
C.	Yes	No

12. In her discussions with Welch, where she asks him to recreate the supporting research for the InnerTech report, has Mackley violated any CFA Institute Standards of Professional Conduct?
    A. No.
    B. Yes, because the request creates a conflict of interest between Mackley and Welch.
    C. Yes, because she failed to preserve the confidentiality of her client's information.

Questions 13–18 relate to Capital Market Expectations and Equity Portfolio Management.

Security analysts Andrew Tian, CFA, and Cameron Wong, CFA, are attending an investment symposium at the Singapore Investment Analyst Society. The focus of the symposium is capital market expectations and relative asset valuations across markets. Many highly-respected practitioners and academics from across the Asia-Pacific region are on hand to make presentations and participate in panel discussions.

The first presenter, Lillian So, President of the Society, speaks on market expectations and tools for estimating intrinsic values. She notes that analysts attempting to gauge expectations are often subject to various pitfalls that subjectively skew their estimates. She also points out that there are potential problems relating to choice of historical time periods to use in developing input estimates.

She then provides the following data to illustrate how analysts might go about generating expectations and estimating intrinsic values.

Index	Value	D_0	$\hat{g}$	Risk-Free	Expected Risk Premium
Singapore	3,750	90	6.0%	2.4%	?
Taiwan	?	450	4.5%	2.7%	1.10 × Singapore's E(Risk premium)

The next speaker, Clive Smyth, is a member of the exchange rate committee at the Bank of New Zealand. His presentation concerns the links between spot currency rates and forecasted exchange rates. He states that foreign exchange rates are linked by several forces including purchasing power parity (PPP) and interest rate parity (IRP). He tells his audience that the relationship between exchange rates and PPP is strongest in the short run, while the relationship between exchange rates and IRP is strongest in the long run. Smyth goes on to say that when a country's economy becomes more integrated with the larger world economy, this can have a profound impact on the cost of capital and asset valuations in that country.

The final speaker in the session directed his discussion toward emerging market investments. This discussion, by Hector Ruiz, head of emerging market investment for the Chilean Investment Board, was primarily concerned with how emerging market risk differs from that in developed markets and how to evaluate the potential of emerging market investments. He noted that sometimes an economic crisis in one country can spread to other countries in the area, and that asset returns often exhibit a greater degree of non-normality than in developed markets.

Ruiz then discusses economic forecasting approaches to developed markets. He makes several statements.

Statement 1: The econometrics model approach offers the advantage of consistent application of relationships throughout all variables, but it is time consuming to initially construct.

Statement 2: In contrast, the economic indicators approach is conceptually easier to understand, but it takes a great deal of time for the user to collect the data.

Ruiz concluded his presentation with the data in the tables below to illustrate factors that should be considered during the decision-making process for portfolio managers who are evaluating investments in emerging markets.

Characteristics for Russia and Brazil

Characteristic	Brazil	Russia
Foreign exchange to short-term debt	93%	182%
Debt as a percentage of GDP	86%	38%

Characteristics for China and India

Characteristic	China	India
Population growth	0.8%	1.3%
Labor force participation growth	1.8%	0.5%
Growth on spending on new capital inputs	1.3%	1.4%
Growth in total factor productivity	0.9%	0.4%
Expected savings relative to investment	Surplus	Deficit

13. When the first presenter refers to skewed estimates and time period selection, she is referring to:
    A. emotional bias and status quo.
    B. emotional bias and data mining.
    C. cognitive errors and status quo bias.

14. Based upon the information provided by So, the equity risk premium in Singapore and the intrinsic value of the Taiwan index are *closest* to:

Singapore E(risk premium)	Taiwan Index Value
A. 6.0%	9,800
B. 6.1%	9,500
C. 8.4%	7,125

15. Regarding Smyth's statements concerning exchange rate links:
    A. both statements are incorrect.
    B. only the statement regarding PPP is correct.
    C. only the statement regarding IRP is correct.

16. Regarding Ruiz's two statements about economic forecasting for developed markets:
    A. only statement 1 is true.
    B. only statement 2 is true.
    C. both statements 1 and 2 are true.

17. With regard to Ruiz's statements concerning emerging market risk, when an economic crisis spreads from one country to other countries in the area, this is known as:
    A. contagion, and non-normality of returns precludes the use of non-parametric models to estimate risk.
    B. contagion, and non-normality of returns makes it more difficult to estimate risk using parametric models.
    C. macro transmission, and non-normality of returns makes it more difficult to estimate risk using parametric models.

18. Based upon the data provided, which of the following statements is *most* correct?
    A. Brazil would be favored for equity investment.
    B. China would be favored for both equity and bond investment.
    C. Russia would be favored for bond investment.

Questions 19–24 relate to Management of Active and Passive Fixed Income Portfolios.

Eugene Price, CFA, a portfolio manager for the American Universal Fund (AUF), has been directed to pursue a contingent immunization strategy. At a minimum return of 6%, $100 million is set aside today to fully fund the five-year liability. The trustees have also stated that they believe an immunization rate of 8% is attainable in today's market. Price has decided to implement this strategy by initially purchasing $100 million in 10-year bonds with an annual coupon rate of 8.0%, paid semiannually.

Price forecasts that the prevailing immunization rate and market rate for the bonds will both rise from 8% to 9% in one year.

While Price is conducting his immunization strategy he is approached by April Banks, a newly hired junior analyst at AUF. Banks is wondering what steps need to be taken to immunize a portfolio with multiple liabilities. Price states that the concept of single liability immunization can fortunately be extended to address the issue of immunizing a portfolio with multiple liabilities. He further states that there are two methods for managing multiple liabilities. The first method is cash flow matching which involves finding a bond with a maturity date equal to the longest liability, buying enough in par value of that bond so that the principal and final coupon fully fund the liability, and continuing this process until all liabilities are matched. The second method is horizon matching which ensures that the assets and liabilities have the same present values and durations.

Price warns Banks about the dangers of immunization risk. He states that it is usually impossible to have a portfolio with zero immunization risk because of reinvestment risk. Price tells Banks, "Be cognizant of the dispersion of cash flows when conducting an immunization strategy. When there is a high dispersion of cash flows about the horizon date, immunization risk is high. It is better to have cash flows concentrated around the investment horizon, since immunization risk is reduced."

19. The initial cushion spread for Price's strategy is *closest* to:
    A. 100 bps.
    B. 200 bps.
    C. 300 bps.

20. The initial dollar safety margin is *closest* to:
    A. $9.21 million.
    B. $34.39 million.
    C. $42.74 million.

21.   If Price's forecast for interest rates in one year is correct, the dollar safety margin, assuming coupons are reinvested at 8% semiannually, will be *closest* to:
A. $3.10 million.
B. $7.58 million.
C. $31.29 million.

22.   Ignoring Price's forecast and instead assuming an immediate (today) increase in the immunized rate to 11%, at what YTM for the bond would Price be required to immediately immunize?
A. 11.0%.
B. 11.7%.
C. 12.5%.

23.   Regarding Price's statements on the two methods for managing multiple liabilities, determine whether his descriptions of cash flow matching and horizon matching are correct.
A. Both statements are correct.
B. Only his statement about horizon matching is correct.
C. Only his statement about cash flow matching is correct.

24.   Price has stated that, because of the need to reinvest coupons, it is usually impossible to totally eliminate immunization risk with coupon-paying bonds. He has also stated that an increased dispersion of asset maturities around the horizon date increases immunization risk. Determine which of these statements is (are) correct.
A. Both statements are correct.
B. Only the statement about the dispersion of cash flows is correct.
C. Only the statement about totally eliminating immunization risk is correct.

Questions 25–30 relate to Asset Allocation, Global Bonds, Risk Management, and Risk Management Applications of Derivatives.

Mary Rolle and Betty Sims are portfolio managers for RS Global Investments, located in Toronto, Canada. RS specializes in seeking undervalued stocks and bonds throughout the North American, Asian, and European markets. RS has clients throughout North America, however, the majority are Canadian (CAD) institutional investors. RS has traditionally managed currency risk in their portfolios by assigning it to their portfolio managers. The manager is allowed discretion for hedging currency risk within the confines of the investor's investment policy statement with the primary goal of reducing portfolio risk.

Rolle and Sims are currently deciding whether to hedge the currency risk of a portfolio of Japanese (JPY) stocks. Rolle explores the possibility of using three different currency hedges. Each is an option contract on the yen-Canadian dollar exchange rate.

Hedge A	Buy CAD Calls
Hedge B	Sell CAD Puts
Hedge C	Sell JPY Puts

RS has a portfolio of European stocks and would like to change its equity risk. They can enter into futures contracts on the Eurostoxx index of large European stocks. The information below provides the characteristics of the futures contract and the portfolio.

Portfolio value in euros	2,000,000
Desired beta value	1.80
Current portfolio beta	0.60
Beta of futures contract	1.02
Value of one futures contract in euros	110,000
Risk-free rate	2.5%

RS is also invested in British and Argentine stocks. RS has taken a position in two main sectors of the British economy. The first sector consists of manufacturers who derive a great deal of their business from exporting to the United States and Canada. The other sector consists of British service firms who are largely immune from international competition, because most of their business is localized and cannot be provided by foreign firms. The main investment in the Argentine stocks consists of firms who provide cellular phone service to Argentine consumers. Rolle and Sims discuss which currency positions RS should hedge.

Upon further analysis, RS has determined it will hedge the currency risk of the Argentine stocks. Their goal is downside protection and modest upside potential for the ARS currency. RS has also received notification from one of its larger clients that a large contribution will be received into the portfolio in six months; the funds are to be synthetically preinvested in a 60/40 allocation to U.K. stocks and bonds.

25. Which of following *best* describes the approach used by RS to manage currency risk?
    A. Currency overlay.
    B. Discretionary hedging.
    C. Active currency management.

26. Regarding hedging the currency risk of the Japanese stock portfolio, which hedge would be *most* appropriate?
    A. Hedge A.
    B. Hedge B.
    C. Hedge C.

27. For RS to change the equity risk of their European stocks, the *most* appropriate strategy is to:
    A. buy 4 equity futures contracts.
    B. buy 18 equity futures contracts.
    C. buy 21 equity futures contracts.

28. Regarding the currency hedge of the British and Argentine stocks, which of the following would RS *least likely* hedge?
    A. The British service firms.
    B. The British manufacturers.
    C. The Argentine cellular phone service firms.

29. To meet its currency risk management goals for the ARS, RS is *most likely* to:
    A. sell the ARS forward to buy CAD.
    B. buy 40-delta and sell 30-delta puts on the ARS.
    C. buy out-of-the-money calls on the CAD and sell out-of-the-money calls on ARS.

30. Which of the following strategies is *most* compatible with RS's requirement to preinvest funds in a 60/40 allocation to U.K. stocks and bonds?
    A. Buy U.K. FTSE stock index futures and sell U.K. bonds futures.
    B. Buy calls and sell puts on U.K. stock index futures, plus buy calls on U.K. bonds.
    C. Buy calls and sell puts on U.K. stock index futures, plus sell calls and buy puts on U.K. bonds.

Questions 31–36 relate to Fixed Income Portfolio Management.

John Rawlins is a bond portfolio manager for Waimea Management, a U.S.-based portfolio management firm. Waimea specializes in the management of equity and fixed income portfolios for large institutional investors such as pension funds, insurance companies, and endowments. Rawlins uses bond futures contracts for both hedging and speculative positions. He frequently uses futures contracts for tactical asset allocation because, relative to cash instruments, futures have lower transactions costs and margin requirements. They also allow for short positions and longer duration positions that are not available with cash market instruments. Rawlins has a total of approximately $750 million of assets under management.

In one of his client portfolios, Rawlins currently holds the following positions:

Bond	Face Amount	Price	Duration Today	Duration in 1 Year
Q	$10m	104.98	10.32	9.46
R	$25m	98.36	8.67	7.83
S	$15m	101.21	7.38	6.51

The dollar duration of the cheapest to deliver bond (CTD) is $13,245.46 and the conversion factor is 1.3698.

In a discussion of this bond hedge, Rawlins confers with John Tejada, his assistant. Tejada states that he has regressed the corporate bond's yield against the yield for the CTD and has found that the slope coefficient for this regression is 1.0. He states his results confirm the assumptions made by Rawlins for his hedging calculations. Rawlins states that had Tejada found a slope coefficient greater than one, the number of futures contracts needed to hedge a position would decrease (relative to the regression coefficient being equal to one).

In addition to hedging specific bond positions, Rawlins tends to be quite active in individual bond management by moving in and out of specific issues to take advantage of temporary mispricing. Between similar bonds, he likes to sell the overpriced bond. Although the turnover in his portfolio is sometimes quite high, he believes that by using his gut instincts he can outperform a buy-and-hold strategy. Tejada on the other hand prefers using statistical software and simulation to help him find undervalued bond issues. Although Tejada has recently graduated from a prestigious university with a master's degree in finance, Rawlins has not given Tejada full rein in decision-making because he believes that Tejada's approach needs further evaluation over a period of both falling and rising interest rates, as well as in different credit environments.

Rawlins and Tejada are evaluating two individual bonds for purchase. The first bond was issued by Dynacom, a U.S. telecommunications firm. This bond is denominated in dollars. The second bond was issued by Bergamo Metals, an Italian based mining and metal fabrication firm. The Bergamo bond is denominated in euros. The holding period for either bond is three months.

The characteristics of the bonds are as follows:

	Yield on Annual Basis	Modified Duration	Maturity	Current Price	Semiannual Coupon Payment
Dynacom Bond	5.00%	5.13	6.0	100	$2.50
Bergamo Bond	9.00%	2.62	3.0	100	€4.50

Three-month periodic (not annualized) cash interest rates are 1% in the United States and 2.5% in the European Union. Rawlins and Tejada will hedge the receipt of euro interest and principal from the Bergamo bond using a forward contract on euros.

Rawlins evaluates these two bonds and decides that over the next three months, he will invest in the Dynacom bond. He notes that although the Bergamo bond appears to have a yield advantage of 1% over the next quarter, the euro is at a three month forward discount of approximately 1.5%. That means that when the currency uncertainty is removed, the Dyancom bond has the higher yield.

Tejada does his own analysis and states that, although he agrees with Rawlins that the Dynacom bond has a yield advantage, he is concerned about the credit quality of the Dynacom bond. Specifically, he has heard rumors that the chief executive and the chairman of the board at Dynacom are both being investigated by the U.S. Securities and Exchange Commission for possible manipulation of Dynacom's stock price, just prior to the exercise of their options in the firm's stock. He believes that the resulting fallout from this alleged incident could be damaging to Dynacom's bond price.

Tejada analyzes the potential impact on Dynacom's bond price using breakeven analysis. He believes that news of the incident could increase the yield on Dynacom's bond by 75 basis points. Under this scenario, he states that he would favor the Bergamo bond over the next three months, assuming that the yield on the Bergamo bond stays constant. Rawlins reviews Tejada's breakeven analysis and states that though he is appreciative of

Tejada's efforts, the analysis relies on an approximation and does not consider secondary effects.

31. The manager wants to completely hedge Bond Q for an expected change in interest rates. The number of futures contracts required is *closest* to:
    A. 82.
    B. 99.
    C. 112.

32. The portfolio's dollar duration today is *closest* to:
    A. $2,964,708.
    B. $4,335,741.
    C. $5,235,741.

33. Suppose that the original dollar duration of the portfolio was $4,901,106 and that the bond prices remain constant during the year. Based on the durations one year from today, and assuming a proportionate investment in each of the three bonds, the amount of cash that will need to be invested to restore the average dollar duration to the original level is *closest* to:
    A. $5,885,167.
    B. $10,888,662.
    C. $12,793,588.

34. Regarding their statements concerning Tejada's regression results, determine if Rawlins and Tejada are correct or incorrect.
    A. Only Rawlins is correct.
    B. Only Tejada is correct.
    C. Both are correct.

35. In their analysis of the Dynacom and Bergamo bonds, the *most likely* basis for the trading of Rawlins and Tejada are:

	Rawlins	Tejada
A.	Yield pickup	Total return approach
B.	Sector rotation	Sector rotation
C.	Total return approach	Yield pickup

36. Regarding Tejada's choice of the Bergamo bond and Rawlins's statement concerning breakeven analysis, determine which statement(s) is (are) correct.
    A. Only Rawlins is correct.
    B. Only Tejada is correct.
    C. Both are correct -OR- both are incorrect.

Questions 37–42 relate to Economic Concepts, Fixed Income Derivatives, Risk Management, and Risk Management Applications of Derivatives.

International Opportunity Investors (IOI) manages substantial euro-priced equity portfolios for two U.S.-based investors, Mark Taylor and Cindy Amsler. Taylor and Amsler have invested in European stocks because of recent media reports suggesting that, due to continued interest rate increases in the United States, European stocks will outperform U.S. stocks over the next few years. Their portfolios are well diversified and similar to the local index portfolio in capitalization weightings.

Ted Tavinsky, IOI's portfolio manager asks his assistant, Tim Treblehorn, to review the relationship between international asset returns and the level of currency risk assumed when investing in foreign securities. The findings, Tavinsky believes, will prove useful in marketing the fund to North American investors. Treblehorn relays two fundamental conclusions to Taylor. First, correlations between international markets have been increasing, and the result has been reduced diversification benefits for international investors. Second, currency risk is typically less than half that of foreign stock risk, but the actual risk assumed is much lower because currency returns and stock returns are not perfectly positively correlated.

Taylor, however, is very concerned that the U.S. downturn may spread to the global economy. He states that he would like to explore the possibility of investing in the emerging market BRIC countries (Brazil, Russia, India, and China). Tavinsky replies that the prospects for the BRIC countries are quite good. Relative to the current G6 countries (U.S., Japan, U.K., Germany, France, and Italy), the stronger economic growth for emerging markets should result in higher stock returns. Furthermore, the increased growth in these markets will increase the demand for capital, which should strengthen their currency values.

Amsler is a novice investor and has hesitantly invested in the overseas markets. In order to calm her fears, Tavinsky and Treblehorn investigate the possibility of hedging using futures contracts on an equity index as well as a euro forward contract. They have chosen futures contracts written on the Eurostoxx equity index for her portfolio because the price changes of the contract have a high correlation with the returns on Amsler's equity portfolio. Amsler's equity portfolio has a market value of €15,000,000 and a beta of 1.15 relative to the local underlying index.

Tavinsky and Treblehorn collect data for spot exchange rates, futures contract prices and betas, as well as U.S. and European interest rates. Tavinsky and Treblehorn are bearish on the European stock market over the next year as noted by their forecasted return for it.

Relevant values are shown in the table below:

Spot U.S. dollar / euro exchange rate	$1.05
One year risk-free rate in Europe	2%
One year risk-free rate in the United States	4%
Price of futures contract written on the Eurostoxx equity index	€120,000
Beta of futures contract written on the Eurostoxx equity index, relative to the local underlying index	0.975
Forecasted return of the local underlying index over one year	−12%
Forecasted spot U.S. dollar / euro exchange rate in one year	$1.12

Tavinsky has told Amsler that he and Treblehorn will calculate the value of her portfolio in hedged and unhedged scenarios. Tavinsky states that if, at the beginning of the year, he were to fully hedge the systematic risk of Amsler's equity portfolio using the index futures, the appropriate futures position to accomplish this would be 125 contracts. Treblehorn states that if they decide to hedge the currency risk of the portfolio as well, the principal for the forward contract that will hedge the currency risk of the hedged equity position will be €15,000,000, using a "hedging the principal" strategy. He adds, though, that in this case, we should hedge more than €15,000,000.

Lastly, Tavinsky and Treblehorn calculate the forecasted return on the portfolio assuming that currency risk is hedged. Assuming that both equity and currency risk are hedged, Tavinsky calculates that the dollar return would be 8.8%. Treblehorn states that the forecasted spot U.S. dollar / euro exchange rate in one year of $1.12 should be used for the forward contract rate.

37. Which of the following is *most* accurate regarding the emerging market BRIC (Brazil, Russia, India, China) countries, assuming a market makes a successful transition to developed market status?
    A. The stock prices and expected returns will increase.
    B. The capital inflows will increase both the value of the currency and the stock prices.
    C. The increasing correlation will mean they no longer be appropriate to hold for developed market investors.

38.   If IOI wants to hedge the portfolios of Amsler as indicated, Tavinsky should go:
A. short the equity index futures contract to hedge equity risk and go long a euro forward contract.
B. long the equity index futures contract to hedge equity risk and go short a euro forward contract.
C. short the equity index futures contract to hedge equity risk and go short a euro forward contract.

39.   Regarding their statements on the amounts needed to hedge the equity and currency risk of Amsler's portfolio, determine whether Tavinsky and Treblehorn are correct or not.
A. Only Tavinsky is correct.
B. Only Treblehorn is correct.
C. Both are correct.

40.   Determine which of the following is *closest* to the dollar return on the unhedged Amsler equity portfolio (if equity futures and currency forwards are not used).
A. An 8% loss.
B. A 12% loss.
C. A 7% gain.

41.   Assuming a futures position based on the expected index value in one year turns out to be a perfect hedge and the currency risk is not hedged, the dollar return on the Amsler equity portfolio is *closest* to:
A. a 9% gain.
B. an 11% gain.
C. a 7% loss.

42.   Regarding Tavinsky's forecasted dollar returns on Amsler's portfolio (assuming equity and currency risk are both hedged) and Treblehorn's statement about the appropriate forward rate:
A. only Tavinsky is correct.
B. only Treblehorn is correct.
C. neither is correct.

Questions 43–48 relate to Risk Management and Performance Evaluation and Attribution.

Jack Mercer and June Seagram are investment advisors for Northern Advisors. Northern provides investment advice for pension funds, foundations, endowments, and trusts. As part of their services, they evaluate the performance of outside portfolio managers. They are currently scrutinizing the performance of several portfolio managers who work for the Thompson University endowment.

Over the most recent month, the record of the largest manager, Bison Management, is as follows. On March 1, the endowment account with Bison stood at $11,200,000. On March 16, the university contributed $4 million that they received from a wealthy alumnus. After receiving that contribution, the account was valued at $17,800,000. On March 31, the account was valued at $16,100,000. They also make a series of statements:

Statement 1: Seagram says the March money-weighted return will be greater than the time-weighted return for the account.

Statement 2: Mercer states that the advantage of the time-weighted return versus money-weighted return is easy to calculate and structurally easy to administer.

Statement 3: Seagram states that the money-weighted return is a better measure of the manager's performance.

Mercer and Seagram are also evaluating the performance of Lunar Management. Risk and return data for the most recent fiscal year are shown here for both Bison and Lunar. The minimum acceptable return (MAR) for Thompson is the 4.5% spending rate on the endowment, which the endowment has determined using a geometric spending rule. The T-bill return over the same fiscal year was 3.5%. The return on the MSCI World Index is used as the market index. The World Index had a return of 9% in dollar terms with a standard deviation of 23% and a beta of 1.0.

	Bison	Lunar
Return	14.1%	15.8%
Standard deviation	31.5%	30.7%
Beta	0.9	1.3
Standard deviation of returns below the MAR	30.1%	30.9%

The next day at lunch, Mercer and Seagram discuss alternatives for benchmarks in assessing the performance of managers.

Statement 4: Mercer states that indexes are often used as benchmarks and benefit the client but not the manager.

Statement 5: Seagram states that in order to be useful in performance attribution, the benchmark must be relevant to the account. That means marketable indexes cannot be used for some clients.

Mercer and Seagram also provide investment advice for a hedge fund, Jaguar Investors. Jaguar specializes in exploiting mispricing in equities and over-the-counter derivatives in emerging markets. Jaguar will periodically provide foreign currency hedges to higher quality, small firms in emerging markets when deemed profitable. This most commonly occurs when no other provider of these contracts is available to these firms. Jaguar is currently selling a large position in Mexican pesos in the spot market. Furthermore, they have just provided a forward contract to a firm in Russia that allows that firm to sell Swiss francs for Russian rubles in 90 days. Jaguar has also entered into a currency swap that allows a firm to receive Japanese yen in exchange for paying the Russian ruble. Because there are often multiple transactions with a single party, net settlements are specified.

43. Calculate the time-weighted return for Bison during March and determine the validity of Statement 1.

Time-weighted	Statement 1
A. 5.9%	Correct
B. 11.4%	Correct
C. 11.4%	Incorrect

44. Statements 2 and 3 are:

Statement 2	Statement 3
A. Correct	Incorrect
B. Correct	Correct
C. Incorrect	Incorrect

45. The M-squared measure for the Bison fund is *closest* to:
   A. 2.2%.
   B. 6.4%.
   C. 11.2%.

46. Mercer and Seagram agree the Sortino ratio is an appropriate method of considering downside risk. Considering that assumption and the other information provided, determine which of the following *best* describes the risk-adjusted performance of the Bison portfolio and Lunar portfolio.
    A. The Lunar portfolio is better diversified and, from a downside risk perspective, has superior performance.
    B. The Bison portfolio is better diversified but, from a downside risk perspective, the Lunar portfolio has superior performance.
    C. The Lunar portfolio is better diversified but, from a downside risk perspective, the Bison portfolio has superior performance.

47. Statements 4 and 5 are:

	Statement 4	Statement 5
A.	Correct	Incorrect
B.	Correct	Correct
C.	Incorrect	Correct

48. Which of the following risks assumed by Jaguar was not explicitly considered?
    A. Credit risk.
    B. Herstatt risk.
    C. Operations risk.

Questions 49–54 relate to Fixed Income Derivatives and Risk Management Applications of Derivatives.

Smiler Industries is a U.S. manufacturer of machine tools and other capital goods. Dat Ng, the CFO of Smiler, feels strongly that Smiler has a competitive advantage in its risk management practices. With this in mind, Ng hedges many of the risks associated with Smiler's financial transactions, which include those of a financial subsidiary. Ng's knowledge of derivatives is extensive, and he often uses them for hedging and in managing Smiler's considerable investment portfolio.

Smiler has recently completed a sale to Frexa in Italy, and the receivable is denominated in euros. The receivable is €10 million to be received in 90 days. Smiler's bank provides the following information:

	Spot	30 days	60 days	90 days	120 days
$/€	1.42	1.43	1.44	1.45	1.46

Smiler borrows short-term funds to meet expenses on a temporary basis and typically makes semiannual interest payments based on 180-day LIBOR plus a spread of 150 bp. Smiler will need to borrow $25 million in 90 days to invest in new equipment. To hedge the interest rate risk on the loan, Ng is considering the purchase of a call option on 180-day LIBOR with a term to expiration of 90 days, an exercise rate of 4.8%, and a premium of 0.000943443 of the loan amount. Current 90-day LIBOR is 4.8%.

Smiler also has a diversified portfolio of large cap stocks with a current value of $52,750,000, and Ng wants to lower the beta of the portfolio from its current level of 1.25 to 0.9 using S&P 500 futures which have a multiplier of 250. The S&P 500 is currently 1,050, and the futures contract exhibits a beta of 0.98 to the underlying.

Smiler will issue $25,000,000 of 20-year par debt in 9 months. The bond will have a duration of 9.9. Ng is concerned that interest rates can fluctuate and wants to hedge the interest rate risk by using the Treasury bond futures contract. The contract price is 75,287 with a duration of 7.11. Ng has also run a regression of yields on 20-year corporate bonds that are comparable to this new issue versus Treasury bonds and finds a stable regression of 1.05.

49. The type of exchange rate exposure generated by the sale to Frexa is:
    A. economic, and the proceeds from a forward contract would be $6.9 million.
    B. economic, and the proceeds from a forward contract would be $14.5 million.
    C. transaction, and the proceeds from a forward contract would be $14.5 million.

50. If Ng purchases the interest rate call, and 180-day LIBOR at option expiration is 5.73%, the annualized effective rate for the 180-day loan is *closest* to:
    A. 6.6982%.
    B. 6.5346%.
    C. 6.3785%.

51. What position should Smiler take to alter the beta of the equity portfolio?
    A. Long 72 futures contracts.
    B. Short 72 futures contracts.
    C. Long 70 futures contracts.

52. Determine the strategy in Treasury bond futures contracts that Ng should take to hedge the interest rate risk of the bond Smiler will issue.
    A. Long 485 contracts.
    B. Short 461 contracts.
    C. Short 485 contracts.

53. When hedging the interest rate risk of the bond Smiler will issue, which of the following is *not* a likely source of hedging error?
    A. The dollar duration for the corporate bond was incorrect.
    B. Interest rates changed more than expected.
    C. The projected basis of the futures contract at the date the hedge is to be removed.

54. Ng is thinking about hedging several foreign exchange positions. Which of the following positions would be the *most* difficult to fully hedge?
    A. Smiler has a loan due in two years that is denominated in yen.
    B. Smiler has an order for German machine parts due in three months, payable in euros.
    C. Ng has an investment in British stocks, which he will be converting to U.S. dollars in one year.

Questions 55–60 relate to Performance Evaluation and Attribution.

Powerful Performance Presenters (PPP) is a performance attribution and evaluation firm for pension consulting firms and has recently been hired by Stober and Robertson to conduct a performance attribution analysis for TopTech. Tom Harrison and Wendy Powell are the principals for PPP. Although performance attribution has come under fire lately because of its shortcomings, Stober believes PPP provides a needed service to its clients. Robertson shares Stober's view of performance attribution analysis.

Stober and Robertson request that Harrison and Powell provide a discussion of performance measures. During a conversation on complements to attribution analysis, Harrison notes the uses of the Treynor ratio. He states that the Treynor ratio is appropriate only when the investor's portfolio is well diversified. Powell states that the Sharpe ratio is useful when you want to find out how the systematic risk of the portfolio is affected when changing its asset allocation.

Stober requests that PPP do some performance attribution calculations on TopTech's managers. In order to facilitate the analysis, Stober provides the information in the following table:

| | Weighting | | Return | |
Composite	TopTech	Benchmark	TopTech	Benchmark
Small-cap value	50%	60%	18.7%	28.6%
Large-cap value	30%	25%	15.8%	12.4%
Financials	20%	15%	12.5%	8.85%

Harrison states one of PPP's services is that it will determine whether TopTech uses valid benchmarks to evaluate the performance of each of its managers. Stober use the performance of the top 10th percentile performance of a broad per group of managers. Stober states that this is a valid benchmark because it is:

- Unambiguous: We inform the managers of this approach so that the managers can verify the securities and security weights of the benchmark they will be compared with.
- Specified in advance: We have and will not change this policy without prior notification.

During a presentation to Stober, Robertson, and other TopTech executives, Harrison and Powell describe how macro attribution analysis can decompose an entire fund's excess returns into various levels. In his introduction,

Robertson delineates the six levels as net contributions, risk-free return, asset categories, benchmarks, investment managers, and allocations effects.

Robertson states that TopTech has performed impressively at the investment managers level for three years in a row. Harrison and Powell then describe the levels in greater detail. Harrison describes the benchmark level as the difference between active managers' returns and their benchmark returns. Powell states that the investment managers' level reflects the returns to active management on the part of the fund's managers, weighted by the amount actually allocated to each manager.

At the request of Stober, Harrison and Powell explore alternatives to the benchmark TopTech is currently using for its small-cap value manager. After some investigation of the small-cap value manager's emphasis, Harrison and Powell derive four potential custom benchmarks and calculate two measures to evaluate the benchmarks: (1) the return to the manager's active management, or A = portfolio return – benchmark return; and (2) the return to the manager's style, or S = benchmark return – broad market return.

The following characteristics are presented below for each benchmark:
(1) the beta between the benchmark and the small-cap value portfolio;
(2) the tracking error (i.e., the standard deviation of A); (3) the turnover of the benchmark; and (4) the correlation between A and S.

	Benchmark A	Benchmark B	Benchmark C
Beta	1.23	1.08	1.53
Tracking error	12%	10%	11%
Benchmark turnover	8%	7%	8%
Correlation between A and S	0.52	0.09	0.33

Harrison and Powell evaluate the benchmarks based on the four measures.

55. Regarding their statements concerning the Sharpe and the Treynor ratios, are Harrison and Powell correct or incorrect?
    A. Only Harrison is correct.
    B. Only Powell is correct.
    C. Both are incorrect.

56. Based on an overall attribution analysis, does TopTech demonstrate superior ability to select sectors?
    A. No, the pure sector allocation effect is –1.8%.
    B. Yes, the pure sector allocation effect is 1.8%.
    C. Yes, the pure sector allocation effect is 3.2%.

57. Based on an overall attribution analysis, does TopTech demonstrate superior ability to select stocks?
    A. No, the within-sector selection effect is –4.5%.
    B. No, the within-sector selection effect is –3.2%.
    C. Yes, the within-sector selection effect is 1.3%.

58. Stober asserts that the benchmark they use for manager permanence evaluation meets two of the characteristics of a valid benchmark. Are these assertions correct or not?
    A. Neither is correct.
    B. Both are correct.
    C. Only the assertion of unambiguous is correct.

59. Regarding their statements concerning macro attribution analysis, determine whether Harrison and Powell are correct or incorrect.
    A. Only Harrison is correct.
    B. Only Powell is correct.
    C. Both Harrison and Powell are incorrect.

60. Of the three benchmarks, determine which would be *most* appropriate for the small cap value manager.
    A. Benchmark A.
    B. Benchmark B.
    C. Benchmark C.

END OF AFTERNOON SESSION

EXAM 1
MORNING SESSION ANSWERS

Question 1

Source: Study Session 4, LOS 8.e, f, g, h, l; LOS 9.a, b, e, i

A.   She is dependent on a yearly employment contract, which reduces ability to bear risk.

Candidate discussion:

2 points. The children are not a good factor because they are provided for financially through college. Her willingness is not a good reason for lower risk because she holds a moderately aggressive stock and bond portfolio.

B.

   i.   Time horizon is one stage, 22 years till retirement to meet her goal. She should also think of a second and longer retirement stage.

   ii. She should seek legal advice regarding the desired education trust for the children.
   - $175,000 within the next year for the education trust. It should come from the taxable account to avoid tax penalties.
   - Save $50,000 annually, with the max allowed going into the tax-exempt portfolio and the balance to the taxable portfolio.

Candidate discussion:

2 points for each item. Regarding time horizon, the one-stage time horizon pertains to her goal of planning for retirement as stated in the vignette. An acceptable alternative answer could also be a two stage time horizon with the first stage consisting of 22 years until retirement and the second stage being retirement. For liquidity, the correct location for the withdrawal is required to receive full points

C.   Investable base:

Tax-exempt account stocks and bonds	450,000
Taxable account	400,000
Less funding education trust	−175,000
	675,000

Annual contribution to tax-exempt portfolio (or to the taxable portfolio if necessary): 50,000 (= 150,000 after-tax income less living of 100,000)

Goal in 22 years: 2,000,000

Required return:

PV = −675,000, PMT = −50,000, n = 22, FV = 2,000,000

CPT I/Y required return = 0.8%

Candidate discussion:

2 points for showing the components and calculating the base; 1 point each for the annual saving amount, goal amount, showing the annuity set up, and for the correct final calculation. It may seem odd that the case had no information regarding inflation and real or nominal return, but a similar question has occurred. There is no value in commenting on whether the return seems realistic because that is not asked for. Focus on answering what is asked.

D. Stocks in the taxable portfolio because their return will mostly be taxed at the lower capital gains rate and the tax can be deferred until sold.

Bonds in the tax-exempt portfolio where Guthrie will not be subject to the otherwise higher tax rates on bonds that derive their return from income.

Candidate discussion:

1 point for correct locations and 2 points for the explanation.

E. Hold in the taxable portfolio because the case states that tax exempt account withdrawals before age 60 are subject to a very high tax penalty.

Candidate discussion:

1 point each for the correct decision and explanation.

QUESTION 2

Source: Study Session 4, LOS 8.k
Study Session 5, LOS 11.b, c, e, f, h, j, l; 12.a
Study Session 8, LOS 17.b

A.   The decision increased her allocation to human capital for two reasons.

1. While underemployed and spending money on the MBA, she was spending financial capital (FC) and decreasing it as a percentage of total wealth (TW).

2. The MBA could increase her future earning potential and its PV [i.e.. her human capital (HC)].

If the increase in HC due to better education exceeded the reduction in FC, her TW increased.

Candidate discussion:

1 point each for: it increased her allocation to HC and for each reason. 2 points for why TW could have increased.

B.   As a private and recent startup, it would be most similar to small-cap equity. It is stock, so it is not like a money market or bond. It is small company, so it is not like large cap.

As a concentrated position, it is included in the aspirational risk bucket.

From a strategic perspective, the employer stock allocation should be reduced. As a percentage, it is too large and represents a concentrated position. Also, it is too risky to have financial assets tied to her employment and human capital. From a tactical perspective, it is restricted stock and cannot currently be sold.

Candidate discussion:

1 point for it being small-cap equity and 2 points for the explanation. 1 point each for it being in the aspirational risk bucket, the SAA, and TAA recommendation.

C.

i.   An estate tax freeze is intended to transfer tax liability on future appreciation to another party. The owner could restructure the company and retain voting preferred stock while transferring nonvoting common stock (and future appreciation) to another party. No immediate funds are generated.

ii.   A collateralized bank loan just uses the stock as collateral to take out a loan.

The loan is more appropriate for two reasons:
* Guthrie is a senior executive but does not have control of the company and, therefore, cannot restructure the stock.
* She wants to diversify, and only the loan provides funds for this purpose.

Candidate discussion:

2 points each for explaining the two strategies. 1 point each for selecting the loan and giving two reasons.

D.

1. MCS can quantify the probability that Guthrie will have sufficient assets to last for her expected lifetime (i.e., it can determine probability of ruin).

2. It can incorporate path dependency issues such as how a change in inflation would affect portfolio value and the need for distributions.

3. It can help Guthrie focus on her primary risk, which is outliving her assets instead of short-term risk analysis focusing on volatility of return.

VonLee should prepare two reports: one showing how long the portfolio will last if Guthrie retires now and another showing how the portfolio can grow over next three years and how long it would then last if retirement is delayed three years. Guthrie can then compare the expected point when the portfolio is exhausted under the two approaches.

Candidate discussion:

1 point each for two reasons, plus 2 points for explaining the two different reports and how they will be used.

E.

The return objective will increase because there is no longer labor income, and Guthrie will be more dependent on the portfolio.

For the same reasons, the ability to bear risk should decline.

Candidate discussion:

1 point each for four items, return needs increase and ability to take risk declines with the same reasons applying to both.

QUESTION 3

Source: Study Session 16, LOS 29.a, d, f, g, h, j, k

A.   Brokers are an agent with a fiduciary responsibility to the customer. They are compensated with an explicit commission.

Dealers are adversaries who make a market and provide liquidity. They trade from their own account and seek to make a profit by selling at the higher asked price and buying at the lower bid price.

Candidate discussion:

1 point each for the four required items.

Answer for Question 3-B

Component	Explain	Cost or negative cost (circle one)	Observable or inferred (circle one)
Market impact	The impact on the market of seeking quick execution	Can be either	Inferred
Delay	The change in the market price if the order is not executed quickly on shares that are subsequently executed	Can be either	Inferred
Unrealized gain/loss	The change in the market price on any part of the order that is never executed	Can be either	Inferred
Explicit cost	Fees and commissions	Cost	Observable

Candidate discussion:

1 point each for the twelve required items.

C.

Trade 1: Market, quick execution is needed to capitalize on proprietary information before the expected downgrade is reflected in market price.

Trade 2: Market, quick execution is needed to restore duration, and Treasury securities would be highly liquid. Failing to match duration leaves the portfolio exposed to the major risk for most bond portfolios, which is interest rate risk.

Candidate discussion:

1 point each for the four required items.

D. VWAP can be gamed by selectively executing or not executing orders received late in the day. For example, if the price is rising during the day and a buy order is received and executed, the price is likely to be above the average price for the day and show a high cost. Don't execute, and cost is hidden.

With IS, the failure to purchase quickly in a rising market will lead to higher delay or missed trade costs.

Candidate discussion:

1 point for explaining how gaming affects VWAP and 1 point each for the two components that might increase in IS analysis.

QUESTION 4

Source: Study Session 3, LOS 5.a, b, c, d; LOS 6.a, b, c, d

A:

Client	Concept best exhibited (circle the most appropriate concept):
1	Loss Aversion
2	Friedman-Savage Double Inflection Function
3	Goal Based Investing
4	Bounded Rationality
5	Efficient Market Hypothesis

Candidate discussion:

2 points each for the five required matches.

B. The terms are similar in that myopic loss aversion is a consequence of loss aversion.
- Loss aversion observes that investors prefer to hold on to securities that have declined but sell those that have appreciated. It is about individuals' behavior.
- Myopic loss aversion postulates that this individual behavior affects overall markets. Investors will underown risky equity keeping stock prices too low and, therefore, the equity risk premium too high.

Candidate discussion:

1 point for explaining that myopic loss aversion derives from loss aversion and 1 point each to describe how they differ.

C. The client shows emotional biases in overestimating his role at his company and assuming very high past returns will continue. Believing there is a perfect asset allocation also sounds like an emotional statement.

Simms needs to educative the client on the need for a new plan because there is a serious problem. The client does not have sufficient capital to meet the planned expenditures.

Candidate discussion:

1 point for determining this is primarily emotional and 2 points for supporting that decision. 1 point each for stating educate and then explaining why education is required.

QUESTION 5

Source: Study Session 6, LOS 13.i, j, k, n

A.

    i.   The objectives are to fund distributions to fund young skiers and maintain the real value of the portfolio.

    ii. $(1.04)(1.035)(1.0075) - 1 = 8.45\%$ to cover 4% real return, 3.5% relevant inflation rate, and 0.75% operating expenses.

    iii. $0.04 \times \$25$ million = $1 million for students and another 0.0075×25 million = 187,500 will be distributed for operating expenses.

Candidate discussion:

1 point each for the two objectives, the three components of return, and the two distribution amounts. Calculating the nominal return target requires knowing the distribution rate. The case states that a real return of 4% is targeted and the real return is what can be sustainably distributed (the distribution rate). While addition of component returns is accepted, compounding for foundations is preferred.

B.   The perpetual time horizon of the foundation increases ability to bear risk.

The need to maintain intergenerational equality and the real value of the portfolio requires taking additional risk.

One other factor:
- Yearly grants can be adjusted quickly, which increases the ability to take risk.
- There is no legally required distribution, which increases the ability to take risk.
- Distribution inflation costs that are higher than the general level of inflation increase the need to take risk.
- The trustee's desire for a minimum annual income return may indicate less willingness to take risk.

Candidate discussion:

1 point each for the three required items.

QUESTION 6

Source: Study Session 6 LOS 13.j, k, n

A.   If rates increase, the earnings on the bond assets will be locked in, but the rate paid on the liabilities will increase. This will reduce earnings and surplus accumulation.

An alternate explanation for the decline in surplus is that the increase in rates will decrease the value of the fixed-rate assets, but the liability costs will float upward and their value will not decrease. The net result is lower surplus.

Candidate discussion:

1 point each for the directional affect on earnings and surplus. 1 point each for explaining both.

B.   Any two reasons related to the ones below:
- Silts is offering two distinct products, life insurance and GICs, even if they are marketed in combination.
- Segmenting allows assets to be selected that match the life insurance characteristics from separate assets to match the potentially upward floating rate on the GIC liabilities.
- Segmenting would reveal the very different characteristics of life insurance and GICs, which should reduce Silt's confusion that what will benefit the customers will automatically benefit the company.
- Segmenting is generally favored by regulators.
- Segmenting allows for analysis of risk and profitability of each product.

Candidate discussion:

2 points each for any two reasons.

C.   If rates fall, the 5-year assets and liabilities are both essentially fixed rate, have similar duration, and surplus should not be significantly affected.

Candidate discussion:

1 point each for explaining how liabilities, assets, and, therefore, surplus is affected.

The key requirement for your answer is to recognize the company liabilities and proposed assets are coupon bearing, due in five years, and therefore have comparable durations. It is true that the liabilities (GICs) have a provision for the coupon rate to reset upward, but that is two years into their life. This means their effective duration is less in an increasing interest rate environment. In that environment, the coupon would reset upward, one time only, and the price would approximate par. In other words, there would be little price downside and duration. However, this consideration has little relevance here. The question deals with declining rates. Theoretically, you could argue this feature makes the effective duration of the liabilities somewhat less than that of the assets. That is a more complex argument and not advised in this question. If you make that argument, you answer must make it clear the coupon reset is out-of-the-money in a declining rate environment and any duration differentials and effect on surplus are going to be small. Theoretically, it can lead to a small increase in surplus in a declining rate environment if D_A exceeds D_L.

QUESTION 7

Source: Study Session 7 LOS 15.l
Study Session 8 LOS 17.h, i, j, k
Study Session 9 LOS 18.a, e

A.   Real rate bonds are a distinct asset class because:
   - All real rate bonds are similar in that their coupon cash flow will increase with rising inflation as their principal increases.
   - They are distinctly different from traditional fixed-rate bonds whose coupon is fixed and whose price declines with rising inflation and interest rates.
   - They offer a diversification benefit.

   They are most directly useful for the DB plans because such plans generally have part of their liabilities directly indexed to future inflation, making real rate bonds a key asset for liability mimicking.

   Candidate discussion:

   1 point each for the five required items.

B.   The analysis should consider the correlation of the addition to the existing portfolio. Add the asset class if the NAC's Sharpe ratio exceeds the product of the Sharpe of the existing portfolio and the addition's correlation to the existing portfolio.

   For NAC 2, he must be correct. The highest correlation is +1, so $0.856 > 1 \times (0.806)$

   For NAC 1, he could be correct or incorrect depending on the correlation. With very high correlation to the existing portfolio, it would not be added. However, with lower correlation, it would be added.

   Candidate discussion:

   1 point each for the two decisions and 2 points each for the supporting explanations.

C.   Hedging currency risk is more important for bonds.
   - Bond and currency returns are generally positively correlated, which makes returns to the firm's clients more volatile. As a result, hedging the currency risk in bonds is more appropriate.

   Or
   - Bond returns and risk are generally lower than for equity, which makes currency volatility proportionately a greater issue for bonds.

   Candidate discussion:

   1 point for stating it is more important for bonds and 2 points for the explanation.

QUESTION 8

Source: Study Session 8 LOS 17.p, r

A.   The asset allocation output of MVO is heavily dependent on the asset class inputs. Small changes in the estimated returns of asset classes can produce large changes in the recommended asset allocation. This instability of the efficient frontier does not inspire confidence and would lead to high turnover and transaction costs as the portfolio is rebalanced. No credit is given for explaining resampling because that was not requested by the question. You just had to realize that instability is the issue resampling addresses.

Candidate discussion:

2 points for stating the issue is input return sensitivity and returns in particular, 2 points for explaining the consequence is variability in recommended asset allocation, and 1 point for why that matters.

B.   Both are used in determining strategic asset allocation.

Black-Litterman starts with standard deviations, correlations, and market asset class weights. From these inputs, consensus expected returns by asset class are derived. The manager can view adjust those consensus expected returns upward or downward if the manager has opinions and then use MVO analysis based on those view-adjusted returns to solve for optimal portfolios.

ALM, in contrast, refers to modeling and analyzing surplus and surplus volatility instead of focusing only on asset return and asset volatility. ALM could, in fact, be done using the Black-Litterman approach or with more basic MVO analysis.

Candidate discussion:

1 point for explaining they are both used in SAA. 2 points each for a discussion of each approach that highlights how they differ.

C.   It makes more sense to include risk free as an asset class in EF analysis.

In EF analysis, "risk free" is treated like any asset class that can be historically analyzed and modeled as having an expected return, a non-zero standard deviation, and correlation with other asset classes.

However, in CAL analysis, the risk-free rate is a borrowing or lending rate with zero standard deviation. A long-term strategic use of leverage is not part of most portfolios, so the results are not a realistic SAA.

Candidate discussion:

2 points for concluding EF is more suitable and 2 points for discussing how it is used in EF versus CML to support that conclusion. An acceptable alternative explanation is: A true risk-free asset has a known return and zero standard deviation. In a multiperiod ongoing portfolio, this does not exist. The risk-free return changes over time and a stable CAL does not exist.

QUESTION 9

Source: Study Session 12 LOS 23.b, i, m, n, r

A.   Worthington is incorrect. As strategies move from passive to semiactive to full active, both active return and tracking risk tend to increase; however, the ratio of the two, the IR, tends to be maximized at semiactive.

Carlos is incorrect. Tracking risk is higher for full-blown active management. Selective hedging would only add value and reduce risk if the manager were always correct, which is an unreasonable assumption.

Candidate discussion:

1 point for each conclusion and 1 point for each discussion of what is incorrect.

B.

Statement by:	Discuss what is correct	Discuss what is incorrect
Worthington	Correct that LCV is the largest positive exposure	Both SCV and LCV have large positive weights, indicating this is a value manager more than LC. The regression also indicates negative weights to LCG and SCG, further suggesting the focus is on value and not market cap.
Carlos	Large positive (1.23 + 1.45) exposure to value offset by large negative (−0.61 − 0.85) exposure to growth, which is consistent with long value and short growth.	The data indicates net long exposure. Comparing to equity returns is more appropriate than money market. Note that if there were equal long and short positions, that would be more consistent with market neutral and comparison to money market returns plus a spread.

Candidate discussion:

1 point each for the two discussions of what is correct and 2 points each for what is incorrect.

C.   Active return is a simple weighted average: $0.8(-0.10\%) + 0.2(2.71\%) = 0.46\%$

Active risk uses the standard portfolio variance formula with the default assumption of 0 correlation:

$0.8^2(0.01^2) + 0.2^2(4.55^2) + 2(0.8)(0.2)(0)(0.01)(4.55) = $ variance $ = 0.8282$

Active risk $= 0.8282^{0.5} = 0.91\%$

IR $= 0.46\% / 0.91\% = 0.51$

Candidate discussion:

For each calculation, 1 point for a correct setup and 1 point for a correct calculation.

D.   This is core-satellite.
- Alternative 1 is most likely an index fund given the small active return and risk.
- Alternative 2 is a small allocation to an active management to add value given the positive active return of Alternative 2.
- If it were a completeness fund approach, then the allocations should have offsetting active return and risk to achieve more index-like characteristics.

Candidate discussion:

1 point for core-satellite and 2 points each for two reasons.

QUESTION 10

Source: Study Session 17 LOS 31.c, e, i, k, l
Study Session 18 LOS 32.c, d

A. True time weight return (geometric linking of subperiods) is most accurate for performance measurement, with subperiods defined by date of ECF.

Period 1 = (116.2 – 86.3 – 15.0) / 86.3 = 17.27%

Period 2 = (107.9 – 116.2) / 116.2 = –7.14%

Monthly return = (1.1727)(.9286) – 1 = 8.90%

Candidate discussion:

1 point each for the three correct calculations.

B. Kozlov could be correct in some cases where other methods will reasonably approximate geometric linking. The other methods include Original Dietz, Modified Dietz, and MIRR.

He is incorrect in this case because the path of returns was erratic: high positive return in the first subperiod but negative in the second.

Candidate discussion:

1 point for theoretically correct and 1 point for why he is incorrect in this case.

C. Benchmark 2. Style and manager value added return should be uncorrelated in order to determine what value added the manager contributes independent of style, which could be obtained with a passive index fund. Benchmark 2 is least correlated with –0.04.

Candidate discussion:

1 point for selecting benchmark 2 and 2 points for using correlation to explain why it was selected.

D. The equity team lost value 8.97 – 9.53% = –56 b.p.

The fixed-income team added value of 17.63 – 15.33% = + 230 b.p.

Candidate discussion:

1 point for each statement of who added or lost value and 1 point for each correct supporting calculation.

E.

    i.   Value added is portfolio return less benchmark return:

           Portfolio return is: 0.176(4.50) + 0.453(6.71) + 0.222(5.99) + 0.149(3.22) = 5.64%

           Value added is: 5.64 – 4.98 = 66 b.p.

    ii.   Pure sector is the sum of over/under weight times benchmark sector return less benchmark total return:

           (0.176 – 0.197)(6.70 – 4.98) = –0.04%

           (0.453 – 0.483)(7.52 – 4.98) = –0.08%

           (0.222 – 0.134)(6.57 – 4.98) = +0.14%

           (0.149 – 0.186)(–4.59 – 4.98) = +0.35%

           Sum = +0.38%

    iii.   Value was added in stock selection for Energy.

           Value was lost in Industrial, Consumer, and Finance.

    Candidate discussion:

    1 point each for: portfolio return, total value added, 4 pure sector subcomponents and the sum, plus 1 point each for correct sectors where stock selection added and lost value.

F.   The 15 b.p. are a residual plug. An attribution model rarely works perfectly. The analysis assumes the weights, and assets did not change during the period. Thus, the 15 b.p. could be interpreted as a trading effect.

    Candidate discussion:

    2 points for indicating it is a residual plug and 1 point for explaining why it might occur or what it might represent.

EXAM 1
AFTERNOON SESSION ANSWERS

To get detailed answer explanations with references to specific LOS and SchweserNotes content, and to get valuable feedback on how your score compares to those of other Level III candidates, use your Username and Password to gain Online Access at *www.schweser.com* and choose the left-hand menu item "Practice Exams Vol. 2."

1.	B	25.	A	49.	C
2.	B	26.	C	50.	A
3.	B	27.	A	51.	C
4.	C	28.	A	52.	B
5.	C	29.	B	53.	B
6.	A	30.	C	54.	A
7.	B	31.	B	55.	C
8.	B	32.	C	56.	B
9.	C	33.	B	57.	C
10.	A	34.	C	58.	C
11.	A	35.	A	59.	C
12.	C	36.	B	60.	B
13.	C	37.	B		
14.	A	38.	B		
15.	A	39.	A		
16.	B	40.	C		
17.	B	41.	A		
18.	C	42.	C		
19.	B	43.	A		
20.	C	44.	B		
21.	B	45.	C		
22.	C	46.	B		
23.	C	47.	B		
24.	C	48.	A		

Candidate discussion: 3 points for each correct answer.

Exam 1
Afternoon Session Answers

QUESTIONS 1–6

Source: Study Session 1

1. **B** In the meeting with Pavlica's children, King disclosed Pavlica's medical condition. Since King learned this information as a result of his professional relationship with the client, he has a duty to keep it confidential, even from her children. By breaking the confidentiality, King has violated Standard III(E) Preservation of Confidentiality. In this case, the trust assets are to be used solely for Pavlica. Even if the children or others had any claim, it would still be a violation to share information about one beneficiary with another. (Study Session 1, LOS 1.b)

2. **B** In a trust relationship, the responsibility of the trustee is to act in accord with the terms of the trust. In this trust, King has full discretion, so he has no need to have approval from Pavlica. However, he does have the responsibility to act in her best interests, and changing the investment policy to take more risk when her needs for immediate funding have increased is not reasonable. It would normally reduce her ability to take risk. With no reasonable basis for the change, King is in violation of Standard III(A) Loyalty, Prudence, and Care to act solely in the best interest of his client and maintain loyalty to Pavlica, not her children. (Study Session 1, LOS 1.b)

3. **B** King has essentially guaranteed a certain level of portfolio performance by stating that Pavlica's spending requirements will definitely be met by the new strategy. This is a violation of Standard I(C) Misrepresentation, which prohibits misrepresentations in dealing with clients. The investment strategy has some inherent level of uncertainty and by implicitly guaranteeing performance, King has misrepresented the strategy. (Study Session 1, LOS 1.b)

4. **C** King has violated Standard VI(B) Priority of Transactions by trading his shares in VNC ahead of his client's shares in VNC. It doesn't matter that in this situation the client came out with a better price. King may not trade ahead of his clients. The purchase of the private placement in ShaleCo is best interpreted as in compliance and not a violation. There is no specific indication that an allocation to a private placement is unsuitable for a client with $7 million. Likewise, there is no indication King knew or expected he would be later appointed to the board. If there were indications the investment was unsuitable, that would be a violation. If he had known he would or might be appointed to the board, he would have had to make a disclosure to avoid a violation. In addition, now that he is a board member, King must disclose this and also be careful not to violate Standard II(A) Material Nonpublic Information. (Study Session 1, LOS 1.b)

5. **C** King may accept the directorship even though it may create a potential conflict of interest, as long as the conflict is prominently disclosed in understandable language to all clients and prospects as well as to his employer. According to Standard VI(A) Disclosure of Conflicts, such disclosure is necessary so that all related parties can assess the impact the potential conflict will have on King's professional activities. If the directorship will provide additional compensation to King, that must also be disclosed and approved by his employer. (Study Session 1, LOS 1.b)

6. **A** Standard VI(A) Disclosure of Conflicts. Performance compensation, such as the one in effect at Rowan Brothers, encourages portfolio managers to act in their own interests instead of their clients' best interest (a potential conflict of interest) and encourages them to take additional risks to attain the 10% goal. Therefore, this compensation scheme must be totally disclosed to all clients and prospects. By not disclosing the fees to current clients (he only discloses the new fee structure to prospective clients), King has violated the Standard. It is not a violation to have such a compensation program, however, as long as it is disclosed. (Study Session 1, LOS 1.b)

QUESTIONS 7–12

Source: Study Session 1

7. **B** Of the three Standards listed, *Performance Presentation* is the only Standard that was not violated during the initial selection process. Keenan used the hedge fund data to create an internal report to rank the hedge fund managers, but Keenan remained in compliance with the *Performance Presentation* Standard because this information was not communicated to clients.

   A is incorrect. Keenan violated the Standard of *Independence and Objectivity.* Investment professionals should consider their clients' best interests to be of supreme importance in their decision-making process. Keenan appears to favor the employees' leveraged co-invest FOF over the retail FOF by selecting the majority of historically higher performing managers for the employees' FOF, at the possible expense of the bank's retail clients.

   C is incorrect. Keenan violated the Standard of *Fair Dealing* by placing the majority of better performing managers in the employees' FOF. (Study Session 1 LOS 2.a)

8. **B** The Standard of *Independence and Objectivity* addresses the acceptance of gifts. It states that while no threshold exists for accepting or not accepting a gift, professionals should refrain from accepting gifts that might compromise, or give the impression of compromising, independence, or objectivity. In particular, Keenan cannot accept lavish gifts that could even appear to compromise his integrity from non clients under any conditions. (Disclosure and approval of his supervisor would only apply to lavish gifts from clients.) Keenan is responsible for selecting a vendor and, although the performance record of Carmichael's firm met Keenan's criteria for inclusion, the use of Carmichael's mountain house is effectively a gift for selection that may be considered by other parties as a compromise of Keenan's independence and objectivity. This violation is further supported by the fact that while Keenan has promised to take Carmichael's children to Walt Disney World at a *future* date, it is a conditional promise, and he instructs Carmichael to keep this offer confidential.

   A is incorrect. Keenan did exercise diligence and has a reasonable and adequate basis, supported by appropriate research, for the recommendation of managers for the FOFs.

   C is incorrect. The mere appearance of preferred treatment to Carmichael here gives rise to a violation of the *Independence and Objectivity* Standard. (Study Session 1 LOS 2.a)

9. **C** The Standard on *Additional Compensation Arrangements* addresses the potential for conflict of interest when an employee receives compensation from someone other than their employer. Written consent from all parties involved (Grant and Keenan's supervisor) must be obtained prior to entering into such arrangements.

   A is incorrect. The small amount of the fee does not relieve his responsibility to get written consent.

   B is incorrect. Verbally disclosing the arrangement to his direct supervisor is not enough; Keenan should have received the written consent from both Grant and his direct supervisor before accepting the fee. (Study Session 1 LOS 2.a)

10. **A**   Keenan violates the *Misrepresentation* Standard because he may not misstate facts or present information in a way that might mislead investors. Misleading clients into believing an investment's principal or return is guaranteed is a violation, and while Keenan does not guarantee a certain return, his presentation would mislead clients by implying the fee structure is sufficiently motivational to yield superior returns.

   B is incorrect. It is a violation to misrepresent a firm's or individual's experience, credentials, or qualifications, but it is not a violation to simply state the number of CFA charterholders on the management team, as long as superior performance is not implied. The information presented indicates that only factual information was provided.

   C is incorrect. Keenan violated the *Misrepresentation* Standard. (Study Session 1 LOS 2.a)

11. **A**   Keenan violated the *Misconduct* Standard by acting in a way that lacks professionalism or integrity, including fraud, deceit, and dishonesty. Had Keenan operated in an honest fashion, he would have excluded Carmichael's fund from the FOF. Keenan also violated his *Loyalty to his Employer*, as that Standard requires Covered Individuals to act for the benefit of their employer, and to refrain from activities that may harm the employer's interest. Retaining a poorly performing manager because of a friendship shows loyalty to the friend, not the employer. (Study Session 1 LOS 2.a)

12. **C**   Based on the facts presented, selecting the new fund for inclusion with the FOF did not violate any Standards.

   A is incorrect. Market manipulation did not occur; investment managers may exploit legal, but asymmetric information.

   B is incorrect. The *Suitability* Standard was not violated as suitability refers to whether an investment is appropriate for a client in light of the client's unique objectives, constraints, and level of understanding. It should be assumed that an investor in a hedge fund is adequately sophisticated and that this type of investment strategy is suitable. (Study Session 1 LOS 2.a)

QUESTIONS 13–18

Source: Study Sessions 6 and 18

13. **C** Neither statement is correct. Rose is wrong because while defined benefit (DB) and defined contribution (DC) do create an obligation to contribute, the risk to the sponsor is not the same. In a DB plan, the obligation is to make promised payouts and if plan assets are not sufficient to meet obligations, more must be contributed. In contrast, in a DC plan, the contribution is based on a formula and once that amount is contributed, the sponsor has no further contribution obligations. The DB plan is considered riskier for the sponsor.

Boatman is wrong because cash balance and ESOP plans are unrelated. The purpose of an ESOP is to hold company stock. But, a cash balance plan is a DB plan that provides participants with a DC plan-like statement showing their balance in the plan. (Study Session 6, LOS 13.e, g)

14. **A** Statement 1 is true; maximizing the Sharpe ratio is an asset only based ratio and it ignores the variability in surplus. If the durations of plan assets and liabilities are different, then changes in interest rates would make the surplus vulnerable.

Statement 2 is false in that MCS could be applied to assets only or to the surplus (assets – liabilities).

Statement 3 is false; asset only tends to focus on asset return and not consider variability of surplus. This commonly leads to an over allocation to equity. By focusing on the correlation between assets and liabilities, the ALM approach will typically lead to a larger allocation to real rate bonds (not smaller), which will better track with inflation indexed benefits. (Study Session 6, LOS 14.c)

15. **A** The assistant is correct regarding crediting rate; that portion of return is typically not taxed. The other statements are incorrect. The underwriting cycle is a profitability cycle triggered by market competition when profitable companies lower insurance premiums to gain market share. It is not triggered by interest rates. Life insurance companies generally have little inflation risk as their policies have a stated nominal amount paid. (Study Session 6, LOS 13.i)

16. **B** This is an easy question based on the GIPS guidelines. The key issue is client perception and a common investment decision process. Equity and Fixed Income (EFI) must report as one firm. While the teams have their own "members," the actual decision process is common and through the IPC, plus the members share authority in managing accounts. Real Estate and Private Equity (REPE) can be separate from EFI, reflecting a different CIO and investment decision process. If REPE wishes to comply with GIPS, more information regarding their investment process is needed to determine if they are one firm or two. The issues of support staff and even legal entity are not the determining factors in defining the firm for GIPS. (Study Session 18, LOS 32.b)

17. **B** Statement 2 is correct. Statement 1 is incorrect. Beginning 2012, external valuations must be performed at least annually, unless the client agrees to a less frequent valuation, but in no case less frequently than every 36 months. The statement was incorrect in not allowing for an exception to the annual valuation. (Study Session 18, LOS 32.o)

18. **C** Both statements 3 and 4 are correct. (Study Session 18, LOS 32.u)

QUESTIONS 19–24

Source: Study Sessions 10, 11, and 15

19. **B** Price of bond in one year: N = 19 × 2 = 38; PMT = 7 / 2 = 3.5; I/Y = 8 / 2 = 4; FV = 100; CPT → PV = –90.32

Value of coupons at end of one year: N = 1 × 2 = 2; PMT = 7 / 2 = 3.5; I/Y = 8 / 2 = 4; PV = 0; CPT → FV = –7.14

The semiannual return is the rate of return between today and the accumulated value one year from now:

N = 2; PMT = 0; PV = –100; FV = (90.32 + 7.14) = 97.46; CPT → I/Y = –1.28%

The bond equivalent yield is –1.28% × 2 = –2.56%. (Study Session 10, LOS 20.f)

20. **C** In the first sentence of the first statement, two of the three statements are correct. The repo rate is directly related to the maturity of the repo (the repo term) and inversely related to the quality of the collateral. The longer the repo term, the higher the repo rate and as the quality of the collateral increases, the repo rate decreases. Although the maturity of the collateral is considered in determining the quality of the collateral, however, it does not act as a separate factor in determining the repo rate. The last part of the first statement is correct.

The first sentence in the second statement is correct, but the second sentence is incorrect. If the availability of the collateral is limited, the repo rate will be lower, not higher. Limited availability makes the collateral more valuable due to its scarcity (e.g., callable bonds, long maturity bullets). (Study Session 11, LOS 22.b)

21. **B** The gross profit on the portfolio is: $200 million × 8% = $16 million.

The cost of borrowed funds is: $60 million × 3% = $1.8 million.

The net profit on the portfolio is: $16 million – $1.8 million = $14.2 million.

The return on the equity invested (i.e., the portfolio) is thus: $14.2 / $140 = 10.14%.

Alternatively, the problem can be solved using:

$$R_p = R_i + [(B / E) \times (R_i - c)]$$

where:
R_p = return on portfolio
R_i = return on invested assets
B = amount of leverage
E = amount of equity invested
c = cost of borrowed funds

Using the figures above: 8% + [(60 / 140) × (8% – 3%)] = 10.14%.
(Study Session 11, LOS 22.a)

22. **C** The duration is calculated with the following formula:

$$D_p = \frac{D_i I - D_B B}{E}$$

where:
D_p = duration of portfolio (or the investor's equity duration in the portfolio)
D_i = duration of invested assets
I = amount of invested funds
B = amount of leverage
E = amount of equity invested

Using the values in the problem:

$$D_p = \frac{(7.2)200 - (0.8)60}{140} = 9.9$$

(Study Session 11, LOS 22.a)

23. **C** Both statements are incorrect. It is true that portfolio managers, especially active managers, complain that using variance and standard deviation to calculate Sharpe ratios biases the results, because the variance includes returns in excess of the hurdle rate (i.e., positive outcomes). The only false part of the first statement is that semi-variance is easy to calculate. Because of the difficulties of calculating all the variances and correlations, neither regular variance nor semi-variance is easily calculated for large bond portfolios.

Although much of the second statement is true, shortfall risk is effectively the flip side of VAR. The output from a VAR calculation is the maximum loss at a given probability. In other words, you specify the probability and VAR provides the amount of loss. With shortfall risk, you provide the amount of loss (or other target amount or return) and shortfall risk provides the probability. They are both deficient in that they do not provide a measure of the magnitude of potential catastrophic losses. To help compensate for this deficiency in VAR, managers sometimes calculate tail value at risk (TVAR) which is VAR plus the expected value in the lower tail. (Study Session 11, LOS 22.c)

24. **C** Castillo is incorrect. The name of a swaption refers to the fixed arm in the underlying swap. A payer swaption, for example, gives the holder the option of entering a swap as the fixed rate payer. To synthetically refinance Shaifer's fixed rate euro debt of 9.5%, Shaifer should buy a receiver swaption which would give Shaifer the option to enter a swap as pay-floating, receive fixed. If Euribor falls below the swap fixed rate of 7.60%, Shaifer will exercise the swaption and pay the lower floating rate while receiving 7.60%. In net, they would pay Euribor plus 1.9% (9.5% + Euribor − 7.6%). In net, they would pay a floating rate, which would be 7.8% in one year, given the projected Euribor of 5.9% in one year. Note: The terms "receiver" and "payer" refer to the pay fixed arm of the swap. A receiver swaption, therefore, is an option to enter a swap as the receive-fixed counterparty.

So Diaz is incorrect because the effective rate is not 7.5% in one year. In essence, Shaifer has called in the old debt at 9.5% and synthetically refinanced its debt to a floating rate, which will be 7.8% in one year. (Study Session 15, LOS 28.h)

QUESTIONS 25–30

Source: Study Sessions 10 and 11

25. **A** Truxel is correct as international bond portfolio duration management has been made easier through the increasing availability of fixed income derivatives. Timberlake is also correct in saying that the European Monetary Union has made it easier to rotate across sectors, because there are now more non-governmental bonds available internationally. (Study Session 11, LOS 22.h)

26. **C** Truxel is incorrect because even moderate duration mismatches are a significant risk. Enhanced and other forms of indexing will match the benchmark duration. Timberlake is correct because Truxel's approach is to match quality and sector (weights) which still leaves room for individual security over/underweighting of improving/deterioration issuers. That is a common way to add value in enhanced indexing by using credit analysis to identify improving/deteriorating credits. (Study Session 10, LOS 20.b)

27. **A** If there is a parallel shift in the yield curve of 60 basis points for Treasury yields, the approximate percent change is the modified duration of the portfolio times 0.6%. The modified duration of the portfolio is a weighted average of the individual sector durations: $(0.12 \times 5.3) + (0.3 \times 5.4) + (0.3 \times 5.5) + (0.28 \times 5.0) = 5.3$. The modified duration of $5.3 \times 0.6\% = 3.2\%$ change in the portfolio value. (Study Session 10, LOS 20.h)

28. **A** The spread durations for non-Treasuries are the same as their effective durations. The calculation and resulting change from a uniform widening of 60 bps in all spreads is the same as if the yield curve had shifted 60 bps with no change in the spreads. (Study Session 10, LOS 20.i)

29. **B** To determine which sector could generate the greatest tracking error, calculate the contribution to the portfolio's duration for each sector and do the same for the index. The sector whose duration contribution deviates the most from the benchmark will contribute the most to potential tracking error. The contribution to duration is the proportion invested in each sector times the sector's duration. For example, for AAA bonds in the portfolio, it is $0.12 \times 5.3 = 0.636$. For AAA bonds in the index, it is $0.35 \times 5.3 = 1.855$. The discrepancy between the portfolio and the index for this sector is $0.636 - 1.855 = -1.219$. This is the largest absolute difference of all the sectors. The calculations for all the sectors are as follows:

Contribution to Effective Duration			
	Portfolio	Index	Difference
AAA	0.636	1.855	−1.219
AA	1.620	1.620	0.000
A	1.650	1.375	0.275
BBB	1.400	0.500	0.900
TOTAL	5.306	5.350	

(Study Session 10, LOS 20.i)

30. C   The following are rationales for trading in the secondary bond market:
   • Yield/spread pickup trades.
   • Credit-upside trades.
   • Credit-defense trades.
   • New issue swaps.
   • Sector-rotation trades.
   • Curve-adjustment trades.
   • Structure trades.
   • Cash flow reinvestment.

   Seasonality is a secondary trading constraint (i.e., reason for not trading).
   (Study Session 10, LOS 21.e)

QUESTIONS 31–36

Source: Study Session 11

31. **B**   To determine the exact forward discount for the base currency in the denominator:

$$f_{d,f} = \frac{F - S_0}{S_0}$$

where:
$f_{d,f}$ = forward premium or discount for currency f relative to d
F = forward rate
S_0 = spot rate

In the formula, be sure to put the currency that you want to make a statement about (whether it is at a premium or discount) in the denominator. Here we are discussing the £.

$$f_{d,f} = \frac{C\$1.60 - C\$1.75}{C\$1.75} = -8.57\%$$

So the British pound is trading at an 8.57% forward discount relative to the Canadian dollar. (Study Session 11, LOS 22.j)

domestic – foreign = 0.8%

32. **C**   The decision to hedge currency risk is not related to the type of asset. It depends on the forward premium or discount (based on IRP) versus manager expectations of currency change. The CAD trades at a forward premium of 4.8 – 4.0 = 0.8%. This is less than the manager's predicted change of +2%. Therefore, do not hedge the CAD by selling it forward. The GBP trades at a forward discount of 4.8 – 11.0 = –6.2%. The manager expects the GBP to depreciate 2%. A 2% loss is better than a 6.2% loss. Do not hedge. (Study Session 11, LOS 22.j)

33. **B**   Rolle should recommend investment in the Tatehiki bond if a hedged position will be taken. The easiest way to make this determination is to examine their excess returns, which is the bond return minus the risk-free rate in the foreign country.

The Knauff company bond return: 8.0% – 5.0% = 3.0%.

The Tatehiki company bond return: 6.0% – 2.0% = 4.0%.

Note that we assume both bonds have similar risk and maturities, and any currency risk is hedged, so the decision is based solely on the excess returns. (Study Session 11, LOS 22.j)

34. **C**   The Knauf bond promises a return of 8% in euros. Since you hedge using current forward rates, which would incorporate the expected 0.2% depreciation in the euro relative to the dollar (the euro will be trading at a forward discount of 4.8 – 5 = –0.2%), you effectively lock in the current forward discount. The expected return to U.S. investors would be 7.8%, the expected return on the bond (8%) less the forward currency differential (–0.2%).

The unhedged return for the Tatehiki bond is its return in yen of 6.0% plus the expected 2.0% appreciation in the yen geometrically linked which equals (1.06)(1.02) – 1 = 8.1%. (Study Session 11, LOS 22.j)

35. **A** This is a forward hedge, but it is more specifically a proxy hedge. The yen is sold forward as a proxy for the won. While riskier than selling the won forward, it can be used if no contracts on the won exist and there is expected to be a stable relationship (high positive correlation) between the won and yen. A MVHR would be based on regressing the Korean bond returns and the won returns to minimize the volatility of returns as received by the non-Korean investor. (Study Session 11, LOS 22.j)

36. **B** Crawfordville is exposed to rising interest rates as the interest rate payments they will make increase with increasing rates. Purchasing a cap would produce one-for-one inflows to offset outflows on their liabilities if rates rise.

    Ryder has bond assets that will decline in value with falling bond prices (rising rates). Bond futures prices are directly linked to bond prices, and purchasing puts on futures will, therefore, produce approximately one-for-one gains (as the options move into the money) to offset losses on the bond assets. While selling calls would produce premium income, there is no link between that initial income received and any subsequent loss on the bonds. Therefore, selling calls on price is not an acceptable alternative to buying puts on price. (Study Session 11, LOS 22.f)

QUESTIONS 37–42

Source: Study Session 13

37. **B** A representative set of checkpoints for selecting an alternative investment manager would include assessing the market opportunity, the investment process, the organization, the people, the terms and structure, the ancillary service providers, and the documents. Low market efficiency is a common feature of many alternative investments. In fact, the reason that alternative investments present market opportunities is that their markets are not efficient. (Study Session 13, LOS 24.b)

38. **B** Historically, private equity returns have generally been higher than stock returns over most periods. Since a source of the return is often associated with IPOs and other market activity, the returns tend to be correlated with stock returns. This lowers the amount of diversification private equity can offer a standard stock and bond portfolio. (Study Session 13, LOS 24.d)

39. **A** The portfolio allocation to this class should be 5% or less with a plan to keep the money invested for 7–10 years and not 2 years as stated in the vignette. Five to ten investments is a recommended range to achieve diversification within the private equity investments. Since five investments times $5 million is less than $30 million (5% of the portfolio), the recommended size is appropriate. (Study Session 13, LOS 24.d)

40. **C** They were both correct. It is true that private equity benchmarks suffer from infrequent repricing. It is also true that many private equity investors create their own benchmarks. (Study Session 13, LOS 24.e)

41. **A** In contrast to VC funds, buyout funds usually have higher leverage, earlier and steadier cash flows, less error in the measurement of returns, less frequent losses, and less upside potential. These differences are the natural consequence of the buyout funds purchasing entities in later stages of development or even established companies where the risks and returns are lower. Due to the large number of failures and poor performers, even though venture capital has more upside potential, the average return to venture capital tends to be lower than the returns to buyout funds. (Study Session 13, LOS 24.i)

42. **C** Farmington indicated that the clients have not expressed a concern even when the market and portfolio have not performed well. This indicates that decision risk, the risk of the client irrationally requesting a change in strategy because of recent investment losses, may not be an issue. Tax issues are always important. Since Carnegie will be investing in private equity, he certainly needs to find out about other closely held investments the Lewis family holds. Finally, the time horizon is too short. These are long-term, illiquid investments, so two years is unreasonable. (Study Session 13, LOS 24.c)

QUESTIONS 43–48

Source: Study Session 4

43. **A** A flat tax structure on income, dividends, and capital gains can be best classified as a flat and heavy tax regime. Note that a common feature of this type of regime is the favorable treatment of interest income. A flat and light regime would extend the favorable treatment to dividends and capital gains. (Study Session 4, LOS 9.a)

44. **B** Given a pretax return of 7%, an annual tax rate of 25%, and annual compounding (note that the account is taxed annually, so we reduce the annual return for taxes):

FV = 1,000,000 [1 + 0.07 (1 − 0.25)]^{15} = 2,154,426

(Study Session 4, LOS 9.b)

45. **C** The reduction in portfolio risk can be expected to reduce expected returns. Since her investment objective is to accumulate assets that will generate income equal to her wage income, the investment horizon will increase. When taxes are paid periodically during the holding period, a longer investment horizon will increase tax drag, and the tax drag will exceed the applicable tax rate. (Study Session 4, LOS 9.e)

46. **B** Given a pretax return of 12%, a 10-year holding period, a tax rate of 35%, and a cost basis of $250,000:

FV = 250,000 [(1 + 0.12)^{10} (1 − 0.35) + 0.35] = 592,200

gain = 592,200 − 250,000 = 342,200

(Study Session 4, LOS 9.b)

47. **B** The gross sale proceeds, tax, $ tax drag, and % tax drag are:

FV = 250,000[(1 + 0.12)^{10}] = 776,462

Tax = (776,462 − 250,000)0.35 = 184,262

$$TaxDrag = \left(\frac{184,262}{(776,462 - 250,000)} \right) = 0.35$$

Because this is a (deferred) capital gains tax situation, the tax drag is equal to the capital gains tax rate of 35%. (Study Session 4, LOS 9.b)

48. **A** The accrual equivalent after tax return is: $R_{AE} = \sqrt[9]{\frac{150,000}{60,000}} - 1 = 0.1071$

Note that 17.7% is the accrual equivalent tax rate [= 1 − (10.7 / 13.0)], but this is not the value that we are looking for in the question. (Study Session 4, LOS 9.c)

QUESTIONS 49–54

Source: Study Session 15

49. **C**   Effective beta is found by comparing the hedged equity return with the return of the stock market. The hedged equity return is the sum of the returns of the stocks held in the portfolio and the gain or loss on the contracts. Because Willow had a favorable view of the equity market and wanted to increase beta, she would have initially purchased S&P contracts and have a gain as the contract price rose:

Equity portfolio gain:	given	$2,199,120
Futures gain:	$(1547.00 - 1526.00) \times 250 \times 187 =$	981,750
Total gain:		$3,180,870

Return on portfolio of $168 million of which 70% ($117.6 million) is invested in stocks:

$3,180,870 / $117,600,000 = 2.7048%

The portfolio's effective beta can be computed by looking at the portfolio's hedged return (2.7%) relative to the market's return (2.2%):

Effective beta: 0.027048 / 0.022 = 1.23

Both of the reasons discussed can cause effective beta to diverge from targeted beta but the facts of the question demonstrate Reason 1 is not plausible while Reason 2 is possible. Reason 2: During the 6-month holding period, the S&P contract changed by +1.38% (1547 / 1526 – 1). This is substantially different from the market change of 2.2%. By itself, that does not prove the contract was initially mispriced because it is the contract price change plus risk free return on a full collateral position that should equal the index return. But it does leave the possibility the contract was initially mispriced. In contrast, Reason 1 is not plausible in this case. The stocks alone generated a return of 1.87% ($2.2 million / $117.6 million). Comparing this to the market return of 2.2% suggests they behaved as if their beta had been .85 (1.87% / 2.2%). This is exactly the same as the initial assumption given in Exhibit 1 so there is no evidence of the beta of her stocks showing mean reversion.

It is not necessary to calculate the initial target beta because it is given in the question data. (Study Session 15 LOS 26.a)

50. **A**   The first step is to determine the amount to be reallocated to bonds. The initial portfolio of $168 million is composed of 70% stocks and 30% bonds. Therefore, stocks total: $117,600,000 (70% × $168,000,000). Townsend's recommended allocation to stocks is 55%, which is $92,400,000 (55% × $168,000,000). The total to be reallocated is therefore $25,200,000. The second step is to calculate the number of contracts purchased. The formula is:

$$\text{Number of contracts} = \left(\text{yield beta}\right)\left(\frac{MD_T - MD_P}{MD_F}\right)\left(\frac{V_p}{P_f \text{Multiplier}}\right)$$

Plugging in values from the above calculation and Exhibit 1:

$$\text{Number of contracts} = \left(\frac{4.3 - 0.25}{5.2}\right)\left(\frac{25,200,000}{96,500}\right)(0.94)$$

Number of contracts = 191.18, or 191 contracts.

The third step is calculating the price of the futures contract six months later: $96,500 × (1 − 0.06) = $90,710.

The final step is to calculate the loss: 191 × ($90,710 − $96,500) = ($1,105,890).

B is incorrect. This number is derived using 203 contracts, which would result from plugging in $90,710 as "f" in the contracts equation rather than $96,500.

C is incorrect. This number is derived using 216 contracts, which would result from dividing (rather than multiplying) by the yield beta of 0.94.
(Study Session 15 LOS 26.d)

Candidate discussion: The case information in Exhibit 1 specifically says to use a duration for cash and hedged positions of 0.25. Always read and follow explicitly given instructions or you will lower your exam score.

The default assumption for cash equivalents is a 0 duration. But the assumption given in this case is also completely logical. You would know that is reasonable from Level II and arbitrage pricing of contracts, as well as from Level III derivatives hedging and synthetic positions. The hedged position targets the risk-free rate at the time and for the period of the hedged. In other words, a six-month hedge would target the six-month risk-free rate. This is initially a 0.5 duration declining to a 0 duration at hedge expiration. Bottom line, assume 0 duration for cash unless given a different assumption (as in this case). Also note that it does not matter if the hedge is on equity, bonds, or any other asset. The net fully hedged position has a duration regardless of whether the underlying asset has a duration.

51. **C**   Townsend thinks bonds are poised to outperform, so increasing modified duration would be an achievable goal using the purchase of bond futures.

A is incorrect. The sales of stock index futures may be designed to lower target beta or stock market exposure. However, Willow would not support that strategy, as she thinks stocks are going up.

B is incorrect. The purchase of S&P futures may be designed to increase stock market exposure (or increase beta). However, Townsend would not support that strategy, as he thinks stock prices are going down. (Study Session 15 LOS 26.d)

52. **B**   Both situations require increasing equity exposure and all beta adjustments use variations of the same basic formula. A synthetic position requires using a future value in the amount for the numerator of the calculation. Situation 1 is $10,000,000 today and not a synthetic position so the numerator value is $10,000,000. Situation 2 is a synthetic position but the $10,000,000 is already the value to be received 6 months in the future. The numerator is the same in both situations resulting in the same number of contracts. Note that if situation 2 had not specified that the $10,000,000 is a future amount, the $10,000,000 would have been increased to a future value at the risk free rate and Situation 2 would have required more contracts. (Study Session 15 LOS 26.b)

53. **B** The company has floating-rate bond obligations that it desires to convert into fixed-rate obligations via a swap mechanism. If the company prefers fixed payments, it must feel that interest rates are going to rise. The terms of the swap are that Elkridge would receive LIBOR from the swap dealer and pay a fixed rate. It also owes its bondholders LIBOR + 1%. To have a net cost of funds of 7.25%, the fixed rate Elkridge would pay would be 6.25%.

Pay to Bondholders:	LIBOR + 1%
Receive from Dealer:	– LIBOR
Pay to Dealer:	6.25%
Net Cost of Funds =	7.25%

A is incorrect. If the company were expecting interest rates to fall, it would keep its floating-rate obligations because the payments would be lower in the future as interest rates decrease. Also, a fixed rate of 8.25% would make the company's net cost of funds 9.25%.

C is incorrect. The company would want to engage in a swap transaction to pay fixed and receive floating if it expected a rising interest rate environment. However, the fixed rate on the swap would be 6.25%, not 8.25%, if the desired cost of funds is 7.25%. (Study Session 15 LOS 26.b)

54. **A** Assuming a new short fixed duration of 2.625, the duration of the swap overall would become –2.5 (0.125 – 2.625). The notional principal would then be calculated as:

$$NP = \left(V_p\right)\left(\frac{MD_T - MD_p}{MD_{swap}}\right)$$

$$NP = \$96,000,000\left(\frac{4.5 - 6.3}{-2.5}\right) = \$69,120,000$$

B is incorrect. This would be the notional if the swap duration were incorrectly calculated as –2.25 and inputted into the notional principal equation as such.

C is incorrect. This answer fails to adjust the short fixed duration to 2.625, giving the same swap duration (–0.75) as the original one-year tenor; the incorrect swap duration is then used in the notional principal equation. (Study Session 15 LOS 26.d)

QUESTIONS 55–60

Source: Study Session 16

55. **C** In a market expected to increase in relatively constant fashion, constant proportion portfolio insurance will outperform the other strategies. In a constant proportion strategy, a fixed proportion (m) of the cushion (= assets – floor value) is invested in stocks. CPPI refers to a constant proportion strategy with m > 1. Buy and hold is equivalent to the constant proportion strategy with m = 1, so its performance would be good, but not as good. A constant-mix strategy (CM) would be the poorest performer, because as the market continually rises, the CM strategy would dictate selling stocks. (Study Session 16, LOS 30.h)

56. **B** In a market expected to oscillate, constant mix strategies (fixed percentage allocation to stocks) outperform the others, since they involve buying/selling stocks when prices fall/rise. CPPI would perform worst in this scenario, with buy and hold performing better but not as well as CM. (Study Session 16, LOS 30.h)

57. **C** Although CPPI strategies offer downside protection, it is their convex nature that provides it. Statements A and B are correct. (Study Session 16, LOS 32.h)

58. **C** The portfolio has increased from $1,000,000 to $1,150,000, representing a 20% increase ($120,000) in equities and a $30,000 increase in debt and cash ($1,150,000 – $720,000 = $430,000). Since equities now represent 62.6% (= 720,000 / 1,150,000) of the portfolio and their strategic allocation is 60%, Tratman should take no action. (Study Session 16, LOS 30.f)

59. **C** Combining the two would most likely lower costs, as the weights would be checked on a specified periodic calendar basis and then only adjusted if a percentage of portfolio rules were also violated. Essentially, two conditions must be met before rebalancing is done, instead of one condition. (Study Session 16, LOS 30.e)

60. **B** Illiquid assets generally have higher costs associated with buying and selling. In that case, too tight of a tolerance band (i.e., corridor) could require high costs. The investor should always strive for a happy medium between the need to rebalance and the associated costs. Answers A and C would support wider corridors. (Study Session 16, LOS 30.f)

Exam 2
Morning Session Answers

QUESTION 1

Source: Study Session 4, LOS 8.g, h and Study session 5, LOS 12.j, l

A. Their willingness is low.
- They have passive wealth from inheritance and an injury settlement, suggesting they have not been willing to take investment risk.
- They indicate low willingness to take risk with statements about avoiding risky securities or not losing more than 5%.
- They are adverse to any debt.

B. Higher ability:
- At age 40 and 39, they have a long time horizon.
- They have substantial portfolio assets of $3.75 million versus needs.
- The portfolio distributions will need to keep up with inflation.

Lower ability:
- They are heavily dependent on the portfolio for distributions (over $100,000) to meet living expenses in excess of salary.
- They have only Barney's salary and Heather appears unable to work due to a job injury.

C.
- Supplement living expenses
- Pay for the children's college education
- Retire at age 65

Investable asset base: $3.75 million

Need from the portfolio:

Last year's living expenses increased for inflation

$$150,000 \ (1.02) = \ 153,000$$

Less AT salary of: $48,750 \ (1 - 0.25) = 36,563$

Net need: 116,437

AT real return: 116,437 / 3,750,000 = 3.1%
+ future inflation (2%) for AT nominal return of 5.1%

D. Liquidity:
- They want an unspecified emergency reserve, approximately 6 to 12 months of living expenses depending on the situation.
- Cover annual distribution needs.

Time horizon: Overall long given their ages.

- Now until retirement in roughly 25 years and then in retirement.
- An additional stage could be while the children are in school. The oldest child is 12.

E. Life insurance needs are modest (low). The Smythes' have relatively little human capital to insure given Barney's modest salary, especially when compared to their financial capital.

They currently have little need for annuities because they do not plan to retire for 25 years.

Candidate discussion:

A. 1 point for low and 1 point each for two reasons.
B. 2 points each for one reason supporting higher and one supporting lower.
C. 2 points for stating the three things they want. 1 point each for correctly calculating the base and need for the coming year; plus 1 point each setting up the real return calculation and then adding future inflation of 2%. Note that inflating last year's need to determine how much money is required this year is a completely separate issue from adding inflation to the distribution (real) return in order to maintain the real value of the portfolio going forward.
D. Liquidity: 1 point each for stating the need to meet ongoing distributions and the desire for a cash reserve. Six months of living expenses would be roughly $75,000. No specific number can be determined for the cash reserve, so no number or any reasonably similar value to that in the suggested solution is acceptable.

Time horizon: 1 point for dividing time horizon into before and after retirement, plus 1 point for the children's college years.
E. 2 points each for the two issues. In both cases, you must conclude lower and support why it is lower. Recall that insurance is a risk sharing and management tool which, in aggregate, reduces the user's total wealth. It will not fix this couple's financial issues. They have little human capital to insure so there is little need for life insurance. The shortfall between spending and salary is not going to be solved by life insurance. Any need for annuities is far in the future.

QUESTION 2

Source: Study Session 3, LOS 6.b, c
Study Session 6, LOS 13.b, c

A. i.   Elliot has a very limited set of data on which he based all his conclusions. He only looked at some charts; this is most directly sample size neglect. If he thought he personally controlled or influenced future returns, that would be illusion of control. Myopic loss aversion refers to systematic underpricing of equities if investors over-focus on their short-term risk, which is not a prediction they will do well in a higher interest rate environment.

   ii.   The return objective is excessive. Assets should be invested for the benefit of plan participants and underfunding addressed through contributions, not through taking higher risk.

   iii. The investment of plan assets for the stated purpose of bolstering profitability is inappropriate, and is a violation of Elliot's fiduciary responsibilities to invest for the benefit of plan participants, not the sponsoring company.

Answer for Question 2-B

	Investment Policy Statement for Matrix Corporation
Objectives	Risk tolerance is below average: • The plan is underfunded at $8.3 billion to $5.5 billion of liabilities to assets. • The age of active employees is high. • The ratio of active to retired lives is low.
	Return objective: To earn the discount rate used in computing the present value of liabilities. A modest increment above this might be acceptable but the bulk of the underfunding should be addressed by plan contributions.

Answer for Question 2-C

Time horizon	Time horizon is short given the older age of the workforce (57.5 years) and the low ratio of active to retired lives. Both indicate significant outflows from the portfolio.
Liquidity	Liquidity requirements are high given the low ratio of active to retired lives and older workforce.
Legal/ Regulatory	A pension plan has significant legal and regulatory requirements with a fiduciary duty to plan participants, ERISA generally applies in the United States.
Taxes	Pension plans in the United States are normally tax exempt.
Unique circumstances	High average employee age; low active to retired lives ratio; significantly underfunded could be considered unusual.

Candidate discussion:
A. 2 points for each critique of Elliot's statement.
B. 6 points for the risk objective and 5 points for the return objective. Given the high point score, a good technique is to support your answer with specific facts from the case.
C. 2 points for each constraint.

©2016 Kaplan, Inc.

QUESTION 3

Source: Study Session 10, LOS 20.b
Study Session 13, LOS 24.e

Answer for Question 3

Comment	Correct or incorrect? (circle one)	Justification
"The popularity bias can cause problems for measuring value-weighted hedge fund benchmark performance. The popularity bias argues that out-performing hedge funds as well as hedge fund styles tend to attract additional funding, so as they grow in popularity their performance tends to have a greater and greater impact on the value-weighted index's measured performance. This creates a double impact on the value-weighted hedge fund index return; the individual funds have good returns, and their increasing size means they have a greater weight in the index. The result is that the index's return has an upward bias. This bias, however, can be counteracted by utilizing two indices, one long and one short. Since most hedge fund managers attempt to generate alpha through both long and short positions, they can have a net zero weight or even a net negative weight. A single, long-only benchmark will not capture the performance of both strategies."	Incorrect	Solution to popularity bias is an equally-weighted index so the outperforming asset does not have a greater weight.
"If an investor is averse to market value risk, the bond benchmark used should have a long maturity so they can lock in a yield to maturity."	Incorrect	Long maturity bond portfolios have more market value risk. A short maturity benchmark would be better.

"The recommended solution to the 'free float' problem in international markets is to determine the amount of shares to be floated by an issuer in the upcoming year and use that to recalculate the issuer's weight in market capitalization weighted indices."	**Incorrect**	The free float problem refers to the fact that many firms have shares that are closely held or otherwise not available for public trading. Only the values of firms' freely traded shares should be included in a market value weighted index.
"For bond investors such as foundations who desire a stable stream of income, long-term bond benchmarks should be used."	**Correct**	No explanation required. **Candidate discussion:** If the client is dependent on cash flows from the portfolio, those cash flows should be dependable. Long term bonds offer the investor a longer and more certain income stream. Investors desiring a stable, long-term cash flow should invest in longer-term bonds and, therefore, utilize long-term benchmarks.

Candidate discussion:
1 point for identifying each statement as correct or incorrect.
2 points for justifying why the statement is incorrect.
0 points possible if the correct/incorrect decision is wrong.

QUESTION 4

Source: Study Session 7, LOS 15.b, c

A.   Systematic risk is related to beta. Alpha is related to unsystematic risk. Barkley computed the true unconditional return of 9.94% by conditioning his estimated returns to the condition of the market and then probability weighting his results rather than just using an average beta.

Candidate discussion: 2 points each for correctly discussing alpha as unsystematic and beta as systematic risk. 1 point for indicating Barkley was correct to condition his estimated return to market conditions.

B.   Smoothing will cause him to underestimate risk because he has only a beginning and ending point but no idea of the true volatility between the two time points. Applying a constant average income return will only further smooth out the perception of risk.

Regime change is a problem because he does not know if there were fundamental changes that caused risk and return to be much different in one portion of the 10-year period from another portion. For instance, there could be a change in government policy that caused returns in the first half to be high but in the second half to be low. Risk could also have changed.

Candidate discussion: 2 points each for the discussion of smoothing and regime change. For 2 points some illustration or elaboration related to the case facts is required.

C.   i.   The historical risk premium was: 9.5 − 6.8 = 2.7%

Using the current bond yield, this is an equity discount rate of 2.7 + 4.8 = 7.5%.

Candidate discussion: 1 point for each correct calculation.

ii.   GK is a variation on yield plus growth as the expected return. The 1% reduction in shares outstanding is stock repurchase, and it supplements the dividend yield of 1.7%. Growth is real plus expected inflation. The expected decline in P/E is a downward revaluation, which reduces expected return.

$E(R)$ 1.7 + 1.0 + 4.1 + 3.3 + [(13.2 − 13.5) / 13.5] = 10.1% − 2.2% = 7.9%

RP Making the equity risk premium: 7.9 − 4.8 = 3.1%

Candidate discussion: 1 point to set up the GK calculation and 1 point each for the two correct numbers requested.

D.   Unfavorable outlook for equity (or very late in the recovery for equities, which means returns are likely to decline)
   - Inflation is rising, which indicates the central bank will reduce monetary growth and increase short-term interest rates, slowing real growth.
   - Consumer confidence has been increasing, indicating the economy is late in the economic cycle.
   - Inventories are increasing, which is likely to lead business to slow production, reducing economic growth.
   - The yield curve is dramatically flattening, which suggests the central bank is restricting monetary growth to slow the economy.
   - Unemployment has fallen suggesting the economy is late in the economic cycle.

Candidate discussion: 2 points for unfavorable and 2 points each for three reasons.

E.

Statement 1—PPP. With the same real rates, A will have 3% higher inflation, and PPP predicts a 3% decline in currency A (i.e., B will appreciate).

Statement 3—SII. With a savings deficit, a country must maintain the value of its currency to continue to attract foreign capital.

Statement 2—RES. By elimination, this can be RES. The higher rates and inflation could reflect strong economic growth that will attract capital, resulting in an increasing currency value.

Candidate discussion:
1 point each for three correct matches and for each correct supporting statement. Note, that it was easier to evaluate statement 1 and 3 before statement 2 because 2 is very vague.

QUESTION 5

Source: Study Session 12, LOS 23.f, i

A. Holdings-based style analysis (HB) examines the portfolio, classifying securities based on characteristics such as capitalization, value, growth, industry, etc.
- Disadvantage: Subjective classification of categories.
- Advantage over returns-based: Detects style drift faster.

Candidate discussion:
4 points possible: 2 points for describing HB; 1 point each for disadvantage and advantage over returns-based style analysis.

B. Regress portfolio returns against style indices' returns:

$$R_P = b_0 + b_1 I_1 + b_2 I_2 + b_3 I_3 + b_4 I_4 + ... + b_n I_n + e$$

$$\sum_{i=1}^{n} b_i = 1.0$$

R^2 = degree to which the model explains portfolio returns
b_i = portfolio sensitivity to index i
R_P = portfolio returns
I_i = returns on index i
e = returns to active management
n = number of indices used

Historical portfolio returns are regressed against various indices to find weightings of the indices (the equation's coefficients) that would have produced the closest tracking to the actual portfolio returns. For example, a 0.30 coefficient to large cap growth stocks indicates a 30% weight to large cap growth. The weights (coefficients) must sum to 1.0.

Disadvantage: Determining number of and which indices to use.

Advantage over HB: Doesn't require looking at portfolio holdings.

Candidate discussion:
7 points possible: 2 points for writing the equation; 1 point for labeling the inputs; 2 points for describing the approach; 1 point for disadvantage; 1 point for advantage over HB.

C. Full replication is simple in concept; all assets in the index are owned and weighted as in the index. It should produce a low tracking error.
- Appropriate if the index securities are liquid and reasonable in number.
- But otherwise it could be very costly to implement.

Stratified sampling divides the index into key categories. For example, if the index is 25% large cap growth, the portfolio will have the same weight, but a sampling of the index's LC growth stocks will be used, not all of them.
- Can be used when full replication is not practical and too expensive.
- But the tracking error will be higher than for full replication.

Optimization seeks similar results to stratified sampling but a computer model is used to find a sample of securities that will match the index's risk sensitivities while producing the lowest tracking error to the index's return.
- Can identify the most important risk factors and minimize tracking error with the optimal number of holdings.
- Like any complex regression analysis, the historical data may not replicate future results and is subject to biases.

Candidate discussion:

12 points possible: 2 point for each definition; 1 point for properly identifying when each should be used, and 1 point for each disadvantage.

QUESTION 6

Source: Study Session 8, LOS 17.g, r

A.   Since the $750,000 will be donated within the next year, it is not considered part of the investable asset base.

Asset base = $5,000,000 – $750,000 = $4,250,000

After-tax real return = 150,000 / $4,250,000 = 3.53%.

Before tax real return:

3.53 / (1 – .25) = 4.71%

The before-tax nominal rate of return: 4.71 + 3.50 = 8.21%.

To obtain Beitia's utility for each of the corner portfolios, use the expected portfolio return, his risk aversion value of 5.0, the variance of the portfolio, and the following formula:

$$U_p = \hat{R}_p - 0.5(A)(\sigma_p^2)$$

Corner Portfolio	Calculation	Utility of Corner Portfolio
1	$0.065 - 0.5(5)0.041^2$	0.0608
2	$0.0775 - 0.5(5)0.058^2$	0.0691
3	$0.097 - 0.5(5)0.078^2$	0.0818
4	$0.135 - 0.5(5)0.106^2$	0.1069

B.   Given his required return of 8.21%, combine the two corner portfolios that bracket the required return. To solve for their weights:

$0.0821 = w_2(0.0775) + (1 - w_2)(0.097)$

$w_2 = 0.764 = 76.4\%$; $w_3 = 1 - w_2 = 23.6\%$

$\sigma_p = 0.764(5.8\%) + 0.236(7.8\%) = 6.27\%$

C. $\quad 0.082 = w_4(0.135) + (1-w_4)(0.04)$

$$w_4 = \frac{(0.082-0.04)}{(0.135-0.04)} = 44\%$$

$$w_{RF} = 1 - w_4 = 56\%$$

standard deviation $= 0.44(10.6\%) + 0.56(0\%) = 4.7\%$

Candidate discussion:

A. (5 points maximum) 1 point each for investable base, after- and before-tax real, adding inflation, and for a correct before-tax nominal calculation. 1 point each for the 4 utility calculations.

Applying the tax gross up before or after inflation can be confusing. It is best addressed by the client and manager making assumptions regarding the effective annual tax rate or in some other manner. In this case, they explicitly agree the inflation component of return is assumed not to be taxed. Therefore, the tax gross up must be done before inflation. The $150,000 is not adjusted for inflation as it is already stated to be expected spending; however, inflation must still be added to real return for nominal return to reflect the effects of inflation in the future. The inflation and real return can be compounded instead of added and it will slightly change the subsequent calculations.

B. (7 points maximum) 1 point for correctly identifying the two corner portfolios to combine; 4 points for correctly determining the corner portfolio weights; 2 points for resulting standard deviation.

C. (6 points maximum) 2 points for selecting portfolio 4; 2 points for weights of risk-free and portfolio 4; 2 points for the portfolio standard deviation.

©2016 Kaplan, Inc.

QUESTION 7

Source: Study Session 6, LOS 13.i

Answer for Question 7

		Investment Policy Statement for A1 Casualty
Objectives	Return	A1 should follow a total return investment objective that maximizes after-tax return and their ability to maintain a competitive policy pricing, reduce volatility in overall profitability, and achieve a reasonable growth in surplus.
	Risk	There are two important factors affecting the risk tolerance of A1 in this case: the uncertain cash flow characteristics of their claims and the stock-to-surplus ratio. The primary objective is to meet policyholder claims, and the overall level of risk tolerance is low. An ALM approach focused on surplus volatility is appropriate.
Constraints	Time Horizon	Short, given that the duration of A1's liabilities is relatively short.
	Liquidity	The timing of the underwriting cycle, combined with the prospect of hurricane-related claims increases liquidity needs.
	Legal/ Regulatory	A1 is subject to legal and regulatory requirements that vary from state to state.
	Taxes	Casualty companies, such as A1, are taxable entities.
	Unique Circumstances	Significant claims outstanding and geographical concentration of policies in Florida and Alabama.

Candidate discussion:

4 points each for the return and risk components.

2 points for the liquidity component.

1 point each for all other components of the IPS.

Note: Parts of this answer are generic to a property/casualty company because the case is mostly non-quantitative. The goal in the answer is to use specifics of the case where pertinent and given.

QUESTION 8

Source: Study Session 18, LOS 32.b, c, d, e, f, k

Answer for Question 8

Maximum 12 points for any four of the following non-compliant items.
1. Only four years presented. Must present at least five years or since inception if less than 5 years.
2. Assets in the composite. Must present the amount of assets in the composite and either total firm assets or the percentage of firm assets represented by the composite.
3. Failing to provide ex post standard deviation. Beginning in 2011, the annualized trailing 36 months standard deviation of the composite and benchmark must be provided.
4. Incomplete disclosure of fees. Must provide a relevant fee schedule.
5. Composite information. Disclose the presence of and access to descriptions of all the firm's composites.
6. Non-discretionary portfolios included in composites. Non-discretionary portfolios must not be included.
7. Incorrect compliance statement. Firms must disclose whether verified.
8. Failing to disclose policies and procedures. Must state that policies and procedures for calculating and presenting performance will be provided if requested.

Candidate discussion: (12 points maximum)
1 point for stating each non-compliant item.
2 points for each correct recommended change.

QUESTION 9

Source: Study Session 17, LOS 31.p

A.

$$\text{Sharpe Ratio} = \frac{\overline{R_P} - \overline{R_F}}{\sigma_P}$$

$$\text{HNW} = \frac{28.2 - 4.4}{45.0} = 0.53$$

$$\text{S\&P 500} = \frac{22.4 - 4.4}{20.0} = 0.90$$

Sharpe → The HNW portfolio significantly underperformed the S&P 500.

$$\text{Treynor Measure} = \frac{\overline{R_P} - \overline{R_F}}{\beta_P}$$

$$\text{HNW} = \frac{28.2 - 4.4}{1.35} = 17.6$$

$$\text{S\&P 500} = \frac{22.4 - 4.4}{1.0} = 18.0$$

Treynor → The HNW portfolio only modestly underperformed the S&P 500.

Candidate discussion:
2 points for correctly computing each of the measures.

B.

The ratios indicate the other portfolio has substantial unsystematic risk. Alpha is based on the CAPM. The CAPM is based on beta, a measure of systematic risk only. Consistent with the CAPM, most alphas are rather small and the return in the portfolio was largely explained by systematic risk. M^2 is based on standard deviation, a measure of both systematic and unsystematic risk. The poor M^2 but positive alpha indicates a large standard deviation, more than is accounted for by beta (systematic risk). Therefore, the portfolio has high unsystematic risk.

Candidate discussion:
1 point for differentiating between systematic and unsystematic risk.
1 point for explaining which type of risk is relevant to each measure.
1 point for determining the portfolio has substantial unsystematic risk.

C. $\quad M^2 \text{ Measure} = R_F + (R_P - R_F)\dfrac{\sigma_M}{\sigma_P}$

$\quad HNW = 4.4 + (28.2 - 4.4)\dfrac{20}{45} = 15.0\%$

The M^2 for any asset will only equal the M^2 for the market if it has the same level of excess return per total risk. That is, they will be the same if the Sharpe ratios are the same.

Candidate discussion:
2 points for computing the measure.
1 point for explaining the requirements for the portfolio's measure to equal the market.

QUESTION 10

Source: Study Session 6, LOS 13.i
Study Session 12, LOS 23.u

Answer for Question 10-A

Scenario	*Affect on bank's policies*
1. Due to pressure from local activists, Opportunity has stepped up lending in low-income areas. Groh expects the default rate on these loans to be higher than the loans currently in their portfolio.	Must reduce risk tolerance of security portfolio to offset increased risk in loans.
2. Opportunity has bought a regional bank with operations in North Carolina, South Carolina, and Georgia. The acquired bank's loan portfolio consists mostly of commercial loans to small, local businesses.	Loan portfolio has better geographical diversification, so risk objective of security portfolio can be increased.
3. A recent downturn in interest rates has caused many of Opportunity's variable-rate mortgages to be refinanced to 15- and 30-year fixed rate mortgages. Opportunity has retained the business of most of its customers who have refinanced.	The shift will increase loan asset duration and require lowering securities portfolio duration to maintain overall asset duration. **Candidate discussion:** Floating rate loans have lower duration than fixed rate loans.

B. Advantage: Compensation will be more performance based and should better motivate the manager.

Disadvantages:
- Manager has an incentive to take bigger risks to earn a higher performance fee.
- Performance-based fee structures are more complicated to administer.

Candidate discussion:
A. 2 points for correctly identifying the influence of *each* scenario.
B. 1 point for identifying the advantage of performance-based fee structures and 1 point for identifying *each* disadvantage of performance-based fee structures.

Exam 2
Afternoon Session Answers

To get detailed answer explanations with references to specific LOS and SchweserNotes content, and to get valuable feedback on how your score compares to those of other Level III candidates, use your Username and Password to gain Online Access at *www.schweser.com* and choose the left-hand menu item "Practice Exams Vol. 2."

1. B	25. A	49. B
2. C	26. C	50. C
3. A	27. B	51. C
4. B	28. B	52. B
5. C	29. C	53. A
6. A	30. C	54. A
7. C	31. A	55. C
8. C	32. C	56. A
9. A	33. C	57. A
10. A	34. A	58. B
11. B	35. C	59. B
12. C	36. C	60. B
13. B	37. B	
14. B	38. A	
15. B	39. B	
16. A	40. A	
17. C	41. C	
18. B	42. C	
19. B	43. A	
20. C	44. B	
21. B	45. A	
22. A	46. B	
23. B	47. B	
24. B	48. A	

Candidate discussion: 3 points for each correct answer.

Exam 2
Afternoon Session Answers

QUESTIONS 1–6

Source: Study Session 1

1. **B** Standard II(B) Market Manipulation prohibits members and candidates from manipulating securities price or volume with the intent to mislead. BIC's principals have suggested to Bair that she artificially inflate the Horizon Fund's price to alter the market's perception of demand for the fund and mislead investors. The fact the principals have informed Bair they will watch her performance is normal course of business for any employee/employer situation and not a violation. If the employers were to create an environment that encourages unethical or illegal actions, that would be a violation; there is no such indication here. Even though Bair may delegate supervisory duties to a compliance officer, it does not relieve Bair of making sure laws, rules, regulations, firm policies, and the Code and Standards are being followed. (Study Session 1, LOS 1.b)

2. **C** Standard I(A) Knowledge of the Law requires members and candidates to know and comply with rules, laws, and regulations that apply to their professional activities. If there is a conflict, members and candidates are expected to adhere to the stricter of applicable laws, rules, and regulations or the Code and Standards. By seeking qualified advice, Bair meets this requirement if she then acts on that advice. Clients in each country are receiving the required service. Note that this is not a case of BIC establishing different levels of service. That is not unethical, though it must be disclosed so that clients can select the level of service they are willing and able to pay for. In this case, these are not levels of service the clients can select but BIC adherence to differing regulations. Most important, there is no group of clients being disadvantaged by BIC. The crossing actually benefits all clients by improving total fund performance. (Study Session 1, LOS 1.b)

3. **A** According to Standard III(B) Fair Dealing, members and candidates are allowed to offer different levels of service but must disclose the existence of different levels of service and allow clients and prospects to choose the desired level. By not disclosing the levels of service to investors in S, Bair is adhering to local law, which is less strict than the Code and Standards. This is in violation of Standard I(A) Knowledge of the Law, which requires she adhere to the stricter of the two. She also violated Standard III(B) by not disclosing the service levels. (Study Session 1, LOS 1.b)

4. **B** According to Standard II(A) Material Nonpublic Information, the member or candidate cannot act on material, nonpublic information. It is recommended the member or candidate attempt to have the subject company disclose the information publicly themselves. If this is not possible, then the appropriate supervisor and/or compliance officer should be made aware of the situation. (Study Session 1, LOS 1.b)

©2016 Kaplan, Inc.

5. **C** Standard II(A) Material Nonpublic Information prohibits acting on material nonpublic information. The investment bankers should have known that the information was material and nonpublic and have violated Standard II(A) by trading on the information. Because the information cannot be used for account management, it cannot be considered front running ahead of the accounts. There is also no indication Sunrise is a client of the investment banking group and, therefore, no fiduciary duty to Sunrise. (Study Session 1, LOS 1.b)

6. **A** The large earnings restatement is certainly material information. Disclosing the information before the conference call does not make the information public even if several analysts overheard the information. Disclosing the information to her compliance officer also does not make the information public. Therefore, Bair has traded on the basis of material nonpublic information and is in violation of Standard II(A). (Study Session 1, LOS 1.b)

QUESTIONS 7–12

Source: Study Sessions 1 and 2

7. **C** Commissions belong to the client and this is an example of *client-directed brokerage* where the client, in this case Stephen Carobilo, is allowed to direct the investment manager to use a specific broker to execute trades. Under the AMC, if the manager believes the trades are not providing best execution, he should inform the client. The client has the right to make the decision in this case. (Study Session 2, LOS 4.c)

8. **C** Bracco is in violation of Standard II(A) Material Nonpublic Information, which states that members and candidates cannot trade or cause others to trade based on material nonpublic information that could affect the value of an investment. Even though Bracco has performed his own research and the information he acquired from McNulty and his colleague was an accident, it was nonetheless material nonpublic information and therefore cannot be traded upon. (Study Session 1, LOS 1.b)

9. **A** Gun is correct. Accounts who incorrectly received shares also lost interest on the funds during the period they held the shares. The underlying principal is accounts should be made whole for the firm's mistake, in this case, with the lost interest. The CFA text is silent on whether the accounts who did not receive the shares initially can keep any interest they incorrectly earned during the period until they are correctly allocated the shares. Ethically it can be removed to "make them whole," although to avoid upsetting clients, the firm may decide to let them keep the interest. In any case, the firm must bear all costs for the firm's mistake. Accounts that do not meet the minimum transaction amount as described in the company's policies and procedures should not receive shares of the IPO, making Bracco's statement incorrect. (Study Session 1, LOS 1.b)

10. **A** McNulty has violated both the Code of Ethics and the Standards of Professional Conduct. The Code of Ethics states in part that members of CFA Institute must act with integrity, competence, diligence, respect, and in an ethical manner with employees and colleagues in the investment profession. The inappropriate behavior has violated the Code. The unethical behavior also violates Standard I(D) Misconduct. The Standard states in part that members and candidates must not commit any act that reflects adversely on their professional reputation, integrity, or competence. His inappropriate behavior, especially drinking heavily with Stiles' management, has violated this Standard. (Study Session 1, LOS 1.b)

11. **B** The information in the notebook is clearly material and non-public, as its public release will affect Stiles' stock price. As such, McNulty should have taken steps to protect it. His drinking and behavior at the party are the obvious blame for his accidentally losing the notebook, but the reasons for losing it are not the point here. Whether he intentionally or accidentally lost the notebook, McNulty has violated Standard III(E), Duties to Clients, by not taking steps to preserve the confidentiality of his client's planned offering. Sampson violated Standard II(A) by sharing material, non-public information with others and trading on it. (Study Session 1, LOS 1.b)

12. **C** Under the AMC, there must be traded allocation policies in place and disclosed to clients. Any policies that are not documented (written) do not effectively exist. A qualified compliance officer must be in place. While the AMC and the Standards of Professional Conduct both require disclosure of actual and potential conflicts of interest, neither require that firm employees be prohibited from trading in securities in which the firm has an interest. (Study Session 2, LOS 4.c, d)

QUESTIONS 13–18

Source: Study Sessions 10, 11, and 15

13. **B** When evaluating bond investment alternatives based on mean reversion analysis only, the bond that is most attractive is the one whose current spread is the largest positive number of standard deviations above the mean.

    Bond issue YY has a current spread that is below its mean so it is not an attractive candidate. For the spread to revert to its mean, it must widen and the bond will depreciate in value.

    The number of standard deviations above the mean is computed as follows:

    Bond Issue VV: (125 − 98) / 28 = 0.96;   Bond Issue XX: (100 − 75) / 15 = 1.67

    Morrison should purchase Bond Issue XX, since the current spread exceeds its mean spread by the greatest number of standard deviations. (Study Session 10, LOS 21.e)

14. **B** Implication of cyclical and secular changes in the corporate bond market include:

    Securities with embedded options will command a premium due to their scarcity, and the percentage of long-term issues will decline. Thus, Morrison is incorrect. Effective duration and aggregate interest rate risk sensitivity will decline.

    Tabler's statement is correct. Credit-based derivatives will be used increasingly to achieve desired exposures to credit sectors, issuers, and structures. (Study Session 10, LOS 21.b)

15. **B** To answer this question you have to bring to mind the price-yield graph for a callable bond. You will remember that the price-yield graph for a callable bond is concave below the coupon rate (i.e., the callable bond experiences negative convexity at very low interest rates). While a non-callable bond will continually increase in value as its required return falls, the value of the option in the callable bond increases as the required return falls and places a cap on the maximum value of the callable bond. Therefore, as rates fall below the coupon rate, the non-callable bond will outperform a comparable callable bond.

    When rates are already below the coupon rate but are increasing, the callable bond will not fall in value as quickly, so it will outperform the non-callable bond. The difference between the values of the callable and comparable non-callable bond is the value of the embedded call option. Thus, as rates fall below the coupon rate, the value of the call option increases in value, consuming an increasing amount of the total value of the bond. When the required return is significantly higher than the coupon rate, the value of the call option goes to zero and both bonds behave as if they are non-callable. (Study Session 10, LOS 21.e)

16. **A** Morrison is correct. Corporate spread curves, which measure the yield spreads between higher and lower rated bonds, tend to change with the economic cycle, so in order to properly conduct this analysis the analyst must carefully examine credit and yield curves. Tabler is also correct. Corporate spread curves narrow during upturns and widen during downturns. The reason for this is that default becomes more likely during a recession and yields on risky corporate bonds increase. Yield spreads decrease during an expansion because default is generally less likely. (Study Session 10, LOS 21.e)

17. **C** Both Morrison and Tabler are correct. <u>There is a positive relationship between the</u> <u>federal funds rate and the repo rate.</u> The high demand relative to supply creates a scarcity value, which leads the lender of the funds to offer a low repo rate to obtain the collateral. (Study Session 11, LOS 22.b)

18. **B** The net interest paid is determined as follows:

Loan payment   –(LIBOR + 120 bp)

– Pay fixed in swap (5.20% + 100 bp)   –6.20%

+ Receive in swap   +LIBOR

Net =   –7.40%

LIBOR paid in the loan is cancelled by the LIBOR received in the swap. In net, the client will pay a fixed rate of 6.20% + 1.20% = 7.40%. (Study Session 15, LOS 28.a)

QUESTIONS 19–24

Source: Study Sessions 11 and 14

19. **B** Statement 1 is correct. VAR measures loss at some specified probability. For example, if the VAR at 5% over 1 year is $5 million, there is a 5% chance during any one year the surplus will decline $5 million or more in the pension plan. The loss in a pension plan value might be due to declining asset value, increasing liability value, or a combination. However, they will in aggregate decrease the plan surplus, making VAR a useful tool to explain potential risk.

    Statement 2 is false because the aggregation of risk values is complex. At the least, the correlation of the risks must be considered. Aggregating credit risk is particularly difficult because potential credit risk is maximized when asset values are high (there is the most to be lost in default), while normal VAR focuses on market value losses and is highest when asset values are low. Hence, the expression VAR is left tail risk and CVAR is right tail risk. This and other factors suggest centralized risk management is generally superior to decentralized risk management. (Study Session 14, LOS 25.d, e, g, i)

20. **C** Statement 3 is incorrect. Current credit risk is defined as any immediate cash flow due to be received. It essentially is an immediate worst case loss and does not consider probability of default. It is binary; a cash flow is due to be received now or it is not.

    Statement 4 is incorrect because the potential credit risk is defined as the value of the bond (or any other item being analyzed) at that time. An investor will receive all future cash flows of the bond, not just par. The PV of those future cash flows (the bond price) is what the investor has at risk at any one point in time. (Study Session 14, LOS 25.d, i)

21. **B** Current credit risk is any amount due now. The contract has three months to expiration, so no funds are currently due. Potential credit risk is the value of the contract, if positive. Value to the long position is calculated as:

    $$\left[S - \frac{f}{(1+i)^t} \right]$$

    S is the current price of the underlying, and F is the initial contract price. Both are 50 in this case, so there must be positive value and potential credit to the long position. Palmer has the short position and negative value and, therefore, no potential credit risk at this time. One party has potential credit risk. (Study Session 14, LOS 25.i)

22. **A** Netting will reduce risk to DSI. It eliminates the possibility that DSI might make a payment to a counterparty with the expectation an offsetting payment will be received. Instead only a net due to pay (if any) on all transactions with the counterparty would be made, which is a much smaller number. EDPCs are a way to reduce counterparty credit risk, but DSI would want to trade with EDPCs of a counterparty to reduce DSI's risk. If DSI sets up their own EDPC, they are reducing risk for their counterparties, not for DSI. Trading in exchange-traded futures will reduce interest rate and counterparty risk for DSI; however, they are not a practical tool to specifically reduce credit risk. They can be used to hedge general interest rate risk but do not address spread change and credit risk. (Study Session 14, LOS 25.j,k)

23. **B**   As credit quality deteriorates, it will be reflected in a relative decline in price, increase in yield, and increase in spread of the bond. The most direct protection will have payoffs to Weaver that are directly linked to change in spread. By definition that means the purchase of a credit spread call that will pay Weaver based on an increase in spread over a reference spread amount. The option includes an RF multiplier, which converts spread change to the relative price change suffered by Weaver when spread increases. In contrast, a default swap would normally only pay if the bond defaults or meets some other defined condition beyond simple widening in spread. The sale of a put provides Weaver an initial fixed premium income but provides no compensation linked to future spread widening that Weaver is concerned with. (Study Session 11, LOS 22.g)

24. **B**   Since the spread has widened, the credit spread forward results in a payoff to the **buyer** of $300,000:

FV = (actual spread − contract spread) × notional principal × risk factor

FV = (0.045 − 0.03) × $2 million × 10 = $300,000

(Study Session 11, LOS 22.g)

QUESTIONS 25–30

Source: Study Sessions 10 and 11

25. **A**   A cross hedge occurs when the hedged item and hedging vehicle are not identical. It is generally based on the assumption that they will be highly correlated. The U.S. client is exposed to the Thai baht. Selling the bhat forward for the Korean won could be interpreted as expecting the USD and won to be highly correlated, or it could be active management and expecting the won to appreciate. Either way, there are uncertainties and cross hedge-type risks.

   While it is a forward hedge in using forward contracts, that is too vague an answer given the other choices. A MVH would be based on regression and would seek to minimize USD returns of the foreign asset. (There are other types of MVH, but this is the one covered in the curriculum.)

   (Study Session 11, LOS 22.j)

26. **C**   In the case of all three foreign countries, the cash rate is lower than the cash rate in the United States, which means that all three currencies will trade at a forward premium to the U.S. dollar.

   The forward differential for each foreign currency relative to the dollar is approximated as the difference between the domestic and the foreign interest rates. Assume the U.S. dollar is currency d, the Thai baht is currency i, the Korean won is currency j, and the Japanese yen is currency k. Forward rates are denoted f, and the cash rates in each currency are denoted c.

   $$f_{d,i} = c_d - c_i = 6.50 - 2.50 \quad = +4.00$$

   $$f_{d,j} = c_d - c_j = 6.50 - 3.20 \quad = +3.30$$

   $$f_{d,k} = c_d - c_k = 6.50 - 4.20 \quad = +2.30 \text{ (Study Session 11, LOS 22.j)}$$

27. **B**   In breakeven rate analysis, the analyst determines the yield change that makes the returns on bonds equivalent. The general rule is to use the larger duration of the two bonds to determine the smallest spread change to produce breakeven. In this case, the facts specify the yield on the Nakhon Metals bond will change, and Powhatan will not change. Therefore, the Nakhon Metals bond duration is used.

   The next step is to determine the initial return advantage. The question specifies ignoring currency, so Nakhon has an annual yield and return advantage of 0.70% (= 5.2% – 4.5%). Nakhon can, therefore, suffer a relative price decline of 0.70% for breakeven. The magnitude of the yield change is provided by rearranging the modified duration formula:

   $$\%\Delta price = -modified\ duration \times \Delta yield$$

   $$\frac{\%\Delta price}{-modified\ duration} = \Delta yield$$

   $$\frac{-0.70\%}{-7.30} = 0.0959\% \text{ or } 9.59 \text{ basis points}$$

   (Study Session 11, LOS 22.k)

28. **B**   Thomas is correct. The prediction is the yen will appreciate 3.5%. Cash rates in Japan are 2.3% lower than in the United States (4.2 − 6.5%), which means the yen will trade at a forward premium of 2.3% to the dollar. The predicted unhedge yen return of 3.5% is superior to a hedged return of 2.3%. (Study Session 11, LOS 22.j)

29. **C**   Both Thomas and Bentley are correct. Both callable bonds and bonds with very long durations trade at a premium due to their scarcity. (Study Session 10, LOS 21.b)

30. **C**   When interest rates are near coupon rates and fall for callables and non-callables, non-callables will increase in value more than callables. This is because the price of a callable is depressed as the value of the embedded option increases with the drop in interest rates. Under scenario A, therefore, non-callables outperform callables.

When interest rates are historically very low and rise for both callables and non-callables, the value of the non-callable will fall faster than the value of the callable bond. Therefore, under scenario B the callable will outperform the non-callable.
(Study Session 10, LOS 21.e)

QUESTIONS 31–36

Source: Study Session 13, 14

31. **A** The only possible answer from the given reasons is a high water mark provision. Since the firm had experienced losses for two years before increasing in value in the previous year, it is likely that the value of the fund had yet to achieve a previous "high water mark" that it must exceed in order for there to be an earned incentive fee.
(Study Session 13, LOS 24.q)

32. **C** CTAs that specialize in systematic trading strategies typically apply sets of rules to trade according to or contrary to short, intermediate, and/or long-term trends. A discretionary CTA trading strategy generates returns on the managers' trading expertise, much like any active portfolio manager. CTAs can also be classified according to whether they trade in financial markets, currency markets, or diversified markets.
(Study Session 13, LOS 24.t)

33. **C** Similar to a term structure of interest rates, the term structure of futures prices shows the relationship at a point in time between futures prices and time to maturity. When the term structure is negative (called backwardation), longer-term contracts have lower prices than shorter-term contracts, so the curve is downward sloping. With the passage of time, the maturity of a long-term contract shortens and its price rises to that of a shorter-term contract. Thus, an investor can go long a long-term contract and profit as time passes, and the steeper the curve (the greater the backwardation), the greater the potential returns. An upward-sloping term structure of futures prices is called contango.
(Study Session 13, LOS 24.n)

34. **A** Cantori says he will research companies who do business in commodities. He feels that using the indirect method of buying the stock of those companies to gain commodity exposure is an efficient and effective method for gaining exposure to commodities. This is not necessarily true because those companies often hedge their exposure to commodities. The other statements are true. Agricultural commodities tend to be negatively correlated with inflation, but the broad commodity indices have been positively correlated with inflation. Also, commodities have not generally outperformed stocks and bonds. They are attractive in that they can provide a comparable return while diversifying the portfolio. (Study Session 13, LOS 24.o)

35. **C** Both are wrong in the details of what they said. Bliss would be correct for OTC instruments such as forwards and swaps which have counterparty risk. But with exchange-traded futures, there is no dealer counterparty risk and the procedures do not apply. Cantori would be correct for currency swaps where notional principal is exchanged. For other types of swaps, the maximum potential credit risk is typically midlife of the swap when there has been time for market conditions to shift and large amounts continue to be at risk of exchange. The currency swap is unique because the large notional exchange remains until the last day of the swap life. (Study Session 14, LOS 26.i, j, k)

36. **C** Treynor is least appropriate because it is based on stock beta which is not going to apply to the commodity markets. Downside risk measures like Sortino and would be the most appropriate. The Sharpe ratio is based on standard deviation which assumes a symmetrical distribution of returns. While it is often used in hedge fund evaluation, there are issues with that application. Treynor is still the least appropriate.
(Study Session 14, LOS 26.l)

QUESTIONS 37–42

Source: Study Sessions 10, 11, and 15

37. **B**   Edwards is incorrect. The value of the note goes down if interest rates increase. An interest rate call seller provides a payment to the buyer of the call when interest rates increase. If interest rates increase, a short position in interest rate calls would decrease in value, so this will not hedge the risk of the note.

Palmer is correct. We know that the note must have a fixed rate because of the length of its duration. A floating rate note will have a duration significantly less than one year. The swap can effectively turn the fixed-rate note into a floating-rate note and reduce the duration of the position. If interest rates rise, Anderson receives the higher floating rate in the swap. (Study Session 15, LOS 28.a)

38. **A**   In order to calculate how much Anderson will receive in dollars as a result of the swap, first calculate the implied notional principal (NP) of a CHF-denominated swap that would produce quarterly cash flows of CHF12,000,000, given the Swiss interest rate of 6.6%:

$$NP\left(\frac{0.066}{4}\right) = CHF12,000,000$$

$$NP = \frac{CHF12,000,000}{\left(\dfrac{0.066}{4}\right)} = CHF727,272,727$$

Next, calculate the dollar-equivalent principal at the current exchange rate and then calculate a dollar cash flow using the dollar interest rate of 2.8%:

$$CHF727,272,727 \times (\$ / CHF1.24) = \$586,510,264$$
$$\$586,510,264 \times (2.80\% / 4) = \$4,105,572 \qquad \text{(Study Session 15, LOS 28.f)}$$

39. **B**   The statement is accurate. Transaction exposure is from transactions already entered into and the amount to hedge is thus known (i.e., hedge the principal). Transaction exposures are the most commonly hedged exposures of a firm. Economic risk, the relationship between changing exchange rates and asset values, is not contractual and the amount to hedge is thus less certain, making it harder to hedge. Translation risk refers to the effect of exchange rate changes on the income statement and balance sheet and is often not hedged. (Study Session 15, LOS 26.f)

40. **A**   Edwards is correct. If management predicts that interest rates will fall, they will not want to be stuck paying a high, fixed rate. To take advantage of falling rates, they can enter a pay-floating swap (or swaption). The fixed receipt from the swap will at least partially offset the fixed payment on the bonds, while the firm ends up paying a net floating rate. If desired, management could enter a second pay fixed swap after rates have fallen to lock in the lower fixed rate. The net duration on the first swap can be calculated as the duration of the fixed arm minus the duration of the floating arm, which is 3.75 − 0.25 = 3.5. The notional principal for the swap can be calculated as follows:

$$NP = \$10,000,000 \left(\frac{4}{3.5} \right) = \$11,428,571$$

Note: Anderson will assume the receive-fixed arm of the swap, so its duration to Anderson is positive. Also, Anderson is not hedging price risk. That is, they are not trying to change the duration of the bond, so we enter the duration, as it is, in the equation.

Palmer is incorrect. Anderson is paying out a fixed rate, so to take advantage of falling rates, they should receive a fixed rate and pay out a floating rate in the swap. Because the fixed side of the swap has a greater duration than the floating side, Anderson's position in the swap will have a net positive duration. (Study Session 15, LOS 28.f)

41. **C**   If $275,000 is invested in the U.S. bond and $155,000 is invested in the British bond, the total value of the portfolio is $430,000. The duration contribution of the U.S. bond is (275,000 / 430,000) × 4.0 = 2.56.

To obtain the duration contribution of the British bond to the U.S. portfolio, we must incorporate its yield beta. The yield beta tells us how much British bond yields will change, if U.S. bond yields change by 1%. Using the yield beta of 1.40, the duration contribution of the British bond is (155,000 / 430,000) × 8.5 × 1.40 = 4.29.

The duration of the entire bond portfolio from a U.S. perspective is then 2.56 + 4.29 = 6.85. (Study Session 11, LOS 22.i)

42. **C**   Both recommendations are incorrect. For an immunized portfolio, asset duration must be adjusted to match the liability duration, in this case, that means lowering asset duration. The interest rate forecast would apply only in active techniques such as contingent immunization. Yield spreads can be considered in selecting bonds for an immunized portfolio; however, the asset must be very low risk in relation to the liabilities. With USD liabilities, bonds denominated in GBP are going to add unacceptable risk. The goal of the immunized portfolio is to pay USD liabilities. (Study Session 10, LOS 20.g, j)

Source: Study Sessions 10, 14, and 15

43. **A** Strategy 1 is correct in concept, but the number of contracts is wrong. The number of contracts that should be sold is 43. The number is calculated as: $[(0 - 6.7) / 7.9]$ $(5,000,000 / 98,752) = -42.94$.

    Strategy 2 will meet the hedging objective if sized correctly, but swap contracts are OTC instruments with no inherent secondary liquidity. Once entered, contracts can be economically offset by entering additional offsetting contracts. However, there is no clean way to exit contracts prior to expiration. The liquidity objective is not met. (Study Session 15, LOS 26.d and LOS 28.d)

44. **B** The portfolio is long the bond. Selling a call and buying a put on the bond will construct a collar and hedge the bond by limiting upside and downside risk. Selection of the strike prices will control the amount of upside and downside retained. In this case, selling puts on interest rates are used instead of selling calls on price. The two are economically comparable because the short call position will lose value when bond price increases as interest rates decrease. The short put on interest rates will also lose value under these conditions. While a bull spread has the same payoff pattern as this collar, it is constructed by using only calls or only puts and does not involve holding the bond. (Study Session 15, LOS 27.e, f)

45. **A** To return the portfolio to its original dollar duration, the manager could purchase additional amounts of each bond. Alternatively, the manager could select one of the bonds to use as a controlling position. Since the dollar duration has fallen and Bond 1 has the longest duration, the manager could use the least amount of additional cash by increasing only the holding in Bond 1 (i.e., using Bond 1 as the controlling position):

$$\text{desired increase in DD} = \text{target DD} - \text{current DD}$$
$$= \$157,200 - \$142,095 = \$15,105$$

$$\text{increase in Bond 1: new DD of Bond 1} = \$35,100 + \$15,105$$
$$= \$50,205$$

$$\text{required new value of Bond 1} = \frac{\$50,205}{\$35,100} \times \$780,000 = \$1,115,667$$

Thus, the manager could purchase another $335,667 (= $1,115,667 − $780.000) of Bond 1. The new portfolio total value will be $4,217,000 + $335,667 = $4,552,667, and the portfolio dollar duration will be back to its original level:

$$\begin{aligned}DD_{new} &= [\$1,115,667(4.5) + \$2,500,000(3.4) + \$524,000(2.7) + \$413,000(1.9)](0.01)\\ &= [\$5,020,501.50 + \$8,500,000 + \$1,414,800 + \$784,700](0.01)\\ &= \$15,720,002(0.01) = \$157,200 = DD_{Original}\end{aligned}$$

(Study Session 10, LOS 20.h)

46. **B**   Potential credit risk is the market value if positive of the position. Market value was not given but can be estimated from the information provided. The options were worth $225,000 when they were purchased several days days ago. The option delta over the period was 0.7. By definition, option delta is change in value of the options for change in value of the underlying. The bonds increased by $250,000, so the options increased by 70% of 250,000 = 175,000; making their estimated ending value the change estimate plus beginning value (175,000 + 225,000 = 400,000). This is their potential credit risk. Note that this is only an estimate as the time value of the options could have also changed. There is no way to estimate the time value change, and over several days it is not likely to be large. (Study Session 14, LOS 25.i)

47. **B**   Thomas is incorrect. If they use bonds with high yields, it is true that the cost of immunization will be cheaper. Expected returns are higher so they will have to purchase fewer bonds. However, such bonds will also have higher credit risk and contingent immunization assumes no default. If one of the bonds defaults, the immunization strategy will not provide the terminal value required.

   Bentley is correct. The risk from nonparallel shifts in the yield curve (immunization risk) can be minimized by concentrating the cash flows around the horizon date. (Study Session 10, LOS 20.g)

48. **A**   If LIBOR does increase, the cost of Kershaw Ross's floating rate loan will increase. In this case the firm will want to pay a fixed rate and receive a floating rate in a swap. The payer swaption will allow them to pay a predetermined, lower fixed rate in a swap.

   If interest rates increase and the fixed rate on swaps in one year (projected at 9.3%) exceeds the swaption fixed rate, the firm will exercise the swaption and pay 8.5%. They receive LIBOR from the swaption and pay in total 8.5% + 1.5% = 10% in the swap and the loan. The firm's first quarterly payment in net will be:

   $10\% \times £5,000,000 \times 90 / 360 = £125,000.$

   Note that if swap fixed rates are less than 8.5% in one year, the firm would not exercise the swaption. The firm could either (a) enter a swap at that time and pay the lower fixed rate or (b) not enter a swap and just pay the floating rate in the loan. (Study Session 15, LOS 28.h)

QUESTIONS 49–54

Source: Study Session 16

49. **B** Gleeson is correct concerning the nature of uncertainty. Market orders have price uncertainty but no execution uncertainty, while limit orders eliminate price uncertainty but have execution uncertainty. However, he is incorrect concerning when these order types should be used. In most cases, information-motivated and liquidity-motivated trades should use market orders to ensure that execution takes place, while value-motivated and rebalancing trades should use limit orders because price is typically more important than the speed of execution. (Study Session 16, LOS 29.a)

50. **C** The quoted spread for the first trade = 22.36 − 22.18 = 0.18. The quoted spreads for the remaining three trades are 0.20, 0.19, and 0.26, so the **average quoted spread** = (0.18 + 0.20 + 0.19 + 0.26) / 4 = 0.2075.

    The mid-quote for the first trade = (22.36 + 22.18) / 2 = 22.27, and the effective spread = (22.33 − 22.27) × 2 = 0.12. The effective spreads for the remaining three trades are 0.20, 0.17, and 0.30, so the **average effective spread** = (0.12 + 0.20 + 0.17 + 0.30) / 4 = 0.1975.

    The **weighted average effective spread** = (900 / 3,000) × 0.12 + (600 / 3,000) × 0.20 + (700 / 3,000) × 0.17 + (800 / 3,000) × 0.30 = 0.1957. (Study Session 16, LOS 29.b)

51. **C** The VWAP for the day = (900 / 3,000) × 22.33 + (600 / 3,000) × 22.43 + (700 / 3,000) × 22.47 + (800 / 3,000) × 22.65 = 22.468, and the trader's goal would be to have an average cost that is less than the VWAP if they are buying. (Study Session 16, LOS 29.f)

52. **B** The benchmark price and decision price at the time the decision to trade is made is 22.36, and the benchmark quantity is 5,000, so the benchmark investment = 22.36 × 5,000 = $111,800. The terminal benchmark value at the cancellation price of 22.65 is 22.65 × 5,000 = $113,250, and the benchmark gain = 113,250 − 111,800 = $1,450.

    The actual portfolio cost at the various execution prices is (900 × 22.33) + (600 × 22.43) + (700 × 22.47) + (800 × 22.65) = 67,404. With commissions of 210, this is a total cost of $67,614. The actual portfolio terminal value = 22.65 × 3,000 = $67,950, and the actual gain = 67,950 − 67,614 = $336.

    The implementation shortfall = (1,450 − 336) / 111,800 = 0.00996 or 0.996%. (Study Session 16, LOS 29.g)

53. **A** In general, implementation shortfall will be positive (i.e., profits will be foregone) if prices are rising when the trader is attempting to buy, or if prices are falling when the trader is attempting to sell, and all of the order is not completed. Cancellation of a buy order prior to a fall in price, or cancellation of a sell order prior to a rise in price will give rise to a negative implementation shortfall (i.e., the trader will be made better off by the cancellation). (Study Session 16, LOS 29.f)

54. **A** Because an algorithmic trading strategy involves mechanical rules to guide trading, one of the concerns is that the portfolio can become over-concentrated. For example, the portfolio could become over-concentrated in sectors that are more liquid and easier to trade when buying, and the opposite problem could occur when selling (i.e., the most liquid assets are sold first, leaving the portfolio over-concentrated in illiquid securities). (Study Session 16, LOS 29.m)

QUESTIONS 55–60

Source: Study Sessions 9, 11, and 17

55. **C** Compute the weighted average R_{DC} of U.K. and German holdings. Each R_{DC} is the product of R_{FC} and R_{FX}. The currency units are given as direct quotes for the foreign currency units.

R_{DC} U.K.: $[1.167 \times (2.2222 / 2.00000)] - 1 = 29.7\%$

R_{DC} German: $[1.067 \times (1.4286 / 1.3333)] - 1 = 14.3\%$

R_{DC} Portfolio: $0.6(29.7\%) + 0.4(14.3\%) = 23.5\%$

(Study Session 9, LOS 18.a)

56. **A** Both the GBP and EUR appreciated. Manager A had a larger weight in the GBP 60% versus 43% and therefore added relatively more value with the GBP. Manager B had a larger weight in the EUR 57% versus 40% and therefore added relatively more value with the EUR. (Study Session 9, LOS 18.a)

57. **A** HIPP is a U.S. investor, so investing in the U.K. index will earn both the local market return (R_{FC}) of the index and change in value of the foreign currency (R_{FX}). R_{FC} is the same regardless of the currency hedging decision, $115/100 - 1 = 15\%$. The only issue is R_{FX}.
    - Choice 1 is to accept the change in value of the foreign currency, the GBP versus the USD. The unhedged currency return is the change in value of the spot exchange rate, making R_{FX} unhedged $2.2222 / 2.0000 - 1 = 11.11\%$.
    - Choice 2 is to hedge the foreign currency by selling the GBP forward to buy the USD and earn the initial difference in F_0 and S_0. F_0 is not given directly, but we know from the case facts that the real risk-free interest rates and inflation rates in the three countries are equal. That means nominal risk-free rates are equal and based on IRP, F_0 and S_0 are equal; making R_{FX} hedged 0%. Choice 1 is superior at 11.11%. This is sufficient analysis to select "A" as the best answer.
    - Choice 3 is a kind of cross hedge where the manager invests in the U.K. index and then sell the GBP forward versus buy the JPY. This forward currency trade and the IRP relationship would lead to "losing" the short-term rate in the U.K. and "gaining" the short-term rate in Japan. Again, there is a 0% return because the nominal risk-free interest rates are equal. But choice 3 then leaves the U.S. investor exposed to the change in value of the JPY versus the USD. The market data is given as JPY/USD and shows that the USD appreciated. That means the JPY depreciated and a cross hedge into the JPY from the GBP earns a negative currency return on the JPY.

    To summarize, the U.S. investor investing in the U.K. index will earn the R_{FC} of 15% in all three currency hedging choices, so the issue is select the best R_{FX} strategy.

    (Study Session 11, LOS 22.j)

58. **B** Statement 1 is an accurate statement. Statement 2 is inaccurate because the benchmark must be appropriate to the investor's objectives and the manager's approach. An investment style benchmark may be best for a growth style or value style international equity portfolio manager. However, if an international equity portfolio manager focuses on a geographic region or a specific industry within a country, then a regional benchmark or industry benchmark would be more suitable. (Study Session 17, LOS 31.i)

No one best style

59. **B** The return from maturity management is the difference between the total return based on the price of each security at the beginning and end of the period calculated using the spot price for its maturity and the actual return on the Treasury proxy portfolio:

Return from maturity management = 8.25% − 7.50% = 0.75%

The bond selection return is measured by calculating the actual total return on the bond portfolio during the period and then subtracting the actual Treasury return, the return from maturity management, and the return from sector/quality management:

Total return on portfolio	8.75%
Less: Actual Treasury return	7.50%
Less: Return from maturity management	0.75%
Less: Return from sector/quality management	0.25%
Return from bond selection management	0.25%

(Study Session 17, LOS 31.n)

60. **B** Statement 3 is inaccurate. Although it is true that bond portfolio returns come from the external interest rate environment and from active management, studies have actually shown that the value added from active management tends to be inconsistent over time. Statement 4 is accurate. (Study Session 17, LOS 31.n)

Practice Exam 3
Morning Session Answers

QUESTION 1

Source: Study Session 3, LOS 7.a, Study Session 4, LOS 9.b, Study Session 5, LOS 12.a, c, e, j

A.   Westin is an Individualist.
   • Successful business owner which tends to be individualistic in approach.
   • High degree of confidence and careful in his decision making.
   • Used to making his own decisions by careful analysis.

Candidate discussion (maximum 4 points)
1 point for stating that Westin is an Individualist.
3 points for stating characteristics of the Individualist personality type exhibited by Westin.

B.   The taxable portfolio is currently valued at $1,500,000. In a worst case stress test, Westin will pay 25% of all gains each year in taxes.

   Future value minus annual taxes = $1,500,000 \times \{1 + [0.08 \times (1 - 0.25)]\}^{25}$
                                     $= \$6,437,806$

   Future value without taxes $= \$1,500,000 \times (1 + 0.08)^{25}$
                                 $= \$10,272,713$

   Difference $= \$10,272,713 - \$6,437,806$
                                 $= \$3,834,907$

   Potential gains $= \$10,272,713 - \$1,500,000$
                                 $= \$8,772,713$

   Proportion of potential investment gains consumed by taxes $= \$3,834,907 / \$8,772,713$
                                                               $= 43.7\%$

Candidate discussion:
1 point for 6,437,806.
1 point for 10,272,713.
2 points for 43.7%.

C.

Year	Salary	PY @ 11% discount rate
1	$200,000.00	$180,180.18
2	$206,000.00	$167,194.22
3	$212,180.00	$155,144.19
4	$218,545.40	$143,962.62
5	$225,101.76	$133,586.94
	Insurance need:	$780,068.15

Discontinue life insurance: Westin has substantial other liquid assets that could provide for his children if he dies prematurely.

Candidate discussion:

2 points for showing the calculation process and 1 point for $780,068. The case facts are specific as to the timing of the flows so other solutions are not accepted in this case.

1 point for discontinue life insurance and 1 point for the critical consideration in Westin's case that his beneficiaries can be cared for from his existing financial capital, which totals $6.5 million, not including Westin Consulting and the home. There is no need to insure his human capital.

QUESTION 2

Source: Study Session 4 LOS 8.g, h

A.   Primary goals:
   - Generate $80,000 real after-tax annually to fund retirement in 25 years. (Other living expenses are covered by salary.)
   - Provide for his children's education starting in 3 years.
   - Provide for his mother's retirement home in 7 years.
   - Retire in 25 years.

   Secondary goal:
   - Set aside funds to buy a boat and a vacation home ($400,000).

   Funds available:
   Assets (Current Values):

Proceeds from life insurance	$1,500,000
Cash in money market account	$500,000
401(k)	$3,000,000
Taxable Portfolio	$1,500,000
Total assets	$6,500,000*

   * $1,000,000 home is excluded from investable assets.

   Less funds set aside of:
   (1) College funding: PV is given as $628,042.
   (2) Helen's retirement funding: $463,462.
   (3) Set aside $400,000 for boat and vacation home.

   Available funds to invest for retirement:
   $6,500,000 − 628,042 − 463,462 − 400,000 = $5,008,496

   $80,000 annual real after-tax return is needed to fund retirement, making the real return requirement $80,000.

   After-tax real return objective: $80,000/$5,008,496 = 1.6%**
   After-tax nominal return of 1.6% + 3.0% = 4.6%.
   Or
   $(1.016)(1.03) − 1 = \textbf{4.648\%}$

   **This can also be solved as a TVM question: Using the calculator: N = 25, PV = −$5,008,496, FV = $5,008,496, PMT = $80,000; solve for I/Y = 1.6%.

   Candidate discussion:
   2 points for correctly stating the return objective.
   3 points for calculating the *Available funds to invest for retirement*.
   2 points for calculating the after-tax nominal return.

B.   Risk tolerance *willingness*:
   Westin's willingness to take risk should not be a significant factor:
   - Successful entrepreneur willing to take calculated risks.
   - Confident in his own abilities.

   Risk tolerance *ability*:
   Westin's ability is moderate to above average:
   - Young age and significant outside income indicating a large amount of human capital.
   - No debt and significant level of assets.
   Overall risk tolerance is above average.

Candidate discussion:

2 points for the correct *Willingness* interpretation.
2 points for the correct *Ability* interpretation.
1 point for the correct overall risk tolerance.

Westin is an entrepreneur who has successfully operated a small business and is confident in his ability. The fact that he accepts a conservative pyramid layer shows he is also willing to take less risk when appropriate. Westin acts more like an institution in regard to willingness to bear risk—willing to take higher or lower risk as appropriate.

Westin's ability to take risk is increased due to his young age, significant outside income and business skills (high human capital), owning a home and business with no debt, and his significant investable assets. He is in the accumulation phase. This is mitigated by the fact that he is the sole support for two children and his mother plus the small business is risky.

A conclusion of either average or above average risk tolerance are both acceptable as long as willingness and ability are correctly discussed.

C.

• The period until retirement in 25 years.
• After Westin retires.

Portfolio return needs for the portfolio will most likely go up in retirement as Westin will not have a salary.

Candidate discussion:

1 point each for the two relevant periods and 1 point for portfolio return need most likely increases in retirement. Note that the question specifically directs you to focus on the portion of the portfolio not in the set aside layer. Therefore, discussing the children's college, Mom's move to a retirement home, the boat and home purchase, or setting aside funds for these items are not relevant to this question. There are also many unknowns that will affect Westin at retirement, such as what he will receive for his business and how his needs will change. What is known is that Westin will no longer have a (current) salary of $200,000 and he will most likely be more dependent on the portfolio.

QUESTION 3

Source: Study Session 4, LOS 8.j, Study Session 4, LOS 9.i, Study Session 13 LOS 24.c

Answer for Question 3-A

Select the most appropriate portfolio for Westin. (Write one letter below)	Justify your selection on the basis of three items from Exhibit 2 and Westin's IPS.
C	C is greater than the required rate of return of 7.4% at 7.73%
	C avoids excessive cash drag at 5% cash equivalents
	A and B have unheeded cash drag while D has a 14.35% standard deviation (not better than 13%)

Candidate discussion:
(4 points total)
1 point for identifying portfolio C.
1 point for each reason why portfolio C was chosen.

All of the portfolios except D have Sharpe ratios in excess of the specified 0.36 (D's Sharpe is: (0.0808 – 0.030) / 0.1435 = 0.354). C has the best Sharpe ratio at 0.367. It may be acceptable to use that as a justification for selecting C but because return to risk ratios are used to select among portfolios that are, all else, acceptable it is not the best reason to select C. You would not use that reason here unless you cannot come up with another one. Identifying a reason to reject each of the other portfolios is one reason for selecting C.

B. Westin's total assets should be considered when performing an asset allocation for his investable assets. Westin's business (human capital) is most likely highly correlated with Private Equity, thus he should not invest in portfolios B or D. REITs act more like equities than a direct investment in real estate making portfolio C an acceptable choice.

Candidate discussion:
1 point for considering total assets in the asset allocation decision.
1 point for noting the positive correlation between Westin's business (human capital) and Private Equity.
1 point for noting that REITs are not equivalent to a direct investment in real estate.

Hyde's concerns about the current asset stem from concentrated positions. Westin's home and business ownership should be considered as a preexisting allocation before deciding to add additional private equity or real estate exposure. In Westin's case, the owner-occupied home and REITs are very different investments. The consulting firm is likely to be highly correlated to a private equity fund since Westin's clients are composed of privately held and venture companies. In addition, the home is a much smaller investment while the value of the private business is larger and really a reflection of Hyde's human capital (it has virtually no tangible assets). He should not invest in additional investments so highly correlated with his human capital.

C. Disagree – return can be maximized through:
- Allocating higher income securities like bonds in tax deferred accounts.
- Allocating lower income / higher capital gain equities in taxable accounts while minimizing turnover.

Candidate discussion: (3 points total)
1 point for *disagreeing*.
1 point for each reason.

Hyde is incorrect. Asset location is another way to maximize after-tax return. For example locating high income bonds in the 401(k) could maximize the advantage of tax free or deferred compounding while lower income equity could be placed in the taxable portfolio and still achieve tax deferral by keeping the turnover rate low.

QUESTION 4

Source: Study Session 13, LOS 24.m

Answer for Question 4-A

Alternative	Type	Comment
Futures contracts	Direct	Long contracts on energy will provide the desired benefit if energy prices increase.
Energy stocks	Indirect	Equity in stocks related to energy have only a lose correlation with energy prices, which provide a poor hedge.
ETFs	Direct	ETFs that purchase futures contracts are a way to gain direct exposure, but the broad commodity market does not target energy prices.

Candidate discussion: (maximum 6 points)
For each alternative, 1 point for direct/indirect; 1 point for comment.

An ETF buying commodity-related stocks would be an indirect commodity investment. But one taking only long commodity futures is direct. It will directly reflect the return of the futures contracts, and that is a direct investment.

Source: Study Session 13, LOS 24.n

B.   The roll return is change in futures minus change in spot prices:

June 15 futures price – May 15 futures price – change in spot price

Contract	Roll return calculation
July	$83.25 – $82.55 – $0.50 = $0.20
October	$82.35 – $81.70 – $0.50 = $0.15
January	$81.75 – $81.20 – $0.50 = $0.05

Candidate discussion: maximum 3 points, 1 point for each correct calculation.

Source: Study Session 13, LOS 24.n

Answer for Question 4-C

Future pricing	Justification
Backwardation	Futures curve downward sloping. Contracts with longer expiration are priced below shorter contracts.

Candidate discussion: (maximum 2 points)
1 point for backwardation.
1 point for justification.

Source: Study Session 13, LOS 24.e, n

D.   Total return = roll return + spot return + collateral return

$$= 6.4 + 10.2 + 7.1 = 23.70\%$$

Candidate discussion: maximum 3 points.

Source: Study Session 13, LOS 24.f, m, o

E.   i.   Inflation: Prices of storable commodities tend to be positively correlated with inflation.

       ii.   Diversification: Historically low correlation with stocks and bonds.

Candidate discussion: maximum 4 points, 2 points for each item.

QUESTION 5

Source: Study Session 13, LOS 24.g

A.   Disagree, the data shows the opposite.

REIFs represent direct real estate performance and had lower (10%) standard deviation. REITs are publically traded shares of companies that invest in real estate assets, hence indirect ownership.

However the data is not comparable because REITs are traded shares and their standard deviation reflects true volatility while REIF values are based on infrequent appraisals, which leads to price smoothing and understated volatility.

Candidate discussion: (maximum 3 points)
1 point for disagree.
2 points for an explanation that discusses smoothing, infrequent pricing, or appraisals for REIF properties.

Source: Study Session 13, LOS 24.e

Answer for Question 5-B

Advantage	Tax deductible expenses. Can use leverage. Direct control of the properties. Can provide targeted geographic diversification. Lower return volatility.
Disadvantage	Large investment for each property purchased. High transaction and operating expenses. High specific risk for each property.

Candidate discussion: (maximum 4 points)
2 points for a brief explanation of each.

Source: Study Session 13, LOS 24.e, f

Answer for Question 5-C

Decision	Justification
Disagree	Von Wilstrom's Fund invests in apartment REITs and had higher return and lower volatility than the apartment REITs' benchmark.

Candidate discussion: (maximum 3 points)
1 point for disagree.
2 points for justification.

QUESTION 6

Source: Study Session 7, LOS 16.a, b

Answer for Question 6-A

Factor	Factor Change (circle direction)
Production efficiency	Increase / (Decrease)
Environmental controls	(Increase) / Decrease
Size of working age population	Increase / (Decrease)

Candidate discussion:

1 point each for correctly identifying the direction of the factor change.

The change (growth) in real economic output is determined by the country's total factor productivity, TFP, the change in capital inputs, K, and the change in the labor force, L. The equation shows how the three variables can be considered separately:

$$\%\Delta Y \cong \%\Delta TFP + \alpha\left(\%\Delta K\right) + \left(1-\alpha\right)\%\Delta L$$

Answer for Question 6-B

$$\%\Delta Y \cong \%\Delta TFP + \alpha\left(\%\Delta K\right) + \left(1-\alpha\right)\%\Delta L$$

where:
$\%\Delta Y$ = percent change in real economic output
$\%\Delta TFP$ = percent change in total factor productivity
$\%\Delta K$ = percent change in capital stock
$\%\Delta L$ = percent change in labor input
α = output elasticity of capital stock
$\left(1-\alpha\right)$ = output elasticity of labor, β

expected sustainable real growth rate $= 1.0\% + \left(0.3\times 4.0\%\right) + \left(0.7\times 0.7\%\right) = 2.69\%$

Candidate discussion:
2 points for correctly calculating the expected sustainable real growth rate; labeling the inputs is not needed.

Answer for Question 6-C

$$V_0 = \frac{D_0}{r - g_L}\left[(1 + g_L) + \frac{N}{2}(g_S - g_L)\right]$$

where:
V_0 = intrinsic value of the index
D_0 = current dividend
r = real required rate of return
g_L = long-term sustainable growth rate
g_S = supernormal growth rate
N = length of growth rate decline period

$$\text{estimated intrinsic value} = \frac{31}{0.09 - 0.0269}\left[(1 + 0.0269) + \frac{10}{2}(0.0925 - 0.0269)\right] = 665.6403$$

Mantrovia's stock market is slightly undervalued because the current value of 645 is less than the estimated intrinsic value of 665.64.

Candidate discussion:
1 point for correctly selecting the H-Model.
2 points for correctly calculating the intrinsic value.
1 point for correctly identifying the market as undervalued; labeling the inputs is not needed.

QUESTION 7

Source: Study Session 17, LOS 31.k

Answer for Question 7-A

Portfolio	Calculation	Return
Sterling	(0.6 × 12.5) + (0.25 × 16.0) + (0.15 × 10.0) = 1 point 1 point 1 point	13.00% 1 point
Benchmark	(0.5 × 10.0) + (0.3 × 18.5) + (0.2 × 9.0) = 1 point 1 point 1 point	12.35% 1 point
Circle one		
Outperform 2 points		

Candidate discussion: maximum 10 points.

Source: Study Session 17, LOS 31.e, l

Answer for Question 7-B

Effect	Calculation	Final Answer
Pure sector allocation effect	1 point (0.6 − 0.5) × (10.0 − 12.35) + 1 point (0.25 − 0.30) × (18.5 − 12.35) + 1 point (0.15 − 0.20) × (9.0 − 12.35) =	−0.375% 1 point
Within-sector selection effect	1 point [0.50 × (12.5 − 10.0)] + 1 point [0.3 × (16.0 − 18.5)] + 1 point [0.2 × (10.0 − 9.0)] =	0.70% 1 point

Candidate discussion:
The pure sector allocation effect measures the manager's ability to over-weight outperforming sectors and under-weight underperforming sectors. It is calculated by multiplying the difference in the weights of sector i in the portfolio and benchmark by the difference between the return for sector i in the benchmark and the overall return on the benchmark and then summing across all sectors:

$$\text{pure sector allocation effect} = \sum_{j=1}^{s} \left(w_{P,j} - w_{B,j} \right) \left(R_{B,j} - R_B \right)$$

The within-sector-selection effect, or security selection effect, measures the manager's ability to select outperforming securities to represent the sectors in the portfolio. It is calculated by multiplying the weight of sector i in the benchmark by the difference between the returns for sector i in the portfolio and benchmark:

$$\text{within-sector selection effect} = \sum_{j=1}^{s} \left(w_{B,j}\right)\left(R_{P,j} - R_{B,j}\right)$$

Candidate discussion: maximum 8 points.

Source: Study Session 17, LOS 31.e, l

C.   3 points—The outperformance is due to the within-sector selection effect; value added by the segment managers.

3 points—The Rawls Group hurt performance with their pure sector asset allocation decisions.

Candidate discussion: maximum 6 points.

QUESTION 8

Source: Study Session 6, LOS 14.b, c

A. 1. High ratio of active to inactive lives suggests a greater allocation to equities for increases in future real wages.

2. High ratio of active to inactive lives suggests a greater allocation to TIPS to cover inflation component of future wages.

3. Small proportion of inactive lives suggests lower allocation to nominal bonds.

Candidate discussion: (maximum 9 points)
For each of the 3 assets: 1 point to state increase or decrease and 2 points for justifying why.

Smith Hospital Corporation has a relatively young workforce with an average age of 31, indicating a fairly long time horizon. In addition, the ratio of active to inactive participants is very high. To meet future pension liabilities, a greater percentage of assets must be invested in equities than in Weekly's proposal. In other words, to meet the increased future liability generated by the real growth component in wages, Smith Hospital Corporation should invest a significant percentage of the plan's assets in equities.

Even though pension benefits are fixed at retirement and do not offer an inflation adjustment, the growth in future wages earned by the large number of active participants will have an inflation component. The significant liability created by this inflation component will require a greater percentage of pension assets invested in Treasury inflation-protected securities (TIPS) or some other type of inflation-protected securities.

The high percentage allocated to nominal bonds would reduce the company's overall risk profile, but the portfolio would likely not generate the returns needed to cover the growing pension liability caused by the inflation component in future wage increases. The percentage allocated to nominal bonds should be reduced. As the percentage of inactive participants rises, a larger proportion of the pension plan's assets can be invested in nominal bonds since employee benefits are fixed after retirement.

Source: Study Session 6, LOS 14.b

B. Real rate bonds: 1.0($20) + 1.0($22) + 0.60($35) = $63 million

Nominal bonds: 1.0($10) + 0.40($35) + 0.25($25) = $30.25 million

Equity: 0.75($25) = $18.75 million

Candidate discussion:
2 points for each of the three calculations.

A fully funded plan will have assets equal to the liabilities of $112,000,000. Based on the information provided, the allocation for each liability exposure should be:

Liability Exposure	PV of Liability (millions)	
Current retirees	$10	100% nominal
Deferred retirees	$20	100% real rate
Active accrued	$22	100% real rate
Future wage inflation	$35	60% real rate and 40% nominal
Future real wage growth	$25	75% equity and 25% nominal
Total	$112	

With an involved calculation, it is smart to do a quick total to check the work. The three allocations total to $112 million, which matches the total in the table.

QUESTION 9

Source: Study Session 6, LOS 14.a, b

A.   i.   Factor 2, a high correlation of assets with plan liabilities defines a low risk or risk-free asset in ALM because assets and liabilities will change in value together, allowing surplus to remain stable.

A.   ii. Only 3 does not directly increase liability noise because it is a gradual change known in advance that can be modeled by the plan actuaries.

Candidate discussion:
For both i and ii, 1 point for a correct selection and 2 points for justification. "i" is a straightforward definition of what is low risk in ALM. A 0.0 sigma and correlation with other assets is the quantitative definition of risk-free in asset only, but not ALM. Equities may be low risk for a portion of plan liabilities in ALM but only if they are highly correlated with the particular liabilities of a given plan. They are not, by definition, risk-free in ALM or asset only. "ii" is somewhat tricky because it is looking for the non-market factor that does not directly create liability noise. Liability noise is an unpredictable change in plan demographics (item 1) or uncertainty in the model used to project the PV of future liabilities (item 2). Item 2 is relevant because the young work force makes the payout dates further in the future and is therefore harder to predict. 3 is an announced change and the actuaries should be able to model the implications.

Source: Study Session 6, LOS 13.a

B.   1.   Plan sponsor: Make required annual contributions; provide investment alternatives.
     2.   Participant: Faces investment risk; determine fund allocations.

Candidate discussion: maximum 4 points.

1. Plan sponsor (SHC)	SHC must contribute only the amount owed to the employee. SHC must provide the employee with a diversified selection of investment alternatives and investment education to help them make appropriate allocation decisions. Sponsor does not face investment risk.
2. Participant (employee)	The employee is responsible for all investment decisions and performance; faces all investment risk. The employee owns the assets and can move them if he or she leaves the company.

QUESTION 10

Source: Study Session 8, LOS 17.n

A.   Returns can be quite high initially as capital flows into the formerly segmented market and bids up stock prices.

Volatility is also initially high, reflecting the risk the integration process will not proceed smoothly or may fail.

Then risk and volatility decline as the market successfully integrates. The now higher stock prices and lower risk lead to lower (but still attractive) expected future returns.

Candidate discussion:
4 points will require you to point out that return and volatility are higher initially and then decline with successful integration. The command word "explain" indicates that you should give some explanation of why this is occurring. For four minutes, it does not need to be longer than our sample answer.

Source: Study Session 8, LOS 17.h, i, l, and Study Session 13, LOS 24.c

Answer for Question 10-B

Circle one	Justify with two reasons
Disagree	1. Correlations have increased (e.g., with large-cap U.S. from 0.71 to 0.81) but they are not 1.0 and there is still a diversification effect. 2. The case for emerging markets also rests on higher returns and those have still been attractive, 19.3% versus 0.5 and 8.2% for U.S. large- and small-cap stocks, respectively. 3. Risk in emerging markets has also been declining from 27.2% to 21.0%, which offsets the rise in correlation.

Candidate discussion:
The question asks for two reasons so only give two of the three provided, 1 point for disagreeing and 2 points each for two reasons. The question specifically directs you to refer to the exhibits; assume you will lose 1 point in each reason if you do not use data directly from the exhibits.

QUESTION 11

Source: Study Session 6, LOS 13.k

Answer for Question 11-A

Objectives	
1. Return	Make distributions in perpetuity to address global social concerns. 5% real distribution, 2% expenses, and 2.75% inflation. $(1.05)(1.02)(1.0275) - 1 = 10.0\%$ required return
2. Risk	Above average risk tolerance given the perpetual nature of the foundation and expectation of continued contributions into the portfolio.
Constraints	
1. Liquidity	No specific liquidity needs are given. A modest cash equivalent reserve is reasonable if desired.
2. Time horizon	Perpetual
3. Taxes	Tax exempt
4. Unique circumstances	• A socially responsible investment screen is required. • 60% minimum of investments in non-U.S. assets. • 5% minimum allocation to each of eight specified asset classes.

Candidate discussion:
3 points for each of the two objectives and 2 points for each of the four constraints. This is a straightforward foundation question. Each of the following issues would likely result in losing 1 point of the possible point score in a template box:
- Failing to state the return objective as being global social funding.
- Adding return components; this is a perpetual foundation.
- Anything other than above average or higher risk tolerance or ability to bear risk.
- Specifying a numeric liquidity need if it implies this was a request of the board.
- Anything other than perpetual as time horizon; it was stated in the case.
- Anything other than tax exempt or tax free.
- Failing to list the three unique directions given by the board.

It is possible you could make one of these "mistakes" and still get full credit. But, if you know the CFA material and read what was given in the case, you should not make one of the "mistakes."

Source: Study Session 6, LOS 13.i, j, k and Study Session 8, LOS 17.r, s

B.   Portfolio A is the only acceptable allocation.
  • It meets the minimum return target of 10%.
  • It allocates at least 5% to all eight asset classes.
  • It has the minimum 60% in international.
  • Best Sharpe ratio of the eligible portfolios.

Candidate discussion:
2 points for selecting Portfolio A and 2 points each for any three of the reasons listed. 0 points if any portfolio other than A is selected. Another reason that could be used is to eliminate all portfolios but A: B for less than the required 10.0% return, D for only 40% international, and E for 0% in natural resources. But then a reason for picking A, not C, must also be given. In that case, the lower Sharpe for C or its higher 50% fixed income allocation could be used to eliminate C.

Source: Study Session 3, LOS 7.c, f, Study Session 6, LOS 13.i, Study Session 8, LOS 17.j, and Study Session 11, LOS 22.l

C.   1. An arbitrary 5% allocation to eight asset classes may not optimize the portfolio's risk and return characteristics; it is naïve diversification.

          2. The SRI screen can also result in sub-optimal asset allocation; SRI can lead to herding or social proof bias.

Candidate discussion:
1 point each for stating two problems and 1 point each for two discussions. The challenge in answering this question is there is only one problem—constraints that lead to inefficient asset allocation. The sample answer is a good way to handle such questions: the same problem is stated in slightly different ways. For "discuss," the answer drew on behavioral finance issues. Alternatively, the answer could have briefly explained how the constraints are likely to shift the efficient frontier downward and to the right. It is only a four-minute question so do not let it slow you down. If you think the answer is just stating the obvious, you are correct.

QUESTION 12

Source: Study Session 16, LOS 29.h

A. 1. VWAP can be gamed.
    2. Does not evaluate missed or delayed trades.
    3. Not good for trades that dominate trading.
    4. Does not account for market movements or trading volume.

Candidate discussion: maximum 4 points, 2 points for any two.
Measuring execution costs by implementing a VWAP benchmark can lead to higher trading costs as traders attempt to time orders based on the benchmark. For example, if a trader buying shares recognizes the security is moving higher as the market closing approaches, he may wait for the next trading day rather than purchase the full position by day's end. The next day the trader is able to finish buying the security in the VWAP range rather than incur a higher price relative to the VWAP the previous day. This is good for the trader's performance measurement, but the portfolio's performance suffers as shares are purchased at higher prices than could have been obtained the previous day.

The VWAP becomes an ineffective measure of trading if the trade orders are delivered to the trading desk just after the opening bell. The trade is compared with a VWAP calculated over the full day, while the actual trade is not. This may help or hurt the trader's measured performance.

Source: Study Session 16, LOS 29.j, k

B. Value trades: Capture over- or under-pricing; limit order.
    Information trade: Speed required to capture the value of information not already incorporated into price; market order.

Candidate discussion: maximum 4 points, 1 point for identifying the order type, and 1 point for describing the motivation.

In a value trade the manager has identified a miss-priced security. Assuming the manager does not have to trade the security, the manager would most likely submit a limit order that can expire unfilled if the limit price is not met.

In an information trade, information has hit the market or the manager has uncovered information that could be incorporated into the security price at any moment. Thus, time is of the essence and the manager will want the trade executed immediately. Market orders are orders to trade as quickly as possible at the best available price.

Source: Study Session 16, LOS 29.n, o

C.

- Attempt to improve performance while meeting fiduciary responsibilities.
- On-going process/multiple trades over time.
- Cannot be measured for single trade.
- Cannot be determined ex ante.
- Must be judged within the context of the investment decision.
- Relationships and practices are integral.
- Written policies for attaining best execution.
- Provide disclosure to clients on how practice best execution.

Candidate discussion: maximum 4 points, 1 point each for any 4 of the items listed.

QUESTION 13

Source: Study Session 3, LOS 6.b, c, d and LOS 7.a and Study Session 4, LOS 8.e

Answer for Question 13

Comment	Is the statement correct or incorrect? (circle one)	Explanation, if incorrect
"Many of our investors use a mental accounting or pyramiding approach to investment planning. Even though this approach might help them achieve a degree of self-control, it is a form of emotional bias that must be overcome for clients to effectively meet their long-term goals."	Incorrect	Mental accounting is a cognitive error.
"An investment policy statement should be reviewed and considered for possible revision when an investor experiences a change in personal circumstances or when external conditions change significantly. For example, a change in tax laws may trigger an investment policy statement review."	Correct	
"We have a lot of clients I would classify as independent individualists. Due to their tendency toward emotional decisions, they can be very difficult to advise."	Incorrect	Independent individualists are primarily subject to cognitive errors.

Candidate discussion: (maximum 9 points)
1 point each for identifying the two incorrect statements.
2 points for each explanation.
3 points for identifying the correct statement.

Because they put goals and related assets into mental accounts, investors' portfolios tend to resemble layered pyramids of assets. As a result, investors subconsciously ignore the correlations of assets and, thus, may not achieve an optimal asset allocation. They also may consider income and capital gains separately rather than as parts of the same total return. Rather than reinvest, they spend current income, which could lead to a decrease in real portfolio value over time. They could also take too much risk in search of high potential current income, as with low-rated, high-risk bonds.

To help the client mitigate mental accounting, have the client look at all investments as if they are part of the same portfolio and then analyze their correlations. This also leads to a clearer perception of the true portfolio allocation, which might be less evident when assets are not considered together.

The second statement is correct. An investment policy statement should be reviewed periodically (yearly) and considered for possible revision when an investor experiences a change in personal circumstances or when external conditions change significantly. Examples of the former include a change in marital status, health, and income. Examples of the latter include a change in tax laws, capital market expectations, and asset availability. A large loss in the portfolio could also trigger an investment policy statement review.

The independent individualist is an active investor who is willing to risk his own capital and give up security to gain wealth. He has moderate to high risk tolerance and suffers from cognitive biases. He is strong-willed, likes to invest, does his own research, and tends to be a contrarian. The independent individualist tends to be difficult to advise but will listen to sound advice. Therefore, the best approach to advising him is regular education on investing concepts relevant to the investor.

Exam 3
Afternoon Session Answers

To get detailed answer explanations with references to specific LOS and SchweserNotes content, and to get valuable feedback on how your score compares to those of other Level III candidates, use your Username and Password to gain Online Access at *www.schweser.com* and choose the left-hand menu item "Practice Exams Vol. 2."

1.	C	25.	B	49.	C
2.	A	26.	A	50.	A
3.	A	27.	C	51.	B
4.	B	28.	B	52.	C
5.	C	29.	C	53.	C
6.	B	30.	B	54.	C
7.	A	31.	C	55.	A
8.	B	32.	B	56.	A
9.	A	33.	C	57.	A
10.	A	34.	B	58.	A
11.	C	35.	A	59.	C
12.	C	36.	C	60.	B
13.	A	37.	B		
14.	B	38.	C		
15.	A	39.	B		
16.	A	40.	A		
17.	B	41.	A		
18.	C	42.	C		
19.	B	43.	C		
20.	A	44.	C		
21.	B	45.	C		
22.	B	46.	A		
23.	C	47.	C		
24.	A	48.	C		

Candidate discussion: 3 points for each correct answer.

Exam 3
Afternoon Session Answers

QUESTIONS 1–6

Source: Study Session 2

1. **C** The IPS review policy is inadequate. It is good that IPS are reviewed at any time upon client request, but it is also likely that clients may be unaware of when such a review might be appropriate. It is incumbent upon the manager to initiate a review of the client's IPS. The Asset Manager Code recommends such reviews on an annual basis, or more frequently if changes in client circumstances justify them. The process for making changes in style/strategy is adequate. (Study Session 2, LOS 4.c)

2. **A** The IPO program creates a substantial conflict of interest between managers and clients. Managers wanting to boost their participation in an IPO would be motivated to place orders in accounts where such an investment might not be appropriate. The employee participation in and of itself might be acceptable, so long as clients' interests were placed ahead of employees'. In this case, there is no evidence of such a priority of transactions, and further, the fact that CA has no exact numbers on the program indicates that the firm is not tracking employee trading activity, which is poor policy. (Study Session 2, LOS 4.c)

3. **A** It is perfectly reasonable for CA to offer certain services or products only to clients meeting specified criteria, such as assets under management. (Study Session 2, LOS 4.c)

4. **B** Riley was incorrect. The pricing methodology should be disclosed to clients, whether one or multiple sources are used. Simpson was correct. Multiple sources are acceptable, so long as full disclosure is made. (Study Session 2, LOS 4.c)

5. **C** This type of trading is clearly market manipulation. Even though the 100 shares may be insignificant, the trade sets the price for the entire position. Such trades, especially entered as buy orders, are an unethical attempt to manipulate prices higher and justify a higher return for the period. However, even a sell transaction made under similar circumstances would be market manipulation. (Study Session 2, LOS 4.c)

6. **B** BTN obviously assists in the investment decision-making process at CA. Using soft dollars to purchase BTN is acceptable. BTR might assist in the investment decision-making process, but managers have not performed any due diligence to verify the quality of the service. With no proven track record or other apparent means of verifying BTR's value, buying the service violates the managers' duty to have a reasonable basis for making investment decisions. Also, the very small capitalization firms may not be suitable for all clients. Unless CA has specific policies and monitoring in place to ensure only soft dollars from appropriate accounts are used to purchase research from BTR, they could also be in violation of Standard III: C, Suitability, as well as AMC Standard B:5.a. (Study Session 2, LOS 4.c)

QUESTIONS 7–12

Source: Study Session 1

7. **A** Mackley has appropriately disclosed the referral arrangement to clients and prospects but improperly uses an association with the CFA Institute for personal or professional gain, which is a violation of Standard VII(A) Conduct as Members and Candidates in the CFA Program. Mackley has misused her authority to select companies to make presentations to her local society. She only selects Kern & Associates to make presentations and excludes their competitors in order to generate referrals for her business. This reflects poorly on the local society and CFA Institute. Mackley may have also violated Standard I(D) Misconduct by engaging in behavior that reflects poorly on her professional reputation. (Study Session 1, LOS 1.b)

8. **B** Welch violated Standard V(C) Record Retention by failing to maintain adequate records to support his investment recommendations. In the absence of another regulation, CFA Institute recommends keeping such records for a minimum of seven years. Certainly, one week is not an adequate record retention policy. Mackley did not violate any Standards by purchasing the stock for all clients with a net worth greater than $6 million. In making her initial purchase of the stock, Mackley did review security information and the suitability of the stock for her clients. As a result, she was in compliance. (Study Session 1, LOS 1.b)

9. **A** The flowers and chocolates are gifts of nominal value and can be accepted even without disclosure to the employer. If the condo offer were a gift, it would be more significant and would require disclosure before acceptance, if possible. However, in this case, it is compensation and not a gift. It is an offer in exchange for future performance. That must be treated as compensation, and that requires prior disclosure to and approval from the employer. Note that "in writing" is not the focus of the Standards, but if it is not in writing, there is no way to document it was done. Outside compensation arrangements need to be treated seriously. (Study Session 1, LOS 1.b)

10. **A** According to Standard VII(B) Reference to CFA Institute, the CFA Designation, and the CFA Program, proper use of the designation would stipulate that CFA and Chartered Financial Analyst always be used as adjectives. Also, the designation may not be written in bold type so that it is more prominent than the rest of the name. (Study Session 1, LOS 1.b)

11. **C** Mackley may have violated Standard VII(B) Reference to CFA Institute, the CFA Designation, and the CFA Program by linking her future investment performance to her status as a CFA charterholder. The violation is borderline as Mackley only implies her participation in the CFA program has contributed to her abilities and does not say it led to past or guarantees future success. However, given the answer choices, the best answer was selected. Mackley has not violated the standard with her references to the CFA program and the examinations. The CFA Institute encourages factual descriptions and indications of the rigorous nature of the program. (Study Session 1, LOS 1.b)

12. **C** According to Standard III(E) Preservation of Confidentiality, Mackley has a duty to keep information about her clients confidential, unless it involves illegal activities, in which case she may need to disclose the information to her supervisor, compliance officer, or regulatory authorities as appropriate. She should not, and there was no valid reason to, have divulged the client information. (Study Session 1, LOS 1.b)

QUESTIONS 13–18

Source: Study Session 7

13. **A** There is no assumption that professional analysts make systematic cognitive errors, but there is evidence they can be overly emotional prior to turning points. Likewise, there is no reason to assume they intentionally try to manipulate the selection of time period data. Nevertheless, there are challenges in determining what past time period is most likely to be similar to the future. (Study Session 7, LOS 15.b)

14. **B** The required return on the Singapore index can be estimated with the dividend discount model.

$$3{,}750 = \frac{90(1.06)}{(R_M - 0.06)} \Rightarrow R_M = 8.544\%$$

The market risk premium for Singapore = 8.544 − 2.4 = 6.144%. The market risk premium for Taiwan = 6.144 × 1.10 = 6.76, so the required return on the market in Taiwan is 6.76 + 2.7 = 9.46%. Thus, we can estimate the intrinsic value of the Taiwan index.

$$\frac{450(1.045)}{(0.0946 - 0.045)} = 9{,}481$$

(Study Session 7, LOS 15.c)

15. **A** The presenter is incorrect on both counts. For any pair of freely traded currencies, interest rate parity is governed by arbitrage and must hold in the short run. IRP is used to determine the relationship between spot and forward exchange rates; however, it is not a valid predictor of actual changes in the spot rate. In fact, IRP dictates that the currency with the higher short-term rate will trade at a forward discount, while the empirical evidence is that currency is more likely to appreciate in value than depreciate. IRP determines f versus S at any one moment in time, but it does not predict what will happen to S over time. On the other hand, the relative form of purchasing power parity is not governed by arbitrage, and currency values can deviate widely from their PPP value in the short run. However, the evidence suggests that PPP is a useful forecasting tool for the long run. (Study Session 7, LOS 15.l)

16. **A** Statement 1 is true. Econometric models are extremely rigorous and time consuming to construct with hundreds of mathematical relationships incorporated. This does mean the input, relationships, and output are internally consistent.

Statement 2 is false because the approach is easy to understand and can be executed quickly. The indicators are readily available in developed markets, and the analyst does not have to do any underlying collection or analysis of raw data. (Study Session 7, LOS 15.n)

17. **B** When an economic crisis, such as that which began in Thailand in 1997, spreads to other countries, this is known as contagion. The fact that emerging market asset returns may exhibit greater non-normality makes it more difficult to apply parametric models (e.g., those based upon the statistical concepts of mean and standard deviation). In such instances, the analyst should consider non-parametric approaches, such as bootstrapping techniques and Monte Carlo simulation to estimate risk. (Study Session 7, LOS 15.m)

18. **C**   All else being equal, the economic statistics presented favor Russia over Brazil for bond investment. Russia has a relatively greater level of foreign exchange relative to short-term debt, implying that short-term ability to pay is greater, and the overall indebtedness relative to GDP is lower.

While India and China each have the advantage in two of the four economic growth statistic categories, in aggregate, the statistics presented favor China for growth and, therefore, equity investment.

estimated long-term growth = population growth + labor force

participation growth + growth in capital spending + growth in total factor productivity

estimated long-term growth for China: 0.8 + 1.8 + 1.3 + 0.9 = 4.8%

estimated long-term growth for India: 1.3 + 0.5 + 1.4 + 0.4 = 3.6%

In addition, China enjoys a relatively more favorable savings to investment balance, implying that the growth may be more sustainable. (Study Session 7, LOS 15.r)

QUESTIONS 19–24

Source: Study Session 10

19. **B** The cushion spread is the difference between the safety net return (minimum acceptable return) and prevailing immunized rate. In this case, the cushion spread is 8% − 6% = 200 basis points. (Study Session 10, LOS 20.j)

20. **A** The liability in five years is fully funded today by 100 million earning 6%. The FV of the liability must, therefore, be:

$$\$100 \text{ million} = \frac{L}{(1.03)^{10}}$$

L = \$100 million$(1.03)^{10}$ = \$134.39 million future value

The amount required to achieve the required terminal value at the current immunization rate of 8% over the five remaining years is \$134.39 million / $(1.04)^{10}$ = \$90.79 million.

So, the dollar safety margin is \$100 million − \$90.79 million = \$9.21 million. (Study Session 10, LOS 20.j)

21. **B** After one year, the value of the portfolio is the price of the bond plus accumulated interest. The price of the bond is computed as follows:

FV = 100; N = 18; I/Y = 4.5; PMT = 4; CPT → PV = 93.92

The accumulated value of the coupon payments is the compounded value of the first coupon at 4% (= 8% / 2) for one 6-month period plus the value of the second coupon payment received at the end of the first year, or:

4(1.04) + 4 = 4.16 + 4 = \$8.16

Thus, the value of the portfolio after one year is 93.92 + 8.16 = 102.08, or \$102.08 million.

The required terminal value is \$134.39 million. The portfolio value necessary to achieve the required terminal value at the prevailing immunization rate of 9%, compounded semiannually, over the four remaining years, is:

\$134.39 million / $(1.045)^8$ = \$94.50 million

So, the dollar safety margin is: \$102.08 million − \$94.50 million = \$7.58 million. (Study Session 10, LOS 20.j)

22. **B** Immunization is required if the dollar safety margin reaches zero. First determine the new PVL at the 11% immunization rate. The present value of \$134.39 million at the immunized rate of 11% (for 5 years) is (\$134.39 million)/$(1.055)^{10}$ = \$78.676 million. The safety margin will be zero if the bond falls to the same value. Calculate the bond's YTM if the bond trades at the value:

FV = 100,000,000; PMT = \$8 / 2 = 4,000,000; N = 10 × 2 = 20; PV = −\$78,676,000; CPT → I/Y = 5.83 × 2 = 11.67%

(Study Session 10, LOS 20.j)

23. **C**   Price has correctly described cash flow matching but has incorrectly described horizon matching. Cash flow matching involves finding a bond with a maturity date equal to the liability payment date, buying enough in par value of that bond so that the principal and final coupon fully fund the last liability, and continuing this process, using a recursive procedure, until all liabilities are matched. Features of multi-cash flow immunization include ensuring that assets and liabilities have the same present values and durations. Horizon matching (a.k.a. combination matching) is a combination of cash flow matching in the early years and multiple liability immunization. (Study Session 10, LOS 20.m)

24. **A**   Immunization risk can only be eliminated by investing in zero-coupon bonds (e.g., Treasury strips) with a maturity and face value equal to that of the liability, so that statement is correct. That strategy is rarely followed, however, due to the high asset cost (low return potential). His statement about the dispersion of cash flows around the horizon date is correct, because the greater the dispersion the higher the reinvestment risk; the less the dispersion the lower the reinvestment risk. Note that using zeros is the extreme example of concentrating the asset maturities and cash inflows at the horizon date. (Study Session 10, LOS 20.g)

QUESTIONS 25–30

Source: Study Sessions 9 and 15

25. **B** An overlay involves the use of a third party to manage the currency risk. Active currency management places greater emphasis on increasing return through currency management, while discretionary puts more emphasis on risk reduction; RS's goal is risk reduction. (Study Session 9, LOS 18.b)

26. **A** RS is a Canadian firm with long currency exposure to the JPY. Using currency options to reduce downside currency exposure RS would buy puts on the JPY (equivalent to buying calls on the CAD). (Study Session 9, LOS 18.g)

27. **C**
$$\text{\# contracts} = \left(\frac{\beta_{target} - \beta_{current}}{\beta_{futures}} \right) \left(\frac{V_P}{V_F} \right)$$

$$= \left(\frac{1.80 - 0.60}{1.02} \right) \left(\frac{2,000,000}{110,000} \right) = 21.39 \ (\text{buy 21 contracts})$$

(Study Session 15, LOS 26.a)

28. **B** The question deals with the impact of correlation between local market and local currency return. Positive correlation increases volatility of domestic return to an investor in a foreign market, increasing the minimum variance hedge ratio and the need to hedge currency risk. Negative correlation has the opposite effect. The question describes investment in British manufacturers as having negative correlation. A decrease in the GBP increases exports, revenue, profits, stock prices, and local market returns. This negative correlation between local currency and local market returns lowers the volatility of domestic returns to a non-British investor in British manufacturers. Neither the British service firms nor Argentinean cell service providers show any correlation (a correlation of 0.0) between local market and local currency returns. (Study Session 9, LOS 18.f)

29. **C** RS has described a collar on the ARS. A collar will provide downside protection if the ARS declines to a strike price below the current exchange rate and retain upside potential until the ARS appreciates to a strike price above the current exchange rate. A collar is created by purchase of an OTM put on the ARS (equivalent to an OTM call on the CAD) and sale of an OTM call on the ARS (equivalent to an OTM put on the CAD). The other answer choices are incorrect. The purchase of 40-delta and sale of 30-delta puts are a put spread that provides downside protection below one strike price but no further protection if the ARS falls below a lower strike price. The forward would remove all upside and downside exposure. (Study Session 9, LOS 18.g)

30. **B** The most straightforward strategy to preinvest is to buy futures (or forwards) on U.K. stocks and bonds. Buying ATM calls and selling puts on U.K. stock indexes or futures is equivalent to buying a future or forward on U.K. stocks, thus all three answers meet the objective of preinvesting in U.K. stocks. The issue becomes which answer best replicates the purchase of U.K. bonds. Selling U.K. bond futures is exactly wrong. Selling the calls and buying puts replicates an incorrect short position in U.K. bonds. Buying the calls would give the upside, but not downside, risk of U.K. bonds. This best replicates the purpose of preinvesting, capturing the upside of the asset. (Study Session 15, LOS 26.d, e and 27.a, b)

QUESTIONS 31–36

Source: Study Sessions 10 and 11

31. **C** To calculate the number of futures contracts necessary for the hedge, we must first obtain the dollar durations for the CTD and Bond Q:

The dollar duration for a given change in interest rates at time t is expressed as:

DD_t = duration$_t$ × assumed change in interest rates × value of asset at time t

DD_{CTD} is given as $13,245.46.

DD_Q = 10.32 × 0.01 × 1.0498 × $10,000,000 = $1,083,394

The number of futures contracts necessary for the hedge can be computed as:

$$\text{\# contracts} = \left(\frac{DD_T - DD_P}{DD_{CTD}}\right)(\text{conversion factor})(\text{yield beta})$$

$$\text{\# contracts} = \left(\frac{0 - \$1,083,394}{\$13,245.46}\right)(1.3698)(1.00) = -112.04$$

Therefore, sell 112 contracts.

(Study Session 11, LOS 22.e)

32. **B** The portfolio's dollar duration is the sum of the individual bond's dollar durations:

$$DD_P = DD_Q + DD_R + DD_S$$

$$= [(1.0498 \times 10,000,000) \times 0.01 \times 10.32]$$

$$+ [(0.9836 \times 25,000,000) \times 0.01 \times 8.67]$$

$$+ [(1.0121 \times 15,000,000) \times 0.01 \times 7.38]$$

$$= 1,083,394 + 2,131,953 + 1,120,395 = \$4,335,742$$

(Study Session 10, LOS 20.h)

33. **C** $DD_P \text{ (in one year)} = 0.01\big[(10m \times 1.0498 \times 9.46) + (25m \times 0.9836 \times 7.83) + (15m \times 1.0121 \times 6.51)\big]$
$= \$3,906,822$

$\text{rebalancing ratio} = 4,901,106 / 3,906,822 = 1.2545$

We must increase the value of the portfolio by the rebalancing ratio, which assumes a proportionate increase in each bond. To do this, multiply the necessary percentage increase by the total value of the portfolio.

$\text{required cash} = 0.2545 \text{ (Total value of Bond Q, Bond R, and Bond S)}$

$\text{required cash} = 0.2545\big[(10m \times 1.0498) + (25m \times 0.9836) + (15m \times 1.0121)\big] = \$12,793,588$

(Study Session 10, LOS 20.h)

34. **B**   Rawlins is incorrect. If the slope coefficient from Tejada's regression was greater than one, the number of futures contracts needed to hedge a position would *increase* because the yield on the underlying bond would be more volatile than the yield on the hedge instrument.

Tejada is correct. The yield beta is obtained from using a regression equation in the following form:

yield on bond to be hedged = a + b(yield on CTD issue) + error

The yield beta, *b*, measures the relationship between changes in yields. If the yield spread between the bond being hedged and the CTD issue is assumed to be constant, the yields must move together and the yield beta must equal one.
(Study Session 11, LOS 22.e)

35. **A**   Rawlins is looking for pure yield pick up. He initially says that when he says he seeks to sell the overpriced (i.e., lower YTM) bond, and his analysis of Dynacom confirms it. Note that considering the currency forward premium or discount does not make it total return analysis because there is no projection involved. The currency discount is a known return from hedging the currency.

Tejada is doing total return analysis because he is considering all factors, including potential price change. (Study Session 10, LOS 21.d)

36. **C**   Bergamo bonds (B) yield 4% more than Dynacom bonds (D). Over three months, B has a yield advantage of 100 bp. However, B is a foreign (EUR) denominated bond, and the EUR trades at a 150 bp discount for three months. On a currency hedged basis, B has a 50 bp return disadvantage, giving D the return advantage of 50 bp.

The breakeven spread change based on D's duration is:

$$-50 \text{ bp} = -5.13(\text{sc}) \qquad \text{sc} = 9.7 \text{ bp}$$

If the yield on D increases more than 9.7 bp, its price will underperform by more than 50 bp, and B will outperform. Tejada forecasts D's yield will increase by 75 bp. He is correct to recommend B.

Rawlins states the analysis does not consider secondary effects, and he is correct. The analysis is based on duration and ignores convexity effects. (Study Session 11, LOS 22.k)

QUESTIONS 37–42

Source: Study Sessions 8, 11, 14, and 15

37. **B**   The expected effects are increasing stock prices as capital flows into the economy, standalone risk declines, and economic growth improves. Initially this produces very high returns but as the integration proceeds, the expected returns become lower to reflect the now lower risk of the economy and market. The inflow of capital is also positive for the currency value. (Study Session 8, LOS 17.n)

38. **C**   Amsler's portfolio is invested in European stocks that are denominated in the euro. She is therefore long European stocks and long the euro. In order to hedge, short positions should be taken in both the European stocks and the euro. If the European equity index or euro decline in value, the short positions in the derivative contracts will rise, therefore offsetting the losses in the underlying equity and currency positions. (Study Session 15, LOS 26.a, f)

39. **B**   Tavinsky is incorrect.

   The correct number of futures contracts can be calculated as:

   $$N_f = \left(\frac{0-1.15}{0.975}\right)\left(\frac{15,000,000}{120,000}\right) = -147.44 \Rightarrow \text{short 147 contracts}$$

   Treblehorn is correct. In a "hedging the principal" strategy, the investor simply sets the principal of the forward contract equal to the beginning principal value of the investment. A more theoretically correct approach is to hedge the ending number of currency units. Because that would require forecasting the return on a risky asset, the simple principal-only approach is normally used. He is correct to use a larger amount here because the underlying risky portfolio is being hedged, making its return target the local risk-free rate. He can reasonably increase the currency hedge size by 2% and improve the expected quality of the hedge. (Study Session 15, LOS 26.a)

40. **A**   If the local market declined by 12% and the portfolio beta is 1.15, the expected local market return is (–12%)(1.15) = –13.8%. The euro is expected to appreciate from $1.05 to $1.12, a 6.7% appreciation. This makes the U.S. investor's expected return (1 – 0.138)(1.067) – 1 = –8.0%.

   A more cumbersome way to confirm this is to apply the –13.8% to the beginning portfolio value. This would translate into a portfolio worth €15,000,000 × (1 – 0.138) = €12,930,000 at the end of the year. The ending position in dollars is worth (€12,930,000)($1.12 / €) = $14,481,600. Since the beginning portfolio value was worth (€15,000,000)($1.05 / €) = $15,750,000, this translates into a U.S. dollar loss of 8.05%. (Study Session 15, LOS 26.a)

41. **A**   If the futures position was a perfect hedge, the euro rate of return on the equity portfolio will be the local risk-free rate of 2%. Combining this with the currency return produces (1.02)(1.067) – 1 = 8.8%.

   Alternatively, apply the 2% to the beginning portfolio value. This would translate into an ending portfolio value of €15,300,000. The dollar equivalent of that portfolio would be (€15,300,000)($1.12 / €) = $17,136,000, which is an 8.8% return ($17,136,000 / $15,750,000 – 1). $15,750,000 was calculated in the previous question answer. (Study Session 15, LOS 26.a)

42. **C**   Tavinsky is incorrect. When all sources of risk are hedged, the U.S. investor can expect to earn the U.S. risk-free rate of 4%.

Math can be used to confirm this. By covered interest rate parity, the forward rate between two currencies must reflect the current spot rate times the ratio of one plus the interest rates:

$$F_{\$/\mathnormal{€}} = S_{\$/\mathnormal{€}} \times \left(\frac{1 + i_\$}{1 + i_\mathnormal{€}} \right)$$

$$= \$1.05 \times \left(\frac{1.04}{1.02} \right) = \$1.070588$$

If a perfect hedge took place using equity futures, then the rate of return on the equity portfolio would be the local risk-free rate of 2%. This would translate into an ending portfolio value of €15,300,000.

If the €15,300,000 is sold in one year at the forward rate of ($1.070588 / €), the value of the portfolio in dollars will be $16,379,996. The starting portfolio value in dollars was (€15,000,000)($1.05 / €) = $15,750,000. So the investor's return in dollars, hedging both equity and currency risk, would be 4% ($16,379,996 / $15,750,000 – 1).

Treblehorn is also incorrect. When the local market and currency risk are hedged, the ending spot exchange rate (or in this case, what is projected to happen to the spot) is irrelevant. The currency was hedged. (Study Session 11, LOS 22.j)

QUESTIONS 43–48

Source: Study Sessions 9, 14, and 17

43. **C** The time-weighted return is 11.4%, and money-weighted return is 6.8%.

To calculate the time-weighted return, calculate the returns for each subperiod and link them:

$(17.8 - 11.2 - 4.0)/11.2 = 23.2\%$ $(16.1 - 17.8)/17.8 = -9.6\%$

$(1.232)(0.904) - 1 = 11.4\%$

Because a cash inflow was received before the lower second subperiod return, the MWR must be lower than the TWR. Calculations are unneeded but can be used to validate that conclusion. MWR is the IRR that equates the PV of future account cash flows and value to the initial value. It is a trial and error calculation although when the subperiods are of equal length, calculator cash flow functions can be used to make the calculation. Ignoring that March is a 31-day month, the approximate IRR is:

Keystrokes on the TI BAII Plus®:

CF 2nd CLRWORK
–11,200,000 ENTER↓
–4,000,000 ENTER↓↓
16,100,000 ENTER
IRR CPT = 3.36

(Study Session 17, LOS 31.c)

44. **C** Statement 2 is incorrect because administration is complicated. Accounts must be valued with every large, external cash inflow or outflow. Essentially this would mean daily valuations. Marking to market daily can be expensive to administer.

Statement 3 is incorrect because TWR is normally required for reporting manager performance. It is not influenced by client external cash flows. Only if the manager controls the timing of ECFs is MWR allowed and, in fact, required. (Study Session 17, LOS 31.c)

45. **C** The M-squared measure for the Bison fund is 11.2%.

M-squared is the theoretical return the portfolio would have earned if the risk (standard deviation) had been the same as the market. It is calculated as:

$3.5\% + [(14.1 - 3.5)/31.5](23.0) = 3.5 + 7.7 = 11.2\%$

(Study Session 17, LOS 31.p)

46. **A** The Sortino ratio compares the excess return over the MAR to downside sigma:

Bison: $(14.1 - 4.5)/30.1 = 0.319$
Lunar: $(15.8 - 4.5)/30.9 = 0.366$

Lunar is superior when considering downside risk. Lunar is also better diversified. This is clear because it has a lower standard deviation but a higher beta. This can only be explained if Bison has a higher degree of unsystematic (diversifiable) risk. While unnecessary in this case, that conclusion can be confirmed by calculating risk-adjusted return ratios: Jensen's alpha, Treynor, Sharpe, and M-squared for each fund.

Jensen's alpha is the return of the portfolio less the return expected based on beta and the SML:

Bison: 14.1 – [3.5 + (9.0 – 3.5)0.9] = 14.1 – 8.5 = 5.6%
Lamar: 15.8 – [3.5 + (9.0 – 3.5)1.3] = 15.8 – 10.7 = 5.1%

Treynor is the portfolios excess return to systematic risk ratio:

Bison: (14.1 – 3.5)/0.9 = 11.8
Lamar: (15.8 – 3.5)/1.3 = 9.5

Because both Jensen's alpha and Treynor are based on systematic risk, they will agree in relative ranking. In this case, Bison is superior.

Sharpe is similar to Treynor but uses total risk (standard deviation):

Bison: (14.1 – 3.5)/31.5 = 0.34
Lamar: (15.8 – 3.5)/30.7 = 0.40

M-squared is the theoretical return the portfolio would have earned if the risk (standard deviation) had been the same as the market:

Bison: 3.5 + [(14.1 – 3.5)/31.5](23.0) = 3.5 + 7.7 = 11.2%
Lamar: 3.5 + [(15.8 – 3.5)/30.7](23.0) = 3.5 + 9.2 = 12.7%

Because both Sharpe and M-squared are based on total risk, they will agree in relative ranking. In this case, Lamar is superior.

Lamar's superior ranking using total risk but inferior ranking using only systematic risk is explained if Lamar is more diversified and has less unsystematic risk.

(Study Session 14, LOS 25.l and Study Session 17, LOS 31.p)

47. **C**   Statement 4 is incorrect. Indexes are often used as benchmarks, but this benefits both the client and manager. For example, a well chosen index clearly communicates expected return and risk characteristics, which reduces potential miscommunications.

Statement 5 is correct. Indexes are not always appropriate as benchmarks. For example, in ALM-based portfolios, the liabilities are the more appropriate benchmark. (Study Session 9, LOS 19.a, b, d, e)

48. **C**   Credit risk was specifically considered when Jaguar limited transactions to higher quality firms as was Herstatt risk when netting was required across multiple transactions with the same firm. Operations risk was not directly referenced. (Study Session 14, LOS 25.d)

QUESTIONS 49–54

Source: Study Sessions 11 and 15

49. **C**   The sale has resulted in transaction exposure; a change in revenues or costs that result from changes in foreign exchange rates. If the size of Smiler's sales to Frexa were to change as a result of a change in the \$/€ rate this would be economic exposure. The third type of exposure is translation exposure, and it occurs when financial statements are converted from foreign currency to home currency.

Assuming Smiler hedges the long position in €10,000,000 by selling euros for dollars at the 90-day forward rate, the proceeds from the forward contract = €10m × 1.45\$/€ = \$14.5 million. (Study Session 15, LOS 26.f)

50. **A**   The cost of the call is 0.000943443 × 25 million = \$23,586.

The future value of this premium at the beginning of the loan period based on current 90-day LIBOR plus the 150 bp spread is:

23,586 × [1 + (0.048 + 0.015) 90 / 360] = \$23,957, making the net loan:

25,000,000 − 23,957 = \$24,976,043

The payoff on the call = (\$25,000,000)(0.0573 − 0.048)(180 / 360) = \$116,250.

The effective dollar interest cost = (\$25,000,000)(0.0573 + 0.0150)(180 / 360) − \$116,250 = \$787,500.

Alternatively, the interest on the loan can also be calculated as the exercise rate plus the spread because the call is in the money at expiration: (0.048 + 0.015) × 180 / 360 × 25,000,000 = \$787,500.

The annualized rate on the loan is $(\$25,787,500 / \$24,976,043)^{365/180} - 1 = 6.6982\%$. The call premium increased the cost of the loan from (4.8 + 1.5 =) 6.3% to 6.698%. (Study Session 15, LOS 27.c)

51. **B**   To decrease beta, the number of contracts to sell is:

$$\text{number of contracts} = \left(\frac{0.9 - 1.25}{0.98}\right)\left(\frac{\$52,750,000}{1,050 \times \$250}\right) = -71.77; \text{ short 72 contracts.}$$

(Study Session 15, LOS 26.a)

52. **C** The question analysis is a bit tricky. Smiler is going to issue a liability but has not yet done so. They are short the liability, which is actually an asset. To hedge bond assets, sell bond contracts.

Another way to reach this correct conclusion is to analyze their risk. If rates rise, the value of the liability will decline, meaning Smiler at issue will receive a smaller amount of funds. They need an offsetting gain to make them whole. Bond futures will decline in value if rates increase, which is a gain to the short position. The number of contracts to sell must include the yield beta (regression coefficient of yield changes) that was given.

$$N_f = \frac{0 - 9.90}{7.11} \times \frac{\$25,000,000}{\$75,287} \times 1.05 = -485.48$$

Smith must sell 485 contracts.

(Study Session 11, LOS 22.e)

53. **C** The futures contract has an expiration date that coincides with the expected date of the bond issuance, so the basis will be zero and does not have to be estimated. However, bond duration can change and, with larger changes in rates, the convexity effect could become significant, making either a more likely source of hedging error. (Study Session 11, LOS 22.e)

54. **C** Ng has an investment in British stocks, which he will be converting to U.S. dollars in one year. The problem with hedging the foreign exchange rate risk of an equity investment is that the investor does not know how much to hedge because the investment's value fluctuates. (Study Session 15, LOS 26.f)

QUESTIONS 55–60

Source: Study Session 17

55. **A**   Harrison is correct. Since the Treynor ratio uses beta, which measures only systematic risk, it is only appropriate for assessing the performance of well-diversified portfolios or individual stocks held in well-diversified portfolios. Recall that unsystematic risk is diversified away in a well-diversified portfolio.

   Powell is incorrect. The Sharpe ratio uses the standard deviation as the measure of risk, which is useful when the portfolio is not well-diversified and reflects unsystematic or firm specific risk. Since the Treynor ratio uses systematic risk as the relevant measure of risk, it may rank portfolios differently than the Sharpe ratio. Consider a portfolio with low systematic risk but high unsystematic and total risk. This portfolio may rank highly using the Treynor ratio but quite low using the Sharpe ratio. (Study Session 17, LOS 31.p)

56. **A**   The pure sector allocation effect is calculated by taking the differences between the portfolio and benchmark weights for each sector and multiplying it by the difference between the benchmark return for that sector and the total benchmark return. The products are then summed across the sectors:

$$\text{pure sector allocation} = \sum_{j=1}^{s} \left(W_{P,j} - W_{B,j} \right) \left(R_{B,j} - R_B \right)$$

   benchmark return = (0.6)(0.286) + (0.25)(0.124) + (0.15)(0.0885) = 0.216

   The pure sector allocation effect = (0.5 − 0.6)(0.286 − 0.216) + (0.3 − 0.25)(0.124 − 0.216) + (0.2 − 0.15)(0.0885 − 0.216) = −1.80%.

   So TopTech does not demonstrate superior ability to choose sectors, because the allocation effect is negative at −1.80%. (Study Session 17, LOS 31.l)

57. **A**   The within-sector selection effect measures the manager's ability to select superior securities to represent each sector in the portfolio. It is the sum of the weight for each sector in the benchmark times the difference in that sector's return in the portfolio and in the benchmark:

$$\text{within-sector selection} = \sum_{j=1}^{s} W_{B,j} \left(R_{P,j} - R_{B,j} \right)$$

   Within-sector selection effect = (0.60)(0.187 − 0.286) + 0.25(0.158 − 0.124) + (0.15)(0.125 − 0.0885) = −0.0594 + 0.0085 + 0.0055 = −0.0454 = −4.54%.

   In sum, in the financial and large cap sectors, the manager chose superior stocks, so they show superior ability there. The overall within-sector selection effect is negative (−4.54%), however, so they do not show a consistent overall ability to select stocks.

   The remaining component of attribution analysis (the allocation/selection interaction effect) can be calculated as the difference between the portfolio and benchmark weights for each sector multiplied by the difference between the return for the sector in the portfolio and the return for the sector in the benchmark. The total allocation/selection interaction effect is the sum of these products:

$$\text{allocation/selection interaction} = \sum_{j=1}^{s}\left(W_{P,j} - W_{B,j}\right)\left(R_{P,j} - R_{B,j}\right)$$

Allocation/selection interaction effect = (0.50 − 0.60)(0.187 − 0.286) + (0.30 − 0.25)(0.158 − 0.124) + (0.20 − 0.15)(0.125 − 0.0885) = 0.0099 + 0.0017 + 0.0018 = 0.0134 = 1.34%.

The total excess return for the manager is then −1.80% + 1.34% − 4.54% = −5.00%.

This should be equal to the excess return calculated using the total returns for the benchmark and the portfolio. The total return for the benchmark is calculated above as 21.6%. For the portfolio it is: = (0.5)(0.187) + (0.3)(0.158) + (0.2)(0.125) = 16.6%. Thus, the excess return calculated using the total returns for the portfolio and the benchmark is 16.6% − 21.6% = −5.0%. (Study Session 17, LOS 31.l)

58. **A**   For a benchmark to be considered valid, it must be: (1) unambiguous; (2) investable; (3) measurable; (4) appropriate; (5) reflective of current investment opinions; (6) specified in advance; and (7) owned. Stober is describing a variation on the median manager approach, using the top 10th percentile instead of the median manager. The problem is that such approaches only meet the measurable standard. The manager and their result can only be known at the end of the period. To be unambiguous and specified in advance, the characteristics of the benchmark would need to be knowable at the start of the period. It is helpful to recall that to be valid in performance attribution, the benchmark should have been investable at the start of the period to be a valid alternative to hiring the active manager. (Study Session 17, LOS 31.f)

59. **C**   Harrison is incorrect. The benchmark level examines the difference between the return to custom benchmarks reflecting the managers' styles and the return to a broad asset category. Essentially the benchmark return measures the return to style bets resulting from the policy weighting in various styles. Harrison actually describes the investment managers level.

Powell is incorrect. Although the investment manager's level does reflect the return from active management, it uses the policy weights established for each manager. Returns due to differences between policy weights and the amounts actually allocated to each manager do not show up until the last level of macro attribution analysis (i.e., allocation effects). (Study Session 17, LOS 31.k)

60. **B**   Benchmark B is the best benchmark for the small-cap value manager. A good benchmark will have a beta relative to the portfolio that is close to one, so the tracking error (i.e., the standard deviation of the excess return of the portfolio relative to the benchmark) will be low. The benchmark turnover should be low so that it is investable by a passive manager. The correlation between the return to the manager's active management (A) and the return to the manager's style (S) should be low. Otherwise, the benchmark has not adequately captured the manager's style.

Benchmark B is the best benchmark using all four measures.
(Study Session 17, LOS 31.i)

Notes

Notes